Oxford Revise

In partnership with

C000107893

Edexcel GCSE (9–1) Maths

Foundation

Suitable for Grades 1–5

Revision Guide

Author: Katie Wood

Series Editor: Naomi Bartholomew–Millar

The Oxford Revise GCSE Maths Series: Our approach

Our no-fuss approach lets you dive straight into exactly what you need to know for the exam. GCSE Grades and check-boxes help you monitor your own progress on every page, and you'll find plenty of further practice on the exact same page in the matching workbook. Best of all, our unique visual approach — with diagrams, mnemonics and handy memory tips — will help you recall even the trickiest points.

OXFORD
UNIVERSITY PRESS

Contents

Strive for 5

So you have the best possible chance of reaching Grade 5, we've carefully studied past exam papers and reports to identify the 7 trickiest question types.

STRIVE FOR 5 Look for this logo to see which topics have most often caught students out in the past.

Pages 111–125: We've provided structured support on these pages for answering the 7 trickiest question types.

Use of calculators

This book provides support with both how and when to use your calculator. Look for these symbols against questions:

Make sure to use your calculator – it's good practice for the exam.

Make sure not to use your calculator – this question would only appear in the non-calculator paper.

If there's no symbol, then the question could appear on either the calculator or the non-calculator paper.

Place value

You can use a number line or a place value diagram to visualise the size of numbers, including decimal numbers.

Key points

- To multiply by 10, move all digits 1 place to the left.
- To divide by 10, move all digits 1 place to the right.
- To multiply or divide by 100, move all digits 2 places, and so on.
- Add zeros as placeholders at the beginning or end of the number if needed.

Dividing by 100 moves everything two spaces to the right

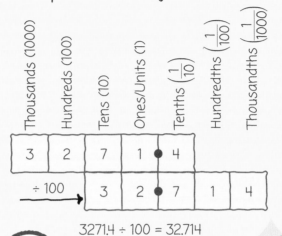

$3271.4 \div 100 = 32.714$

Confidence bar

Sorted!

☑

☑

☑

Had a look

Worked example

Grade 2

a) Write the value of the digit 7 in the number 25.371 **[1 mark]**

b) Calculate 1.06×1000 **[1 mark]**

c) Complete with < or > **[1 mark]**

0.29 ☐ 0.209

Solution

a) The 7 is in the hundredths column, so its value is $\frac{7}{100}$

b) To multiply by 1000, move all the digits 3 places to the left: $1.06 \times 1000 = 1060$

c)
```
   0.209                              0.29
◁─┼──*─┼──┼──┼──┼──┼──┼──┼──┼──*─┼──▷
 0.2 0.21 0.22 0.23 0.24 0.25 0.26 0.27 0.28 0.29 0.3
```

So 0.29 > 0.209

There are two ways of remembering the < and > signs.

The 'Less than' sign looks like the letter 'L':

Less than

Smaller numbers go next to the smaller end:

2 < 4

small end

Worked example

Grade 3

Given that $82 \times 0.61 = 50.02$ work out the value of 0.82×6.1 **[1 mark]**

Solution

$82 \div 100 = 0.82$

$0.61 \times 10 = 6.1$

Therefore $0.82 \times 6.1 = 50.02 \div 100 \times 10$

$= 50.02 \div 10$

$= 5.002$

Exam corner

Grade 2

1. a) Write in size order, starting with the smallest.
0.74, 0.704, 0.7, 0.744 **[I got ___ /1 mark]**

b) State the value of the digit 3 in the number 5.203 **[___ /1 mark]**

Grade 3

 2. Given that $12 \times 28 = 336$ calculate the value of 1.2×0.28

[___ /1 mark]

Examiner's tip!

The examiner is expecting you to use the calculation you are given. Don't use long multiplication, as you'll just waste time.

Order of operations

It is important to use the correct order of operations when doing calculations, otherwise you might get the wrong answer.

Key points

- Use **BIDMAS** to remember the correct order of operations.
- Division and multiplication can be done either way around.
- Addition and subtraction can be done either way around.

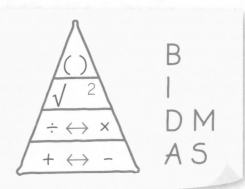

Confidence bar

Sorted!

☑
☑
☑

Had a look

Worked example

Grade 3

 Use your calculator to find the value of $\dfrac{54-6}{(6+2)\times 4}$ **[1 mark]**

Solution

Type (5 4 – 6) ÷ ((6 + 2) × 4)

The answer is $1\frac{1}{2}$

$$(54-6) \div ((6+2) \times 4) \qquad 1\frac{1}{2}$$

Calculator tip

On most new scientific calculators, you can just use the fraction button and copy exactly what you see on the page – no need for extra brackets!

Calculator tip

You will have buttons on your calculator to convert mixed numbers into either decimals or fractions.

S ⇔ D $a\frac{b}{c} \Leftrightarrow \frac{d}{c}$

You can add and subtract in either order:

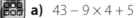 43 – 36 + 5 is the same as
43 + 5 – 36

Worked example

Grade 3

Calculate the value of these expressions without a calculator.

a) $43 - 9 \times 4 + 5$ **b)** $32 - 6^2 \div 2$ **[2 marks each]**

Solution

a) $43 - 9 \times 4 + 5 = 43 - 36 + 5$ Do the multiplication first.
$= 12$

b) $32 - 6^2 \div 2 = 32 - 36 \div 2$ Calculate the 6^2 first.
$= 32 - 18$ Then do the division.
$= 14$

Exam corner

Grade 3

1. Use your calculator to find the value of $\dfrac{14 + 3^2 \times 2}{25 - 7 \times 2}$
   Give your answer as an improper fraction. **[I got ___ /2 marks]**

2. Calculate the value of these expressions without a calculator.
   a) $7 - 2 + 3$ **[___ /1 mark]**
   b) $2 \times 3^2 + 2(\sqrt{3 \times 9 - 2})$ **[___ /3 marks]**

Grade 3

When there is no symbol between a number and a bracket or a square root, you must multiply.

Rounding and truncating

Whole numbers and decimals can be rounded to the nearest 10, 100, 1000 and so on. Decimal numbers can also be rounded in different ways.

Use this flow-chart to help you round numbers.

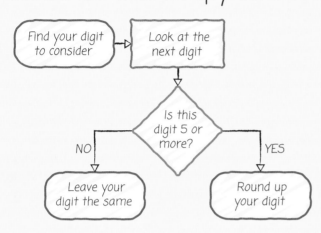

For example: try rounding 0.147 to 2 decimal places.

Your digit to consider is the 2nd decimal place, so 4

Look at the next digit, 7

YES, this is 5 or more.

Round up the 4 to a 5

Answer: 0.15

Worked example

Grade 2

Round 297.25 to
a) the nearest 100
b) the nearest 10
c) the nearest whole number
d) 1 decimal place. **[1 mark each]**

Solution

a) 297.25 = 300 to nearest 100
b) 297.25 = 300 to nearest 10
c) 297.25 = 297 to nearest whole number
d) 297.25 = 297.3 to 1 decimal place

Key points

An alternative to rounding is **truncating**. This is where you just 'cut off' digits after the place value you are interested in.

For example, if you are 15.7 years old, you just say 15

Worked example

Grade 2

How many 180 ml glasses will 2500 ml of water fill? **[1 mark]**

Solution

$2500 \div 180 = 13.88...$

Truncating this, it will fill 13 glasses.

Exam corner

Grade 2

1. Round the number 79.53 to
   a) the nearest whole number **[I got ___ /1 mark]**
   b) 1 decimal place. **[___ /1 mark]**

Grade 2

2. Sue is paid £12.63 per hour.
   How much is she paid for 3.5 hours? **[___ /2 marks]**

- Sometimes you'll have to decide for yourself how to round an answer.
- Money is often rounded to 2 decimal places, i.e. to the nearest penny.

Significant figures

Imagine you won £5480 217 in a competition. What would you say in a text? You would probably round to the most significant part of the number, so £5 000 000, or perhaps £5 500 000

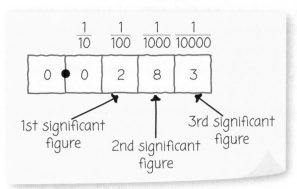

$\frac{1}{10}$ $\frac{1}{100}$ $\frac{1}{1000}$ $\frac{1}{10000}$

| 0 | • | 0 | 2 | 8 | 3 |

1st significant figure
2nd significant figure
3rd significant figure

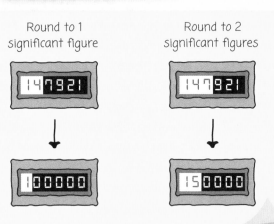

Round to 1 significant figure

| 1 4 7 9 2 1 |

↓

| 1 0 0 0 0 0 |

Round to 2 significant figures

| 1 4 7 9 2 1 |

↓

| 1 5 0 0 0 0 |

Key points

- The first digit that is not 0 is the most significant. You always read from the left, so this is the first digit for numbers larger than (or equal to) 1
- To round to a number of **significant figures**, find the digit to consider then look at the next digit to decide whether to round up or down.

  Round up if 5 or more.

  Round down if less than 5
- Check your answer makes sense – you might need to add zeros at the end.

You need the '.0' in '15.0' to make it 3 significant figures.

Worked example
Grade 3

Round 0.0283 to
a) 1 significant figure   **[1 mark]**
b) 2 significant figures.   **[1 mark]**

Solution

a) 0.0283 = 0.03 to 1 significant figure

b) 0.0283 = 0.028 to 2 significant figures

Worked example
Grade 3

Calculate the area of the rectangle. Give your answer to 3 significant figures.   **[2 marks]**

Solution

Area = 16.7 × 0.9
    = 15.03
    = 15.0 cm² to 3 significant figures

16.7 cm

0.9 cm

 See page 73 for more on area.

Exam corner
Grade 3

1. Round £9644 to

   a) 2 significant figures   **[I got ___ /1 mark]**

   b) 1 significant figure.   **[___ /1 mark]**

Take care rounding up the 9. You might want to draw a number line to help.

Grade 3

2. A recipe for 48 cupcakes uses 1.65 kg of sugar. How much sugar is in 1 cupcake? Give your answer to 2 significant figures.   **[___ /2 marks]**

Estimation

Estimation is a handy technique for quickly checking whether a more complex calculation is likely to be correct or not.

Grade
4–5

Key points

To **estimate** the result of a calculation:

- First round all the numbers to 1 significant figure.
- Use the correct order of operations (BIDMAS) to work out the estimated value.

To estimate the result of $562 \div 64.2$ round everything to 1 significant figure.

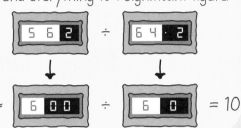

$$\approx \boxed{6\ 0\ 0} \div \boxed{6\ 0} = 10$$

See page 4 for more on significant figures.

Worked example

 A school of 580 students has 22 classes. Estimate the mean number of students per class. **[2 marks]**

Grade 4

Solution

Mean number of students per class $= \dfrac{580}{22}$

$$\approx \dfrac{600}{20}$$

$$= 30$$

Mean $= \dfrac{\text{total of all values}}{\text{number of values}}$

So, in this question,

Mean $= \dfrac{\text{number of students}}{\text{number of classes}}$

Worked example

Grade 4

 Estimate the value of $\dfrac{11 \times 5.7 - 23.4}{0.54}$

Show all your working. **[2 marks]**

Solution

First round each number to 1 significant figure.

$$\dfrac{11 \times 5.7 - 23.4}{0.54} \approx \dfrac{10 \times 6 - 20}{0.5}$$

$$= \dfrac{60 - 20}{0.5} = \dfrac{40}{0.5} = 80$$

Examiner's tip!

In the exam, remember to write down all of the rounded values, and show each step of your working.

Exam corner

Grade 4

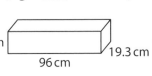 **1.** Simon used his calculator to find the value of $22.5 + 1.9 \times 4.3$

He gave the answer 104.92. Does this seem approximately correct? Explain your reasoning. **[I got ___ /2 marks]**

 2. A cuboid measures 96 cm x 22.1 cm x 19.3 cm. Estimate the volume of the cuboid. **[___ /3 marks]**

Grade 5

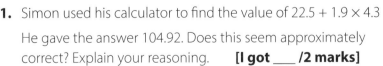

22.1 cm

96 cm

19.3 cm

See page 81 for more on volume.

Error intervals

The **error interval** of a number is the range of values (from minimum to maximum) it could have been before it was rounded or truncated.

Grade 5

Key points

- If a measurement, *m*, is **rounded** to a given unit:
  add and subtract half a unit for the maximum and minimum.
- If a measurement, *m*, is **truncated** to a given unit:
  add 1 unit for the maximum (the minimum is the given measurement).
- Error interval for *m* is written:
  minimum ≤ *m* < maximum

3.7 has been **rounded** to 1 decimal place. What is the error interval?

3.6   3.65   3.7   3.75   3.8

Error interval is 3.65 ≤ *m* < 3.75 so *m* is greater than or equal to 3.65 but strictly less than 3.75 (3.75 would be rounded up).

3.7 has been **truncated** to 1 decimal place. What is the error interval?

3.6   3.65   3.7   3.75   3.8

Error interval is 3.7 ≤ *m* < 3.8

m is greater than or equal to 3.7 but strictly less than 3.8 (never actually equal to 3.8).

See page 37 for more on inequalities (<, ≤, ≥, >)

Worked example
Grade 5

The length of an aeroplane is *l* metres.
l is 76 to the nearest metre.
Give the error interval for *l*.   **[2 marks]**

Solution

The minimum possible length is 75.5 m.

The maximum possible length is 76.499999... m (i.e. the greatest value less than 76.5 m).

Error interval is 75.5 ≤ *l* < 76.5

Worked example
Grade 5

The mass of an apple, *a* g, is given as 80 g.
Give the error interval for *a* in each of these situations:

a) the mass was rounded to the nearest 10 g
b) the mass was rounded to the nearest integer
c) the mass was truncated to an integer.   **[1 mark each]**

Solution

a) 75 ≤ *a* < 85   b) 79.5 ≤ *a* < 80.5   c) 80 ≤ *a* < 81

Read the question carefully!

- Rounded to the nearest 10 ⇒ add/subtract 5 for the minimum/maximum.
- Rounded to nearest integer ⇒ add/subtract 0.5 for the minimum/maximum.
- Truncated to an integer ⇒ add 1 for the maximum (minimum is the given integer).

Exam corner

1. The time, *t*, taken for a child to complete a simple task is recorded as 27 s to the nearest second.
   Give the error interval for *t*.   **[I got ___ /2 marks]**
   Grade 5

2. The capacity, *c*, of a glass is given as 230 ml.
   Give the error interval in each of these situations:
   Grade 5
   a) the capacity was rounded to the nearest ml   **[___ /2 marks]**
   b) the capacity was truncated to 2 significant figures.
      [___ /2 marks]

Calculating with negative numbers

You can do calculations involving negative numbers by using a number line.
You need to remember some simple rules.

Adding a positive number moves to the right: $+(+5) = +5$

Subtracting a negative number moves to the right: $-(-5) = +5$

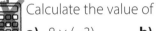
-9 -8 -7 -6 -5 -4 -3 -2 -1 0 1 2 3 4 5 6 7 8 9

Subtracting a positive number moves to the left: $-(+5) = -5$

Adding a negative number moves to the left: $+(-5) = -5$

Worked example **Grade 1**

 Calculate the value of $-1 - 3 - (-6)$

[1 mark]

Solution

Work from left to right:

$-1 - 3 - (-6) = -4 - (-6)$

$= -4 + 6$ Move right 6

$= 2$

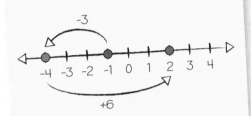

Start at -1

Move 3 left to -4

Move 6 right to 2

Key points

- Use these rules for multiplying with negative or positive numbers:

  positive × positive = positive

  positive × negative = negative

  negative × positive = negative

  negative × negative = positive

- The same rules work for division!

Worked example **Grade 2**

 Calculate the value of

a) $8 \times (-3)$ **b)** $(-5)^2$ **c)** $-28 \div 4$

[1 mark each]

Solution

a) $8 \times (-3) = -24$

b) $(-5)^2 = (-5) \times (-5) = 25$

c) $-28 \div 4 = -7$

Exam corner **Grade 1**

1. The temperature in a city during the day is 3 °C. At night it is −12 °C. Calculate how much colder it is at night.   **[I got ___ /1 mark]**

2. Calculate the value of

   a) -4×5 **[___ /1 mark]**

   b) $(-6)^2 \div (-3)$ **[___/2 marks]**   **Grade 3**

   c) $-5 \times 2 - (-7)$ **[___/2 marks]**

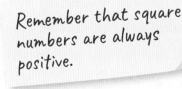

Remember that square numbers are always positive.

Calculating with decimals

With decimal numbers, you can use the usual written methods for addition, subtraction, multiplication and division, just as you do with integers.

Key points

When adding or subtracting decimal numbers using the column method,
- line up the decimal points
- fill in with zeros after the point.

When dividing by a decimal:
- write the division as a fraction and multiply by 10 (or 100 or 1000 . . .) to get an integer denominator
- calculate using long or short division.

When multiplying with decimals:
- ignore the decimal point
- put the point back in the correct place.

For 14.7 + 6.842: *fill in with zeros after the point.*

$$
\begin{array}{r}
1\ 4 . 7\ 0\ 0 \\
+\ 6 . 8\ 4\ 2 \\
\hline
2\ 1 . 5\ 4\ 2 \\
{\scriptstyle 1\ 1}
\end{array}
$$

fill in with zeros after the points.

Worked example

Grade **3**

Calculate the value of
a) 6.2 × 0.48   **b)** 11.07 ÷ 0.9   **[2 marks each]**

Solution

a) Work out 62 × 48 using long multiplication:

$$
\begin{array}{r}
6\ 2 \\
\times\ 4\ 8 \\
\hline
4\ 9\ 6 \\
{\scriptstyle 1} \\
2\ 4\ 8\ 0 \\
\hline
2\ 9\ 7\ 6 \\
{\scriptstyle 1}
\end{array}
$$

So 6.2 × 0.48 = 2.976

The decimal point moved 3 digits to the right to make 6.2 × 0.48 into 62 × 48, so move it back to the left in the final answer.

b) $11.07 \div 0.9 = \dfrac{11.07}{0.9}$ Write as a fraction, then make the denominator an integer by multiplying both sides by 10

$= \dfrac{110.7}{9}$

$9\overline{)1\,1^{2}0\,.^{2}7}$ → 12.3

So 11.07 ÷ 0.9 = 12.3

To work out 0.024 × 56.9 imagine the decimal point is a football that you can kick out of touch. You just need to remember how many digits you've kicked it past...

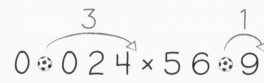

$$0 \cdot 0\ 2\ 4 \times 5\ 6 \cdot 9$$

So 4 digits in total.

Now use long multiplication to work out

24 × 569 = 13 656

Kick the point back over 4 digits to get the final answer:

$$1 \cdot 3\ 6\ 5\ 6$$

The answer is 1.3656

Exam corner

 1. A group of eight friends go to a restaurant. They spend £136.46 on food and £52.02 on drinks. They share the bill equally between them.

How much does each friend pay?   **[I got ___ /3 marks]**   Grade **3**

2. Calculate the value of $\dfrac{3.114 - 0.54}{0.18}$. Show all your working.

[___ /3 marks]   Grade **3**

Use estimation to check your answers are sensible.

In the Worked example:

6.2 × 0.48 ≈ 6 × 0.5 = 3

11.07 ÷ 0.9 ≈ 10 ÷ 0.9 which is a little over 10

Introduction to fractions

You can find equivalent fractions by multiplying or dividing the numerator and denominator of a fraction by the same number. You can write improper ('top-heavy') fractions as mixed numbers.

Key points

- You can simplify a fraction by dividing the numerator and the denominator by the highest common factor (HCF).
- If the numerator is bigger than the denominator then it's an

  improper fraction, e.g. $\frac{13}{6}$

- Improper fractions can be converted to

  mixed numbers, e.g. $\frac{13}{6} = 2\frac{1}{6}$

Remember this...

Numerator is North

$$\frac{\text{Numerator}}{\text{Denominator}}$$

Denominator is Down

See page 16 for more on HCF.

Confidence bar

Sorted!

☑

☑

☑

Had a look

In questions like this, try simplifying the fractions.

With $\frac{14}{70}$, you might have simplified in two steps:

$$\frac{14}{70} = \frac{7}{35} = \frac{1}{5}$$

But it's quicker to divide by the HCF of 14 and 70, which is 14

Worked example

 a) Explain how you know that $\frac{14}{70} < \frac{2}{5}$ **[2 marks]**

b) Convert $2\frac{3}{5}$ to an improper fraction.   **[1 mark]**

c) Convert $\frac{17}{3}$ to a mixed number.   **[1 mark]**

Solution

a) $\frac{14}{70} = \frac{1}{5}$ which is less than $\frac{2}{5}$
(÷14)

b) $2\frac{3}{5}$ can be represented as:

 $\frac{5}{5} +$

$\frac{5}{5} +$

$\frac{3}{5} = \frac{(2 \times 5) + 3}{5} = \frac{13}{5}$

c) $\frac{17}{3}$ means the same as $17 \div 3$

$17 \div 3 = 5 \text{ r2} = 5\frac{2}{3}$

Exam corner

1. Write these fractions in order, starting from the smallest.

$\frac{1}{3}$ $\frac{16}{40}$ $\frac{3}{18}$

[I got ___ /2 marks]

2. A bag contains $7\frac{2}{5}$ kg of sand. Write this amount as an improper fraction.

[___ /1 mark]

The denominator always stays the same when you convert between improper fractions and mixed numbers.

Proportions of amounts

You can use multiplication and division to find a fraction or a percentage of an amount without using a calculator.

Key points

Fractions of amounts

To find, e.g., $\frac{2}{5}$ of 30:

- DIVIDE the amount by the denominator: $30 \div 5 = 6$
- MULTIPLY the result by the numerator: $6 \times 2 = \mathbf{12}$

Percentages of amounts

To find, e.g., 26% of 160, use one or more of these strategies:

divide by 100 to find 1%: 1% is $160 \div 100 = 1.6$

divide by 10 to find 10%

divide by 4 to find 25%: 25% is $160 \div 4 = 40$

divide by 2 to find 50%

Then add up as needed:

$26\% = 25\% + 1\% = 40 + 1.6 = 41.6$

Remember this...

Rearrange the percent symbol to remember that % means out of 100

 % means out of 100

Confidence bar

Sorted!

☑
☑
☑

Had a look

Worked example

Grade 3

 Which is greater, **A** 68% of 400 or **B** 75% of 360? **[3 marks]**

Solution

A 10% of $400 = 400 \div 10 = 40$

So, 60% of $400 = 6 \times 40 = 240$

1% of $400 = 400 \div 100 = 4$

So, 8% of $400 = 8 \times 4 = 32$

68% of $400 = 240 + 32 = \mathbf{272}$

B 25% of $360 = 360 \div 4 = 90$

So, 75% of $360 = 90 \times 3 = \mathbf{270}$

Answer: 68% of 400 is greater

Worked example

Grade 2

David earns £350 and gives $\frac{3}{7}$ of it to charity. How much does he give to charity? **[2 marks]**

Solution

DIVIDE by the denominator:

$\frac{1}{7}$ of $350 = 350 \div 7 = 50$

MULTIPLY by the numerator:

$\frac{3}{7}$ of $350 = 3 \times 50 = 150$

David gives £150 to charity.

Remember this...

In maths, the word **of** means **multiply (×)**.

So in this question, you could also say $\frac{3}{7}$ of £350 is $\frac{3}{7} \times £350$

Exam corner

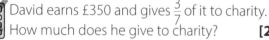

1. Mira went shopping with £90. She spent $\frac{2}{9}$ of her money on clothes and $\frac{7}{15}$ on books. How much money did she have left? Show all your working. **[I got ___ /4 marks]** *Grade 3*

2. A gardener planted 60 basil seeds and 150 coriander seeds. 85% of the basil seeds and 32% of the coriander seeds germinated. Which plant did he have the most of? Show all your working. **[___ /3 marks]** *Grade 3*

Examiner's tip!

STRIVE FOR 5

Try to choose the most efficient method for the numbers in your question.

See pages 118–119 for more practice

Calculating with fractions 1

You need to be able to multiply and divide fractions without using a calculator.

Key points

- To multiply two fractions, multiply the numerators and multiply the denominators.
- To divide by a fraction, multiply by its **reciprocal**.

  The **reciprocal** of a number is $\dfrac{1}{\text{number}}$

- Make sure you cancel any common factors in the final answer.

You can use KFC to remember how to divide a fraction by another fraction:
Keep the first, Flip the other, and Change the sign:

so $\dfrac{2}{7} \div \dfrac{5}{6}$

becomes $\underset{\text{Keep}}{\left(\dfrac{2}{7}\right)} \times \underset{\text{Flip}}{\left(\dfrac{6}{5}\right)}$

Change

Confidence bar

Sorted!

Had a look

Worked example

Grade 3

 Calculate these and give your answers in their simplest form.

a) $\dfrac{3}{4}$ of $\dfrac{5}{6}$ **b)** $2\dfrac{7}{9} \times \dfrac{3}{10}$ **[5 marks]**

Solution

Remember, **of** means **multiply**

a) $\dfrac{3}{4}$ of $\dfrac{5}{6} = \dfrac{3}{4} \times \dfrac{5}{6}$

$= \dfrac{15}{24}$

$= \dfrac{5}{8}$ Cancel common factor of 3

b) $2\dfrac{7}{9} \times \dfrac{3}{10} = \dfrac{25}{9} \times \dfrac{3}{10}$ Convert $2\dfrac{7}{9}$ to an improper fraction.

$= \dfrac{75}{90}$

$= \dfrac{5}{6}$ Cancel common factor of 15

Worked example

Grade 3

Calculate these and give your answers in their simplest form.

a) $\dfrac{3}{8} \div \dfrac{7}{10}$ **b)** $5 \div \dfrac{1}{3}$ **[4 marks]**

Solution

a) $\dfrac{3}{8} \div \dfrac{7}{10} = \dfrac{3}{8} \times \dfrac{10}{7}$ Keep the $\dfrac{3}{8}$

Flip the $\dfrac{7}{10}$ to $\dfrac{10}{7}$
Change $\div$ to $\times$

$= \dfrac{30}{56}$

$= \dfrac{15}{28}$ Cancel common factor of 2

b) $5 \div \dfrac{1}{3} = 5 \times \dfrac{3}{1}$ Keep the 5

Flip the $\dfrac{1}{3}$ to $\dfrac{3}{1}$
Change $\div$ to $\times$

$= 5 \times 3$

$= 15$

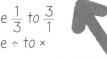

You can think of an integer as a fraction over 1. So $5 = \dfrac{5}{1}$

Exam corner

Grade 3

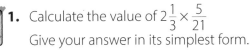 **1.** Calculate the value of $2\dfrac{1}{3} \times \dfrac{5}{21}$

Give your answer in its simplest form.   **[I got ___ /3 marks]**

 **2.** Calculate the value of $\dfrac{3}{4} \div \dfrac{5}{14}$

Give your answer as a mixed number in its simplest form.

[___ /3 marks]

Grade 3

 Convert mixed numbers to improper fractions first.

Calculating with fractions 2

In order to add or subtract fractions, you must find a **common denominator**.

Key points

You can only add or subtract fractions when the denominators are the same.

STEP 1: Find the lowest common multiple (LCM) of the denominators.

STEP 2: Scale the fractions so they have the LCM as their denominator.

STEP 3: Add or subtract the numerators, but don't change the denominator.

You can think of an upside-down picnic table to help you to add fractions. The lines show you which numbers to multiply:

Multiply 7 by 9 to find the denominator.

Then multiply 1 by 9, then 2 by 7, to find the numerator.

$$\frac{1}{7} + \frac{2}{9} = \frac{9 + 14}{63} = \frac{23}{63}$$

Remember to simplify your answer if possible.

Confidence bar

Sorted!

Had a look

It helps to write mixed numbers as improper fractions first.

Worked example

Grade 4

A jug contains $\frac{7}{8}$ litre of lemonade. How much lemonade is left in the jug after $\frac{1}{6}$ litre is poured out? **[3 marks]**

Solution

$$\frac{7}{8} - \frac{1}{6} = \frac{21}{24} - \frac{4}{24}$$

$$= \frac{17}{24}$$

The LCM of 6 and 8 is 24

$\frac{7}{8} = \frac{21}{24}$ and $\frac{1}{6} = \frac{4}{24}$

Subtract the numerators once the denominators are the same.

$\frac{17}{24}$ litre of lemonade is left in the jug.

 See page 16 for more on LCM.

Worked example

Grade 4

Two wires of length $2\frac{3}{4}$ m and $1\frac{2}{3}$ m are joined together. How long is the new length of wire? Give the answer as a mixed number. **[3 marks]**

Solution

$$2\frac{3}{4} + 1\frac{2}{3} = \frac{11}{4} \times \frac{5}{3}$$

$$= \frac{33 + 20}{12}$$

$$= \frac{53}{12} = 4\frac{5}{12}$$

The new length of wire is $4\frac{5}{12}$ m.

Use the upside-down picnic table method.

 See page 9 for more on mixed numbers and improper fractions.

Exam corner

1. Calculate the value of

a) $\frac{6}{7} - \frac{2}{7}$ **[I got ___ /1 mark]**

b) $\frac{3}{8} + \frac{1}{4}$ **[___ /2 marks]**

Grade 3

2. A tub of sweets weighs $1\frac{8}{9}$ kg. An additional $\frac{5}{6}$ kg of sweets is added to the tub, then a child takes $\frac{1}{18}$ kg of sweets out of the tub.

What does the tub of sweets weigh now? Give your answer as a mixed number in its simplest form. **[___ /4 marks]**

Grade 4

Examiner's tip!

It's easy to make mistakes when working with different types of fractions, so think carefully and check your answers make sense.

Fractions, decimals, percentages

Fractions, decimals and percentages are different ways of writing the same number. You can convert between them without using a calculator.

Grade
2-4

Key points

You should learn these common fractions, decimals and percentages:

$\frac{1}{2} = 0.5 = 50\%$ $\frac{1}{4} = 0.25 = 25\%$

$\frac{1}{8} = 0.125 = 12.5\%$ $\frac{1}{5} = 0.2 = 20\%$

$\frac{1}{10} = 0.1 = 10\%$ $\frac{1}{3} = 0.\dot{3} = 33.\dot{3}\%$

$0.\dot{3}$ means 0.333333... and is called a **recurring decimal**.

Converting numbers

Divide numerator by denominator

Fraction e.g. $\frac{32}{100} = \frac{8}{25}$

Decimal e.g. 0.32

Write it out of 100 and simplify

Multiply by 100%

e.g. 32% Percentage

Confidence bar

Sorted!

Had a look

Worked example

Grade 3

Put these numbers in order, starting with the smallest:

$\frac{2}{3}$ 65% $\frac{17}{25}$ 0.6

[3 marks]

Solution

Convert all the numbers to percentages so they are easier to compare.

$\frac{2}{3} = 66.\dot{6}\%$ Learn this one too!

$\frac{17}{25}$ is the same as $\frac{68}{100}$ which is 68%

$0.6 = 60\%$

Write the order using the original numbers:

0.6   65% $\frac{2}{3}$ $\frac{17}{25}$

Worked example

Grade 3

Write the fraction $\frac{5}{16}$ as a percentage. **[3 marks]**

Solution

First convert to a decimal by dividing the numerator by the denominator:

$$16 \overline{)5.^50^20^40^80} = 0.3125$$

Now multiply by 100% to convert to a percentage:

$0.3125 \times 100\% = 31.25\%$ So $\frac{5}{16} = 31.25\%$

Calculator tip

You can convert between fractions and decimals on a calculator.

$S \Leftrightarrow D$

You can also enter a percentage using the % button and get the fraction.

Exam corner

Grade 2

1. **a)** Write the number 0.061 as
   i) a fraction   **ii)** a percentage.   **[I got __ /2 marks]**
   b) Write 5% as a fraction in its simplest form.   **[__ /2 marks]**

2. Passengers on a train are travelling for work, school or leisure. $\frac{3}{8}$ of the passengers are travelling for work and 13% for school. Work out the percentage of the passengers who are travelling for leisure.   **[__ /3 marks]**

Grade 4

Examiner's tip!

STRIVE FOR 5

It's easiest to convert all values to percentages in this type of question.

STRIVE FOR 5 See pages 118-119 for more practice.

Powers and roots

You can use your calculator to find roots and powers, but you should learn some of the easy ones from memory.

Grade
2–3

Key points

- The power of a number is the number of times it is multiplied by itself, e.g. $2^5 = 2 \times 2 \times 2 \times 2 \times 2$

- The square root ($\sqrt{}$) of a number can be squared to give the number, e.g. $\sqrt{9} = 3$ since $3^2 = 3 \times 3 = 9$

- The cube root $\left(\sqrt[3]{}\right)$ of a number can be cubed to give the number, e.g. $\sqrt[3]{27} = 3$ since $3^3 = 3 \times 3 \times 3 = 27$

5^2 is 5 squared
This is the area of the square.

5^3 is 5 cubed
This is the volume of the cube.

Confidence bar

Sorted!

☑
☑
☑

Had a look

Worked example

Grade 2

 Write down $\sqrt[3]{75}$ to 1 decimal place. **[2 marks]**

Solution

Enter into your calculator:

$\sqrt[3]{75}$

4.217163327

$\sqrt[3]{75} = 4.2$ to 1 decimal place.

See page 3 for more on Rounding.

Calculator tip

Find the buttons for

square root

and cube root

on your calculator.

You should learn these powers of small numbers:

$1^2 = 1$	$1^3 = 1$
$2^2 = 4$	$2^3 = 8$
$3^2 = 9$	$3^3 = 27$
$4^2 = 16$	$4^3 = 64$
$5^2 = 25$	$5^3 = 125$
$10^2 = 100$	$10^3 = 1000$

See page 19 for more on powers of 10

Worked example

Grade 3

 Work out the value of $6\sqrt[3]{8} + 5^2 \times 4$ **[3 marks]**

Solution

First work out the powers and roots:

$$6\sqrt[3]{8} + 5^2 \times 4 = 6 \times 2 + 25 \times 4$$
$$= 12 + 100$$
$$= 112$$

Exam corner

Grade 2

1. Find the side length of a cube with a volume of 9.261 cm^3. **[I got ___ /1 mark]**

2. Without using a calculator, find the value of $5 + \sqrt{100 - 4^3}$ **[___ /3 marks]**

Grade 3

In BIDMAS the I is for Indices. This includes all powers and roots. So calculate indices before any addition or subtraction.

See page 2 for more on BIDMAS.

Calculating with indices

A power of a number can also be called the **index** (plural **indices**). Indices can be positive or negative numbers.

Key points

INDEX LAWS

- Any number to the power 0 is 1
- If you multiply numbers with the same base, you add the powers.
- If you divide numbers with the same base, you subtract the powers.
- If you raise a power to another power, you multiply the powers.
- A power of –1 gives the reciprocal.

EXAMPLES

$7^0 = 1$

$7^5 \times 7^3 = 7^8$

$7^5 \div 7^3 = 7^2$

$(7^5)^3 = 7^{15}$

$7^{-1} = \dfrac{1}{7}$

Confidence bar

Sorted!

Had a look

$BASE^{index}$

In the number 7^5

7 is the base

5 is the power or index

If there is no power, assume it to be 1, so $5 = 5^1$

Worked example

Grade 5

a) Simplify

   i) $5^8 \times 5$ **ii)** $(5^4)^6$ **iii)** $5^2 \div 5^3$ **[3 marks]**

b) Simplify $(5^3 \div 5^{-4})^2$ **[2 marks]**

c) Find the value of

   i) $\left(\dfrac{2}{3}\right)^2$ **ii)** 5^{-2} **[2 marks]**

Solution

a) i) $5^8 \times 5 = 5^9$ Add the powers: $8 + 1 = 9$

   ii) $(5^4)^6 = 5^{24}$ Multiply the powers: $4 \times 6 = 24$

   iii) $5^2 \div 5^3 = 5^{-1}$ Subtract the powers: $2 - 3 = -1$

b) $(5^3 \div 5^{-4})^2 = (5^7)^2$ First subtract the powers within the bracket: $3 - -4 = 3 + 4 = 7$

   $= 5^{14}$ Then multiply the powers: $7 \times 2 = 14$

When dealing with fractions, you can apply the power to the numerator and the denominator separately.

c) i) $\left(\dfrac{2}{3}\right)^2 = \dfrac{2^2}{3^2} = \dfrac{4}{9}$

   ii) $5^{-2} = (5^2)^{-1}$

If you have a negative power, write using brackets like this with a power of –1 on the outside.

   $= 25^{-1}$

   $= \dfrac{1}{25}$ A power of –1 gives the reciprocal.

Exam corner

1. Simplify

   a) i) $8^7 \div 8^3$ **ii)** $(8^{-5})^2$ **[I got __ /2 marks]**

   b) $8 \times 8^{-4} \div 8^{-5}$ **[__ /2 marks]**

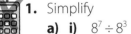

2. Find the value of

   a) i) 13^0 **ii)** 6^{-1} **[__ /2 marks]**

   b) $\left(\dfrac{1}{3}\right)^{-2}$ **[__ /2 marks]**

Grade 4

Grade 5

Examiner's tip!

'Simplify' means you can leave in index form.

'Find the value' means find the actual numerical answer (which may be a fraction).

Factors and multiples

You need to remember the difference between the **factors** and the **multiples** of a number.

Finding the Factors and Multiples of a number

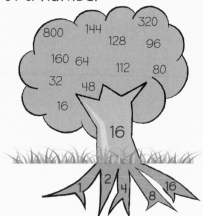

Multiply the number to find the Multiples.

Factors Form the number.

Worked example

From this list of numbers:

　　4　　7　　24　　28

Grade 2

select
a) a multiple of 14
b) a factor of 14　　**[2 marks]**

Solution

a) 28 is a multiple of 14 (since 2 × 14 = 28).

b) 7 is a factor of 14 (since 2 × 7 = 14).

Confidence bar

Sorted!

☑

☐

☐

Had a look

Key points

- **Factors** can be multiplied by each other to form the number.

- A **multiple** is found by multiplying the number by another integer (a number in the times table).

- The **highest common factor (HCF)** of two numbers is the biggest number that is a factor of both.

- The **lowest common multiple (LCM)** of two numbers is the smallest number that is a multiple of both.

Worked example

Grade 3

a) What is the highest common factor of 18 and 12?　　**[3 marks]**
b) What is the lowest common multiple of 8 and 20?　　**[2 marks]**

Solution

a) Factors of 18: ① ② ③ ⑥ 9 18
Factors of 12: ① ② ③ 4 ⑥ 12
Circle the numbers that appear in both lists.
The biggest circled number is 6
The HCF of 18 and 12 is 6

b) Multiples of 20: 20 ④⓪ 60 ...
Multiples of 8: 8 16 24 32 ④⓪ ...
You can now stop looking for multiples of 8 because 40 is in both lists.
The LCM of 8 and 20 is 40

Exam corner

Grade 3

1. a) What is the highest common factor of 98 and 70?　　**[I got ___ /3 marks]**
b) What is the lowest common multiple of 80 and 120?　　**[___ /2 marks]**

2. Part of a bathroom wall is to be covered in square tiles.
The area to be covered measures 63 cm × 42 cm.
What is the largest size of square tiles that will completely cover this area?　　**[___ /2 marks]**

Grade 3

Examiner's tip!

STRIVE FOR 5

Watch out for questions like this, about factors or multiples. Here you need to find the HCF of 63 and 42

STRIVE FOR **5** See pages 112–113 for more practice.

Prime factor decomposition

A number is **prime** if it has exactly two factors: itself and 1. Every whole number can be written as a **product of prime factors** in a unique way.

Key points

To write a number as a **product of prime factors**:

- Use a factor tree to split the number into pairs of factors.
- Each time you reach a prime number, circle it and move to another number.
- Write out the number as a product of all the prime numbers, using index form.
- This is also called the **prime factor decomposition** of the number.

Finding the prime factor decomposition of 120

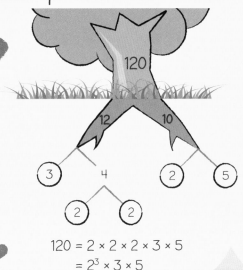

$120 = 2 \times 2 \times 2 \times 3 \times 5$
$\qquad = 2^3 \times 3 \times 5$

See page 14 for more on index form.

Worked example

 Grade **4**

 Write 189 as a product of its prime factors.

Solution

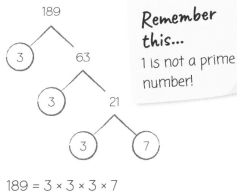

Remember this...
1 is not a prime number!

$189 = 3 \times 3 \times 3 \times 7$
$\qquad = 3^3 \times 7$

Try finding the prime factors of 189 by completing this factor tree instead:

Your final answer should be the same.

Worked example

 Grade **5**

 The prime factor decomposition of a number is:
$$2^3 \times 3 \times 5 \times 7^2$$
Explain whether the number is a multiple of

a) 7   b) 10   c) 9   **[3 marks]**

Solution

a) Yes, the number is a multiple of 7, since 7 is a prime factor.

b) Yes, the number is a multiple of 10, since both 2 and 5 are prime factors and $2 \times 5 = 10$

c) No, the number is not a multiple of 9, since 9 is not a factor (3 is a prime factor but 3^2 is not).

Exam corner

 Grade **4**

1. Write these numbers as a product of their prime factors. Use index notation.

    a) 54   **[I got __ /2 marks]**   b) 650   **[__ /2 marks]**

 Grade **5**

2. A number is a multiple of 6, 14 and 50. What is the smallest possible value of the number? Write your answer using prime factors.   **[__ /2 marks]**

STRIVE FOR **5** See pages 112–113 for more practice.

Finding HCF and LCM

Grade 4-5

You can use prime factors to work out the highest common factor (HCF) or the lowest common multiple (LCM). This is very useful for big numbers.

Key points

To find the HCF and the LCM of two numbers:

STEP 1: Find all the prime factors.

STEP 2: Draw a Venn diagram showing the prime factors of both numbers.

STEP 3:

- Multiply the numbers in the intersection to find the HCF.
- Multiply the numbers in the union (i.e. all the numbers shown) to find the LCM.

Finding the HCF & LCM of 150 and 225

Step 1: $150 = 2 \times 3 \times 5 \times 5$
$225 = 3 \times 3 \times 5 \times 5$

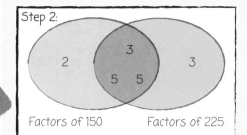

Step 2:

Factors of 150   Factors of 225

Step 3: HCF = $3 \times 5 \times 5 = 75$
LCM = $2 \times 3 \times 5 \times 5 \times 3 = 450$

Confidence bar
Sorted!
☑
☑
☑
Had a look

See page 109 for more on Venn diagrams.

Worked example

Grade 5

Two numbers have prime factor decomposition $2^2 \times 3 \times 5^2$ and $2^3 \times 5 \times 11^2$

Find

a) the highest common factor   **[3 marks]**

b) the lowest common multiple.   **[2 marks]**

Leave your answers in index form.

Solution

Draw a Venn diagram to show the prime factors.

a) HCF = $2 \times 2 \times 5$
       = $2^2 \times 5$

b) LCM = $5 \times 3 \times 2 \times 2 \times 5 \times 2 \times 11 \times 11$
         = $2^3 \times 3 \times 5^2 \times 11^2$

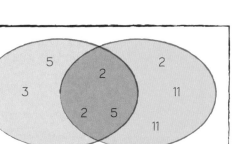

Exam corner

Grade 5

1. $A = 3 \times 5^2 \times 13$ and $B = 3^2 \times 13^2 \times 17^2$

   a) What is the highest common factor of A and B?   **[I got __ /3 marks]**

   b) What is the lowest common multiple of A and B?   **[__ /2 marks]**

      Leave your answers in index form.

Grade 5

2. The Venn diagram shows the prime factors of two numbers.
The highest common factor of the two numbers is 14.
The lowest common multiple of the two numbers is 420.
What are the two numbers?   **[__ /4 marks]**

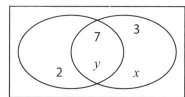

STRIVE FOR 5   See pages 112-113 for more practice

Standard form

You can use a power of 10 to write a very large or a very small number in **standard form**. This makes it easier to understand the size of the number.

Key points

Standard form is written in this way:

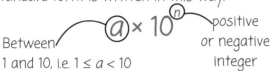

Between 1 and 10, i.e. $1 \leq a < 10$ | $(a) \times 10^{n}$ | positive or negative integer

Converting from standard form to ordinary number:

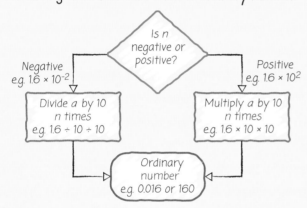

Converting from ordinary number to standard form:

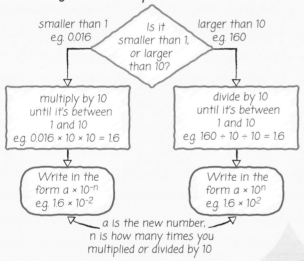

Worked example

Grade **3**

Confidence bar

Write these as ordinary numbers.

a) 5.06×10^{5}
b) 1.7×10^{-3} **[2 marks]**

Solution

a) Multiply by 10 five times:
$5.06 \times 10^{5} = 506\,000$

b) Divide by 10 three times:
$1.7 \times 10^{-3} = 0.0017$

Sorted!

☑

☑

☑

Had a look

Remember this...

A positive power gives a big number.

A negative power gives a small number.

(**not** a negative number)

Worked example

Grade **4**

Write these numbers in standard form.
a) 0.000324 b) $6\,941\,000$ **[2 marks]**

Solution

Work out how many times you need to multiply or divide the number by 10 to get it between 1 and 10

a) You multiply 0.000324 by 10 four times to get 3.24, so $0.000324 = 3.24 \times 10^{-4}$

b) You divide $6\,941\,000$ by 10 six times to get 6.941, so $6\,941\,000 = 6.941 \times 10^{6}$

Exam corner

Grade **4**

1. The length of a bacterial cell is 2.01×10^{-6} metres.
   a) Write the length in metres as an ordinary number. **[I got ___ /1 mark]**
   b) Write the length in centimetres using standard form. **[___ /1 mark]**

2. The average distance between Saturn and Uranus is 1.45×10^{9} km. The average distance between Saturn and Jupiter is $64\,600\,000$ km. Show whether Uranus or Jupiter is closer to Saturn. **[___ /2 marks]**

Grade **4**

Examiner's tip!

Check your answers by doing the reverse, e.g. put ordinary numbers back into standard form.

Calculating with standard form

You need to practise the methods of adding, subtracting, multiplying and dividing numbers in standard form.

Key points

- To add or subtract numbers in standard form, convert to ordinary numbers first.
- To multiply or divide numbers in standard form, regroup then use index laws.

To multiply or divide numbers in standard form:

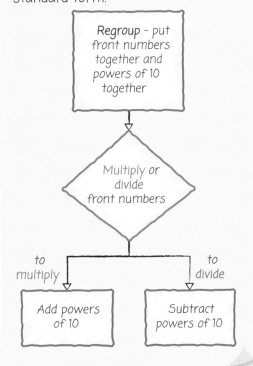

Regroup - put front numbers together and powers of 10 together

Multiply or divide front numbers

to multiply → Add powers of 10

to divide → Subtract powers of 10

Worked example

Calculate the value of
$8.9 \times 10^{-4} - 6 \times 10^{-6}$ **[2 marks]**
Give your answer in standard form.

Solution

$8.9 \times 10^{-4} = 0.00089$

$6 \times 10^{-6} = 0.000006$

$\begin{array}{r} 0.000890 \\ -0.000006 \\ \hline 0.000884 \end{array}$ which is 8.84×10^{-4}

Confidence bar

Sorted!

☑
☑
☐

Had a look

 See page 15 for more on index laws.

Worked example

 Given that
$a = 6 \times 10^5$ and $b = 3 \times 10^{-2}$
calculate the value of
a) ab **[2 marks]**
b) $a \div b$ **[2 marks]**
Give your answers in standard form.

> 18 is not between 1 and 10 so you need to change this further to get standard form.

Solution

a) $ab = (6 \times 10^5) \times (3 \times 10^{-2})$
$= (6 \times 3) \times (10^{5 + (-2)})$
$= 18 \times 10^3$
$= 1.8 \times 10^4$

b) $a \div b = (6 \times 10^5) \div (3 \times 10^{-2})$
$= (6 \div 3) \times (10^{5 - (-2)})$
$= 2 \times 10^7$

Exam corner

1. Calculate the value and give your answers in standard form:
   a) $4.2 \times 10^7 - 6.1 \times 10^6$ **[I got __/3 marks]**
   b) $(9 \times 10^{-7}) \times (8 \times 10^5)$ **[__ /3 marks]**

2. The area of Wales is approximately $2.1 \times 10^4 \, km^2$.
   The population of Wales is approximately 3×10^6.
   Calculate the average area per person, giving your answer as an ordinary number. **[__ /3 marks]**

> In question 1 a), if you're feeling confident, you could write both numbers with the same power of 10, instead of converting into ordinary numbers. Use 10^7

Terms and expressions

Algebra allows you to think about numbers you don't know. To use algebra, you need to be able to write and work with algebraic expressions.

Key points

- An algebraic **expression** is a collection of letters and numbers, e.g. $8 + 7x - 5y$
- Each part of an expression is called a **term**, e.g. 8, $7x$ and $5y$ are terms.
- Write x instead of $1x$
- Write $2x$ instead of $2 \times x$ or $x2$
- Write $\frac{x}{2}$ instead of $x \div 2$
- You find the value of an expression by **substituting** values for each of the letters.

Remember this...

equation

expression   expression

$$8 + 7x - 5y = x - \frac{x}{2}$$

term   term   term   term   term

Confidence bar

Sorted!

☑
☐
☐

Had a look

Worked example

Grade 2

Miguel has p songs on his mobile phone.
Adam has twice as many songs as Miguel.
Josh has 30 more songs than Adam.

a) Write an expression for the number of songs Adam has. **[1 mark]**

b) Write an expression for the number of songs Josh has. **[1 mark]**

Solution

a) Adam has 2 times the number of songs that Miguel has, so the expression is $2p$

b) Josh has 30 more songs than Adam has, so the expression is $2p + 30$

Worked example

Grade 3

Find the value of each of these expressions when $a = 4$, $b = -2$ and $c = 10$

a) $3a - 7$ **[1 mark]**

b) $ab + 2c$ **[2 marks]**

c) $\dfrac{a - b}{2}$ **[2 marks]**

Solution

a) $3a - 7 = 3 \times 4 - 7$
$= 12 - 7$
$= 5$

b) $ab + 2c = 4 \times (-2) + 2 \times 10$
$= -8 + 20$
$= 12$

c) $\dfrac{a - b}{2} = \dfrac{4 - (-2)}{2}$
$= \dfrac{4 + 2}{2}$
$= \dfrac{6}{2}$
$= 3$

Exam corner

Grade 2

1. At a football stadium, burgers cost £4 and pies cost £3
   Sandra buys x burgers and y pies for her family.

   a) Write an expression for the total cost. **[I got ___/1 mark]**

   She pays with a £20 note.

   b) Write an expression for the change she receives. **[___/1 mark]**

Grade 3

2. Find the value of each of these expressions when $s = 8$ and $t = -3$

   a) $5 - s$ **[___/1 mark]**   b) $4s + 5t$ **[___/2 marks]**

   c) $3st$ **[___/2 marks]**

Always start by writing out the expression with the values substituted in.

STRIVE FOR 5   See pages 114–115 for more practice.

Simplifying expressions

You can simplify expressions by collecting terms with the same letter.

Key points

- Terms with the same letter are called **like terms**.
- You can simplify expressions by collecting together and adding or subtracting the like terms.

To simplify an expression, find the like terms:

Remember the + or - sign in front of each term.

This simplifies to **2a + 3b + 4**

Worked example

Grade 2

Shaikha has x apples and y oranges

Jameela has three times as many apples as Shaikha and 5 more oranges.

Write an expression for the total amount of fruit. Give your answer in its simplest form. **[3 marks]**

Solution

Jameela has $3x$ apples and $y + 5$ oranges.

The total amount of fruit is:

This simplifies to $4x + 2y + 5$

Worked example

Grade 3

Simplify
a) $7n - n + 12n$ **[1 mark]**
b) $p - 3q + 5q + 7p$ **[2 marks]**
c) $2ab + 3a^2 - 5ba + 4a^2$ **[2 marks]**

Solution

a) $7n - n + 12n = 18n$

b) $\boxed{p}$ $\left(-3q\right)$ $\left(+5q\right)$ $\boxed{+7p}$

   $p + 7p = 8p$

   $-3q + 5q = 2q$

   The expression simplifies to $8p + 2q$

c) $\boxed{2ab}$ $\left(+3a^2\right)$ $\boxed{-5ba}$ $\left(+4a^2\right)$

   $2ab$ and $5ba$ are like terms (ab and ba mean the same).

   $3a^2$ and $4a^2$ are like terms.

   The expression simplifies to $-3ab + 7a^2$

Exam corner

Grade 2

1. Simplify
   a) $3m - 7m + 8m$ **[I got __/1 mark]**
   b) $7t - s + 3 - t - 4 - 5s$
      [__/3 marks]

2. Write a simplified expression for
   a) the perimeter of the T-shape shown. **[__/2 marks]**

   Grade 4

   b) the area of the T-shape.
      [__/2 marks]

To find the perimeter, add up the lengths of all the sides.

To find the area, multiply length by width for each rectangle then add together.

For more on perimeter and area, see page 73

STRIVE FOR **5** See pages 114–115 for more practice.

Formulae

Formulae can be used to represent real-life situations. You need to be able to substitute numbers into a formula.

Key points

- A **variable** is a letter whose value can change.
- A **constant** is just a number.
- A **formula** (plural formulae) is a rule linking two or more variables with an equals sign.
- A formula can be written in words or using algebra.

formula written in words

$$\text{speed} = \text{distance} \div \text{time}$$

variable   variable   variable

formula written using algebra

$$s = \frac{d}{t}$$

where s = speed, d = distance, t = time

Worked example

Grade 3

A formula for the cost, C, of a boiler repair (in £) is

$$C = 50 + 32t + p$$

where t is the time taken in hours and p is the cost of parts.

Calculate the cost of a boiler repair that takes 2 hours and uses parts that cost a total of £45

[2 marks]

Solution

The question tells you that $t = 2$ and $p = 45$

Substitute these values into the formula:

$C = 50 + 32t + p = 50 + 32 \times 2 + 45$
$ = £159$

Worked example

Grade 3

For each formula, work out the value of y when $x = 3$

a) $y = 5x^2 + 4$ **[2 marks]**
b) $y = x(2x - 1)$ **[2 marks]**

Solution

a) $y = 5x^2 + 4 = 5 \times 3^2 + 4$
$ = 5 \times 9 + 4$
$ = 45 + 4$
$ = 49$

b) $y = x(2x - 1) = 3(2 \times 3 - 1)$
$ = 3(6 - 1)$
$ = 3 \times 5$
$ = 15$

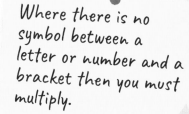

Where there is no symbol between a letter or number and a bracket then you must multiply.

Exam corner

Grade 3

1. Troy gets £7 pocket money per week. He earns an additional £2 per chore he completes.

   Write a formula for P, Troy's total pocket money in a given week, in terms of c, the number of chores completed. **[I got __/2 marks]**

2. A formula for the volume of a square-based pyramid is

   $$V = \frac{l^2 h}{3}$$

   where l is the side length of the base and h is the height of the pyramid. Calculate the volume of a pyramid with $l = 9$ cm and $h = 24$ cm. **[__/2 marks]**

Grade 3

When using a formula, always start by writing out the formula with the values substituted in.

Equations and identities

When using algebra, you need to understand the difference between equations and identities.

Key points

- An **equation** is only true for certain values, e.g. $x + 5 = 8$ is only true for $x = 3$
- An **identity** is true for all values, e.g. $2x + 3x = 5x$ is always true for any value of x, so you can write
$2x + 3x \equiv 5x$ (though $2x + 3x = 5x$ is also fine)

Remember this...

Equation	Identity
$=$	$\equiv$
equal for certain values	equal for all values

Confidence bar

Sorted!

☑

☑

☑

Had a look

Worked example

Grade 4

Decide which of these words best describe each part **a** to **d**:

expression   formula   equation   identity

a) $A = bh$ **[1 mark]**
b) $2x + 5y - 3x = 5y - x$ **[1 mark]**
c) $2x + 7 = 15$ **[1 mark]**
d) $8x + 3y$ **[1 mark]**

See pages 21 and 23 for more on expressions and formulae.

Solution

a) $A = bh$ is a formula; you can substitute the values of b and h and find the value of A

b) $2x + 5y - 3x$ simplifies to $5y - x$, so you could write $2x + 5y - 3x \equiv 5y - x$; it is an identity.

c) $2x + 7 = 15$ is an equation; it is only true for $x = 4$

d) $8x + 3y$ is an expression.

Worked example

Grade 4

Explain whether this identity is true or false.

$$3t^2 + t \equiv 4t^2$$

[2 marks]

Solution

The identity is false, because t and t^2 are not like terms so cannot be simplified in this way.

Exam corner

1. Which of the following are identities?

Grade 4

$3x + 2 + x - 5 = 4x - 3$	$5x - 7 = x + 5$
$2x - 4 - 3x = 5x - 4$	$6 - 2x = -2x + 6$

Try simplifying one side to see if it's the same as the other side.

[I got ___/2 marks]

2. For each part, write down whether it is best described as an expression, a formula, an equation or an identity.

Grade 4

a) $s = ut + \frac{1}{2}at^2$ **b)** $3s - 2t + 4$ **c)** $2s + t = t + 2s$

[___/3 marks]

Functions

A function is an expression that enables you to use an input to calculate an output.

Key points

- A **function** can be written as a formula, e.g. $y = 6x - 4$, or using a **function machine**.
- The function tells you how to find an output (e.g. y) from an input (e.g. x).
- To find the input using a function machine, work backwards and change all the operations.

An example of a function machine for the equation $y = 6x - 4$:

input → $\boxed{\times 6}$ → $\boxed{- 4}$ → output

To work backwards:

input ← $\boxed{\div 6}$ ← $\boxed{+ 4}$ ← output

Confidence bar

Sorted!

☑

☑

☑

Had a look

Worked example

Grade 2

Here is a function machine.

$x →$ $\boxed{\times 2}$ → $\boxed{+ 7}$ → y

a) Work out the value of y when $x = 7$

[1 mark]

b) Work out the value of x when $y = 15$

[2 marks]

c) Write down a formula for y in terms of x

[1 mark]

Solution

a) Put $x = 7$ into the machine.

$7 →$ $\boxed{\times 2}$ → 14 → $\boxed{+ 7}$ → 21 So, $y = 21$

b) Put $y = 15$ into the machine and work backwards, remembering to change all the operations.

$4 ←$ $\boxed{\div 2}$ ← 8 ← $\boxed{- 7}$ ← 15 So, $x = 4$

c) $y = 2x + 7$

Exam corner

1. Here is a function machine

$x →$ $\boxed{- 5}$ → $\boxed{\square 3}$ → y

Given that $y = 12$ when $x = 9$,

Grade 2

a) write the missing symbol in the function machine

[I got __/1 mark]

b) work out the value of y when $x = 3$

[__/1 mark]

c) work out the value of x when $y = 6$

[__/2 marks]

d) write down a formula for y in terms of x

[__/1 mark]

2. Here is a number machine.

Grade 3

input → $\boxed{+ 4}$ → $\boxed{\div 3}$ → $\boxed{- 13}$ → output

a) Find the output when the input is 17

[__/2 marks]

b) Find the input when the output is −12

[__/2 marks]

c) Write down the output when the input is x

[__/2 marks]

A function machine can also be called a number machine.

Examiner's tip!

Remember that your working can gain you some marks even if the final answer is wrong. So always write out each step of your working.

Solving linear equations

An equation such as $3x + 1 = 7$ is called a linear equation. You can solve it to find x using the balance method.

Key point

Use the **balance method** to solve equations.

This means always doing the same thing to both sides of the equation.

To solve the equation $3x + 1 = 7$:

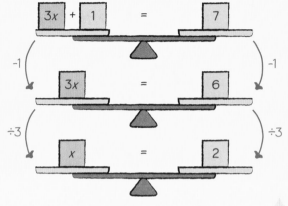

The solution is $x = 2$

Confidence bar

Sorted!

Had a look

Worked example

Solve

a) $\frac{a}{7} = 9$ **[1 mark]**

b) $b - 12 = -3$ **[1 mark]**

c) $5c + 17 = 32$ **[2 marks]**

Solution

a) $\frac{a}{7} = 9$

$\frac{a}{7} \times 7 = 9 \times 7$ Multiply both sides by 7

$a = 63$

b) $b - 12 = -3$

$b - 12 + 12 = -3 + 12$ Add 12 to both sides.

$b = 9$

c) $5c + 17 = 32$

$5c + 17 - 17 = 32 - 17$ Subtract 17 from both sides.

$5c = 15$

$\frac{5c}{5} = \frac{15}{5}$ Divide both sides by 5

$c = 3$ You can check your solution by substituting back into the original equation.

$5 \times 3 + 17 = 15 + 17 = 32$ ✓

Grade 2

Worked example

Grade 4

A workshop produces two types of toy: model cars and model boats.

In one hour, it produces 4 model cars and x model boats. If it produces 72 toys total in an 8-hour day, form an equation and find the number of model boats it makes in 1 hour.   **[4 marks]**

Solution

$(8 \times 4) + (8 \times x) = 72$ The workshop produces $4 + x$ toys in 1 hour, so multiply this by 8 for the number of toys in 8 hours.

$32 + 8x = 72$ Simplify the equation.

$8x = 40$ Subtract 32 from both sides.

$x = 5$ Divide both sides by 5

So it makes 5 model boats in 1 hour.

Exam corner

Grade 3

Grade 4

1. Solve

   a) $13x = -65$ **[I got__/1 mark]**

   b) $\frac{m}{5} = 11$ **[__/1 mark]**

   c) $3y + 7 = 31$ **[__/2 marks]**

   d) $6p + 15 = 3$ **[__/2 marks]**

 2. Esme earns £9 per hour in a cafe. One day she works for h hours and receives £18 in tips. Her total pay for the day is £58.50

Form an equation and solve it to find the number of hours Esme worked.   **[__/3 marks]**

STRIVE FOR 5 See pages 114–115 for more practice.

Harder linear equations

The balance method works for solving harder linear equations like $2x + 5 = 8 + x$

To solve the equation $2x + 5 = 8 + x$:

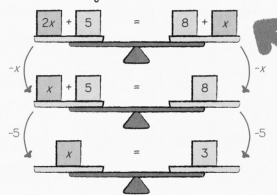

The solution is $x = 3$

Key points

- If an equation has an unknown term on both sides, first change the equation so the unknown term appears on only one side.
- If an equation involves a fraction, multiply both sides by its denominator.

Confidence bar

Sorted!

Had a look

Worked example

Grade 4

Solve $\frac{3 - 2x}{4} = x$ **[3 marks]**

Solution

$\frac{3 - 2x}{4} \times 4 = x \times 4$ Multiply both sides by the denominator.

$3 - 2x = 4x$

$3 - 2x + 2x = 4x + 2x$ Add $2x$ to both sides.

$3 = 6x$

$\frac{3}{6} = \frac{6x}{6}$ Divide both sides by 6

$\frac{1}{2} = x$

This is the same as writing $x = \frac{1}{2}$

Worked example

Grade 5

The square and the triangle have the same perimeter.

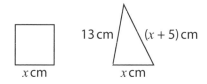

13 cm $(x + 5)$ cm

x cm x cm

Form an equation and solve it to find the value of x **[4 marks]**

Solution

Perimeter of square = $4x$

Perimeter of triangle = $x + (x + 5) + 13 = 2x + 18$

The equation is $4x = 2x + 18$

$4x - 2x = 2x - 2x + 18$ Subtract $2x$

$2x = 18$

$\frac{2x}{2} = \frac{18}{2}$ Divide by 2

$x = 9$

Exam corner

Grade 4

1. Solve

   a) $3x + 6 = 20 - 4x$ **[I got ___/2 marks]**

   b) $\frac{x + 6}{5} = 8$ **[___/2 marks]**

   c) $\frac{3x}{4} - 3 = 9$ **[___/2 marks]**

2. Lucy thinks of a number, multiplies it by 4 and adds 15. The result is the same as when she subtracts her original number from 5

   Form and solve an equation to find Lucy's number.   **[___/3 marks]**

Grade 5

Start by adding 3 to both sides of the equation, so the fraction is on its own on one side of the equation.

STRIVE FOR 5 — See pages 114-115 for more practice

Rearranging formulae

A formula can be rearranged to make a different letter the **subject**. The subject of an equation is a variable that sits by itself on either the left or right-hand side of the equals sign.

Key points

Rearranging a formula is very similar to solving an equation.

You can use the **balance method** to get the letter you want as the **subject** on its own.

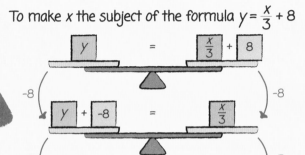

To make x the subject of the formula $y = \frac{x}{3} + 8$

The answer is $x = 3y - 24$

Confidence bar

Sorted!

 ✓

 ✓

☐

Had a look

Worked example

Grade **4**

Rearrange $v = u + 3a$ to make

a) u the subject   **[1 mark]**

b) a the subject.   **[2 marks]**

Solution

a) $v = u + 3a$

   $v - 3a = u + 3a - 3a$ Subtract 3a from both sides.

   $v - 3a = u$

   which you can also write as $u = v - 3a$

b) $v = u + 3a$

   $v - u = u - u + 3a$ Subtract u from both sides.

   $v - u = 3a$

   $\dfrac{v - u}{3} = \dfrac{3a}{3}$ Divide both sides by 3

   $\dfrac{v - u}{3} = a$

   which you can also write as

   $a = \dfrac{v - u}{3}$

Worked example

Grade **5**

Rearrange $y = 2\sqrt{x} - 5$ to make x the subject.   **[3 marks]**

Solution

$y + 5 = 2\sqrt{x} - 5 + 5$ Add 5 to both sides.

$y + 5 = 2\sqrt{x}$

$\dfrac{y + 5}{2} = \dfrac{2\sqrt{x}}{2}$ Divide both sides by 2

$\dfrac{y + 5}{2} = \sqrt{x}$

$\left(\dfrac{y + 5}{2}\right)^2 = (\sqrt{x})^2$ Square both sides.

$\left(\dfrac{y + 5}{2}\right)^2 = x$ You can re-write as…

$x = \left(\dfrac{y + 5}{2}\right)^2$

Exam corner

Grade **4**

1. Rearrange each of these formulae to make x the subject.

   a) $y = 7x + 2$ **[I got __/2 marks]**

   b) $y = \dfrac{3x + z}{4}$ **[__/3 marks]**   **c)** $y = 4 - x$ **[__/2 marks]**

2. You are given the formula $E = \frac{1}{2}ms^2$.

   s represents the speed of a particle.

Grade **5**

   a) Rearrange the formula to make s the subject.   **[__/3 marks]**

   b) Calculate the speed of the particle when $E = 8$ and $m = 4$ **[__/2 marks]**

Examiner's tip!

STRIVE FOR **5**

Check your answer by substituting it into the original formula.

Here, substitute your answer for s, along with $m = 4$. If you get $E = 8$ then your value is correct.

STRIVE FOR **5** See pages 114–115 for more practice.

Expanding single brackets

A number or letter directly in front of a bracket is multiplied by all the terms inside the brackets. This is called **expanding** the brackets.

Key points

- To expand single brackets, multiply each term inside the brackets by the term in front of the bracket.
- If there is a letter in front of the bracket, use the laws of indices to simplify.

$$5(3x + 4) = 15x + 20$$

Or you can use a multiplication grid:

×	3x	4
5	15x	20

Confidence bar

Sorted!

Had a look

Worked example

Grade 3

Expand

a) $4(3a - 7)$ **[1 mark]**

b) $b(1 + 5b)$ **[1 mark]**

Solution

a) Work out each multiplication:

$4 \times 3a = 12a$

and $4 \times -7 = -28$

$4(3a - 7) = 12a - 28$

> Be careful to include the negative sign in the answer.

b) Work out each multiplication:

$b \times 1 = b$

and $b \times 5b = 5b^2$

$b(1 + 5b) = b + 5b^2$

> 📄 See page 15 for the laws of indices.

Worked example

Grade 4

Expand and simplify fully

$x(2x + y) - 3y(1 - x)$ **[3 marks]**

Solution

Expand each pair of brackets:

$x(2x + y) = 2x^2 + xy$

$-3y(1 - x) = -3y + 3xy$

Now simplify by collecting like terms:

$2x^2 \boxed{+ xy} - 3y \boxed{+ 3xy} = 2x^2 + 4xy - 3y$

The expression is now fully simplified.

> Remember that 'like terms' must contain all the same letters **and** all the same indices.
>
> For example, x and $5x$ are like terms, but x and x^2 are not, because the indices are different.
>
> p^2q and $\dfrac{p^2q}{3}$ are like terms, but p^2 and $\dfrac{p^2q}{3}$ are not because they don't both contain q

Exam corner

1. Expand the brackets in each expression   **Grade 3**

    a) $5(2x + 4)$ **[I got __/1 mark]**

    b) $x(3x - 1)$ **[__/2 marks]**

2. This shape is made up of two rectangles. Show that the area is given by the expression $4xy + 20x$ **[__/4 marks]**   **Grade 4**

x

$y - 1$

$3x$

$y + 7$

> Use brackets to write an expression for the area of each rectangle first.

Factorising into single brackets

You can sometimes **factorise** an expression by finding the **common factor** of all the terms. The common factor can be a number or letters, or both.

Grade

4–5

Key points

- Factorising is the opposite of expanding brackets.
- You can factorise an expression by writing the HCF in front of the brackets then working out what must go inside.

See page 29 for expanding brackets.

Confidence bar

Sorted!

Had a look

Worked example

Grade 4

Factorise these expressions fully.

a) $6x + 9y$ **[1 mark]**

b) $15xy^2 - 5x^3y$ **[2 marks]**

Solution

a) The HCF of $6x$ and $9y$ is 3, so this goes in front of the brackets:

$$3(\bigcirc + \bigcirc)$$

Needs to multiply by 3 to give $6x$ Needs to multiply by 3 to give $9y$

The solution is $3(2x + 3y)$

b) The HCF of $15xy^2 - 5x^3y$ is $5xy$, so put this in a grid:

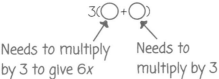

$\times$		
$5xy$	$15xy^2$	$-5x^3y$

Now work out what goes in the top row:

$\times$	$3y$	$-x^2$
$5xy$	$15xy^2$	$-5x^3y$

The solution is $5xy(3y - x^2)$

You can use a multiplication grid to help with factorising trickier expressions.

Identify the highest common factor (HCF) and use this to complete the terms in the top row.

- You could also factorise this as $5(3xy^2 - x^3y)$ or as $xy(15y - 5x^2)$ but these would not be 'fully factorised', so you would lose a mark.

- Expand the brackets to check your answer.

$$5xy(3y - x^2) = 15xy^2 - 5x^3y$$

Exam corner

Grade 4

1. Factorise these expressions fully.

   a) $6x - 2x^2$ **b)** $14ab + 21a^2$

   c) $xy^2z + xy^2z^2 + xy^2$ **[I got__/6 marks]**

2. A rectangle has area $12t^2 - 9t$

   Write down possible expressions for the length and the width of the rectangle.   **[__/2 marks]**

Grade 5

Write the area as the product of two factors.

Expanding double brackets

Grade 4

You need to be able to expand double brackets such as $(x + 1)(x - 2)$. This means multiplying the two expressions to get rid of the brackets.

Key points

- To expand double brackets, multiply both terms in the first set of brackets by both terms in the second set of brackets.
- You will get four terms, which you should then simplify if possible.

 See page 29 for expanding single brackets.

Remember this...

You can use the FOIL method to expand double brackets:

First - multiply the First term in each bracket.
Outer - multiply the Outer two terms.
Inner - multiply the Inner two terms.
Last - multiply the Last term in each bracket.

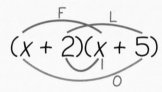

$$(x + 2)(x + 5)$$

It looks like a smiling face with big eyebrows.

Confidence bar

Sorted!

☑
☑
☑

Had a look

Worked example

Expand and simplify.

a) $(x + 2)(x + 5)$ **[2 marks]**
b) $(3 + y)(1 - y)$ **[2 marks]**
c) $(x + y)^2$ **[2 marks]**

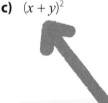

This is NOT $x^2 + y^2$.
Write as $(x + y)(x + y)$ then expand in the usual way.

Grade 4

Solution

a)
$$(x + 2)(x + 5) = x^2 + \underbrace{5x + 2x}_{\text{simplify these}} + 10$$
$$= x^2 + 7x + 10$$

b) If you prefer, you can use a multiplication grid:

×	3	+y
1	3	y
-y	-3y	-y²

$$(3 + y)(1 - y) = 3 + y - 3y - y^2$$
$$= 3 - 2y - y^2$$

c)
$$(x + y)(x + y) = x^2 + \underbrace{xy + yx}_{\text{these are like terms}} + y^2$$
$$(x + y)^2 = x^2 + 2xy + y^2$$

Exam corner

Grade 4

Expand the brackets and simplify if possible.

a) $(a + 1)(b + 2)$ b) $(x + 3)(x - 4)$ c) $(2x - 1)(3x - 2)$ d) $(3x + 2)^2$

[I got___/8 marks]

31

Factorising into double brackets

Expressions of the form $x^2 + bx + c$ can sometimes be factorised using a double set of brackets.

See page 31 for how to expand double brackets.

Grade 5

Confidence bar

Sorted!

☑

☑

☐

Had a look

Key points

To factorise an expression $x^2 + bx + c$:

STEP 1: Draw brackets and write x in each: $(x \quad)(x \quad)$

STEP 2: Find two numbers (positive or negative) **that add to give b and multiply to give c.**

STEP 3: Write these numbers in, then check your answer by expanding the brackets.

To factorise $x^2 + 2x - 15$,

find two numbers that add to give 2 and multiply to give -15

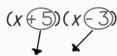

$$(x + 5)(x - 3)$$

$$5 + (-3) = 2$$
$$5 \times (-3) = -15$$

Exam corner

Grade 5

1. Factorise these expressions.

   a) $x^2 + 9x + 14$ [I got __/1 mark]

   b) $x^2 + 8x - 20$ [__/2 marks]

   c) $x^2 - 3x - 18$ [__/2 marks]

   d) $x^2 - 10x + 9$ [__/2 marks]

2. The area of a square is given by **Grade 5**

   $$x^2 - 10x + 25$$

   Find an expression for the length of one side of the square. [__/2 marks]

Examiner's tip!

Watch out for questions like Question 2 about factorisation: they're sometimes disguised. Here you need to factorise the expression you've been given to find the length of each side.

Worked example

Grade 5

Factorise

a) $x^2 + 7x + 12$ **b)** $x^2 + 2x - 3$ **[4 marks]**

Solution

a) Start with the brackets: $(x \quad)(x \quad)$

You need two numbers that multiply to give 12:

1 and 12   or   2 and 6   or   3 and 4

Think whether any of these pairs add to give 7:

$3 + 4 = 7$

So, $x^2 + 7x + 12 = (x + 3)(x + 4)$

b) You can use a multiplication grid if you prefer.

Put in the terms you know. Then you need two numbers that multiply to give -3:

-1 and 3   or   1 and -3

Try filling in a grid with these pairs:

×	x	-3
x	x^2	$-3x$
1	x	-3

or

×	x	3
x	x^2	$3x$
-1	$-x$	-3

The first grid gives $x^2 - 3x + x - 3$ which simplifies to $x^2 - 2x - 3$ ✗

The second grid gives $x^2 + 3x - x - 3$ which simplifies to $x^2 + 2x - 3$ ✔

So, $x^2 + 2x - 3 = (x + 3)(x - 1)$

Difference of two squares

If you have an expression such as $x^2 - 9$ where both terms are square numbers and one is negative, then this is called the **difference of two squares**.

Key points

- An expression of the form $a^2 - b^2$ is the difference of two squares (DOTS).
- You can factorise it as $(a + b)(a - b)$
- When you multiply out the brackets, the middle terms, $-ba$ and $+ab$, cancel out. This leaves just two squared terms, $a^2 - b^2$

Checklist for factorising quadratic expressions:

1. Are there two terms, and do they have a common factor?

   If yes: single brackets. E.g. $x^2 + 3x = x(x + 3)$

2. Are there 3 terms, one of which includes x^2?

   If yes: double brackets. E.g. $x^2 + 6x + 5 = (x + 5)(x + 1)$

3. Are there two terms with a minus sign, and they're both square numbers?

   If yes: two brackets containing square roots. E.g. $x^2 - 16 = (x + 4)(x - 4)$

See pages 30 and 32 for more on these types of factorising.

Worked example

Grade 5

Factorise $x^2 - 9$ **[1 mark]**

Solution

x^2 and 9 are both square terms, so this is DOTS.

The square root of x^2 is x

The square root of 9 is 3

So, write these in the brackets, one with + and one with –

$x^2 - 9 = (x + 3)(x - 3)$

Exam corner

Grade 5

Factorise these expressions fully.

a) $x^2 - 100$ **[I got __/1 mark]**

b) $x^2 + 8x$ **[__/1 mark]**

c) $49x^2 - 1$ **[__/1 mark]**

d) $x^2 - 8x + 15$ **[__/2 marks]**

e) $24x - 12x^2$ **[__/1 mark]**

f) $x^2 - y^2$ **[__/1 mark]**

Worked example

Grade 5

Factorise these expressions fully.

a) $x^2 - 3x + 2$ **[2 marks]**

b) $5x^2 - 15x$ **[2 marks]**

c) $x^2 - 25$ **[1 mark]**

Solution

a) This has three terms including x^2, so use double brackets.

   Think of two numbers that multiply to give 2 and add to give -3:

   $(-2) \times (-1) = 2$ and $(-2) + (-1) = -3$

   $x^2 - 3x + 2 = (x - 2)(x - 1)$

b) This has two terms with common factors, so use single brackets.

   The HCF of $5x^2$ and $15x$ is $5x$

   $5x^2 - 15x = 5x(x - 3)$

c) Both x^2 and 25 are square terms and there's a minus sign, so it is DOTS.

   The square root of x^2 is x and the square root of 25 is 5

   $x^2 - 25 = (x - 5)(x - 5)$

Solving quadratic equations

You need to know how to solve quadratic equations by factorising.

Grade 5

See page 33 to recap the different ways of factorising.

Key points

- Quadratic equations are equations that contain an x^2 term. Examples are:
  $$x^2 - 4x = 0 \qquad x^2 + 2x + 1 = 0 \qquad x^2 - 9 = 0$$
- You can sometimes solve quadratic equations to find x by factorising.

Confidence bar

Sorted!

☑

☑

☑

Had a look

Solving quadratic equations by factorising

$$x^2 + 6x - 7 = 0$$

$$(x + 7)(x - 1) = 0$$

$$x + 7 = 0 \quad \text{or} \quad x - 1 = 0$$

$$x = -7 \quad \text{or} \quad x = 1$$

You are asked to solve a quadratic, e.g. $x^2 + 6x = 7$

↓

Rearrange the equation to get zero on one side

↓

Factorise into single or double brackets

↓

Put each factor equal to zero, e.g. $x + 7 = 0$ or $x - 1 = 0$

↓

Write down the two values of x

Exam corner

Grade 5

Solve each of these quadratic equations.

a) $x^2 + 6x + 8 = 0$

[I got ___/3 marks]

b) $x^2 - 121 = 0$

[___/2 marks]

c) $2x^2 - 6x = 0$

[___/3 marks]

d) $x^2 + x = 12$

[___/4 marks]

Remember to rearrange the equation to get zero on one side.

Worked example

Grade 5

Solve each of these quadratic equations.

a) $x^2 - 5x + 6 = 0$ **[3 marks]**

b) $3x^2 + 12x = 0$ **[3 marks]**

c) $x^2 - 64 = 0$ **[2 marks]**

Solution

a) $x^2 - 5x + 6 = 0$

   $(x - 3)(x - 2) = 0$ Factorise into double brackets.

   $x - 3 = 0$ or $x - 2 = 0$ Put each factor equal to zero.

     $x = 3$ or $x = 2$

b) $3x^2 + 12x = 0$ Notice the common factor in both terms.

   $3x(x + 4) = 0$ Factorise into single brackets.

   $3x = 0$ or $x + 4 = 0$ Put each factor equal to zero.

     $x = 0$ or $x = -4$

c) $x^2 - 64 = 0$

   $(x + 8)(x - 8) = 0$ DOTS

   $x + 8 = 0$ or $x - 8 = 0$ Put each factor equal to zero.

     $x = -8$ or $x = 8$

Simultaneous equations 1

Two equations involving two variables (such as x and y) that you want to solve together (to find x and y) are called **simultaneous equations**.

Key points

You can use the **elimination method** to solve simultaneous equations:

STEP 1: Number the equations (1) and (2).

STEP 2: Multiply one or both equations (if necessary) by a number.

STEP 3: Add or subtract the equations to eliminate one of the variables.

STEP 4: Solve your new equation to find the value of one variable.

STEP 5: Substitute this value into one of the original equations. Solve to find the other variable.

Confidence bar

Sorted!

Had a look

At **STEP 3**, use the STOP method:

Same Take Opposite Plus

If the signs are the Same then Take away (i.e. subtract the equations).

If the signs are Opposite then Plus (i.e. add the equations).

For example, look at the sign before 2y in these equations:

Same so Take	Opposite so Plus
$5x + 2y = 16$ (1)	$5x + 2y = 16$ (1)
$3x + 2y = 12$ (2)	$3x - 2y = 12$ (2)
(1) – (2): $2x = 4$	(1) + (2): $8x = 28$

📄 See page 43 for how graphs can be used to solve simultaneous equations.

Worked example

Solve this pair of simultaneous equations.

$2x + 3y = 25$

$6x - 2y = -2$ **[3 marks]**

Solution

STEP 1: $\quad 2x + 3y = 25$ (1)

$\qquad (6x) - 2y = -2$ (2)

STEP 2: Multiply equation (1) by 3:

$\qquad (6x) + 9y = 75$ (3)

STEP 3: Now there is a $6x$ term in both equations (2) and (3). There's no sign in front of the $6x$ terms which means the signs are positive, so the signs are the Same and you Take away:

$\qquad$ (3) – (2): $11y = 77$

STEP 4: Solve to give $y = 7$

STEP 5: Substitute into equation (1): $2x + 21 = 25$

$\qquad$ Solve to give $x = 2$

Examiner's tip!

STRIVE FOR 5

Always check your values of x and y by substituting into the original equations.

Exam corner

Solve the simultaneous equations.

a) $\quad x + 4y = 48$

$\quad 3x + 4y = 56$ **[I got __/3 marks]**

b) $\quad x + 2y = 11$

$\quad -3x + 5y = 44$ **[__/3 marks]**

STRIVE FOR 5 See pages 114–115 for more practice.

Simultaneous equations 2

You may be given information and have to work out what the simultaneous equations are, so that you can solve them.

Key points

- To form simultaneous equations from a word-based problem, first give a letter to each of the variables.
- Use the elimination method to solve the equations.
- Give the values of the variables in the context of the question.

See page 35 for the elimination method.

Confidence bar

Sorted!

Had a look

Worked example

Grade 5

The cost of 3 adult tickets and 2 child tickets to a theme park is £155.

The cost of 2 adult tickets and 5 child tickets is £195.

a) Form a pair of simultaneous equations to describe this situation. **[2 marks]**

b) Solve your equations to find the cost of an adult ticket and the cost of a child ticket. **[4 marks]**

Solution

a) Use a = cost of adult ticket and c = cost of child ticket.

The equations are $3a + 2c = 155$ (1)

and $2a + 5c = 195$ (2)

b) Multiply (1) by 2: $\quad 6a + 4c = 310$ (3)

Multiply (2) by 3: $\quad 6a + 15c = 585$ (4)

Both of the $6a$ terms are positive, so subtract the equations.

(4) − (3): $11c = 275$

$\qquad c = 25$

Substitute into equation (1): $3a + 50 = 155$

$\qquad\qquad 3a = 105$ so $a = 35$

The cost of an adult ticket is £35 and the cost of a child ticket is £25

> You could have multiplied (1) by 5 and (2) by 2 to get the same number of c in each equation instead.

> Remember STOP:
> Same Take Opposite Plus

Examiner's tip!

STRIVE FOR 5

Remember to relate your answer back to the original question.

Exam corner

Grade 5

1. The perimeter of the rectangle is 28 cm and the perimeter of the triangle is 22 cm.

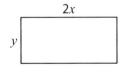

a) Form a pair of simultaneous equations. **[I got __/2 marks]**

b) Find the value of x and y. **[__/3 marks]**

Grade 5

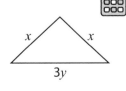

2. The cost of 5 bottles of milk and 2 packs of cheese is £10.30
The cost of 2 bottles of milk and 3 packs of cheese is £10.94
Form and solve simultaneous equations to find the price of a bottle of milk and the price of a pack of cheese. **[__/5 marks]**

See pages 114–115 for more practice.

STRIVE FOR 5

Solving inequalities

In an **inequality**, the left-hand side is not necessarily equal to the right-hand side but can be less than or greater than it. The solution to an inequality is usually a range of values.

Key points

- You can solve an inequality by treating the inequality sign like an equals sign and using the balance method.
- The one difference to remember: do not multiply or divide by a negative number because this would affect the direction of the inequality sign.
- The solution to an inequality can be shown on a number line.

See pages 26 & 27 for the balance method.

Confidence bar

Sorted!

☑

☐

☑

Had a look

A hollow circle shows that the number is <u>not</u> included.

A filled-in circle shows that the number <u>is</u> included.

Remember this...

If the x is on the Little side of the inequality, the arrow points Left. If the x is on the wide side, it points right.

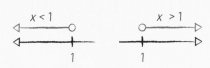

Exam corner

Grade **4**

1. **a)** Show the solutions to $0 < x \le 3$ on a number line.

    [I got ___ /2 marks]

   b) Write down all the possible integer values of x

    [___ /1 mark]

2. Solve these inequalities and display the solutions on number lines.

   Grade **5**

   a) $x + 9 > 12$ **[___/2 marks]**

   b) $-3x \le 12$ **[___/3 marks]**

   c) $2x + 13 \ge 25$ **[___/3 marks]**

Don't divide by a negative number! Instead, add 3x to both sides.

Worked example

Grade **5**

Solve this inequality and display the solution on a number line.

$8 - 2x > 12$ **[3 marks]**

Solution

$8 - 2x + 2x > 12 + 2x$ You want the 2x term to be positive.

$8 > 12 + 2x$

$8 - 12 > 12 - 12 + 2x$

$-4 > 2x$

$\dfrac{-4}{2} > \dfrac{2x}{2}$

$-2 > x$

which you can also write as $x < -2$
Note -2 is not included so leave the circle hollow.

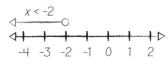

Drawing linear graphs

A **linear** graph is a straight line, which can be vertical, horizontal or sloping.

Key points

- The equation of a graph is a rule that is true for all the points on the graph.
- You can use a table of values to find points on the graph.
- Equations such as $y = 3$ are horizontal lines.
- Equations such as $x = 3$ are vertical lines.
- Equations such as $y = x$ and $y = 2x + 5$ are sloping lines.

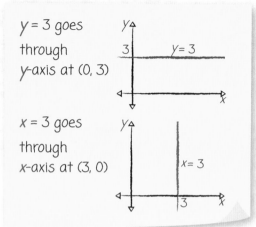

$y = 3$ goes through y-axis at $(0, 3)$

$x = 3$ goes through x-axis at $(3, 0)$

See page 40 for $y = mx + c$, the equation of a straight line.

Confidence bar

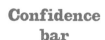
Sorted!

Had a look

Try starting from the right and spotting the pattern.

Exam corner

Grade 2

1. Draw the graph of   **a)** $x = 4$ **b)** $y = 1$

   [I got __/2 marks]

2. **a)** Fill in the table of values for $y = 3x + 1$

   [__/2 marks]

x	−1	0	1	2
y			4	

   Grade 3

   b) Draw an x-axis from −3 to 3 and a y-axis from −3 to 9. Draw the graph of $y = 3x + 1$ **[__/2 marks]**

If your points don't lie on a line, then you know one of them is wrong!

These are coordinates. The first number is the x-value and the second number is the y-value.

Worked example

Grade 3

a) Fill in the table of values for the equation

$y = 2x - 3$ **[2 marks]**

x	−2	−1	0	1
y		−5		

b) Draw the graph of $y = 2x - 3$ **[2 marks]**

Solution

a) Substitute the values of x into the equation to find y

When $x = -2$, $y = 2 \times (-2) - 3 = -7$

When $x = 0$, $y = 2 \times 0 - 3 = -3$

When $x = 1$, $y = 2 \times 1 - 3 = -1$

x	−2	−1	0	1
y	-7	-5	-3	-1

b) Plot each of the points from the table:

$(-2, -7)$, $(-1, -5)$, $(0, -3)$ and $(1, -1)$

Use a ruler to draw a straight line through all the points.

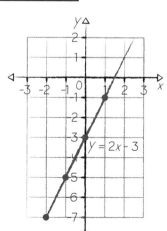

Finding gradients

You need to be able to calculate the gradient of a straight line.

Key points

- The **gradient** of a straight line is a measure of its slope.
  Find two points on the line where you can read the exact coordinates, then:

  $$\text{Gradient} = \frac{\text{vertical change}}{\text{horizontal change}}$$

- A line through the origin with gradient m has equation $y = mx$

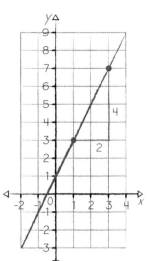

Gradient $= \dfrac{4}{2} = 2$

Remember this...

A gradient can be positive or negative.

uphill   *downhill*

Positive gradient   **N**egative gradient

when you **P**ush uphill   points downhill

Worked example

a) Calculate the gradient of this line.

[1 mark]

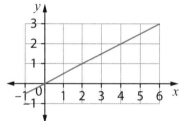

b) Write down the equation of the line.

[1 mark]

Solution

a) Find two points where you can read the exact coordinates

$$\text{Gradient} = \frac{\text{vertical change}}{\text{horizontal change}} = \frac{1}{2}$$

b) Equation is $y = \frac{1}{2}x$ or $y = 0.5x$

Exam corner

Calculate the gradient of each of these lines and write down its equation.   **[I got __/4 marks]**

a)   **b)**

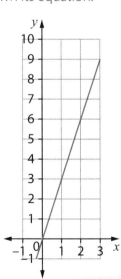

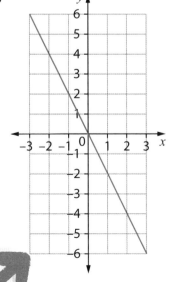

Watch out!
This line has a negative gradient.

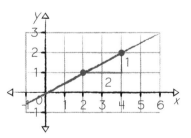
See page 40 for more on equations of lines.

Equation of a straight line

You need to be able to work out the equation of a straight line, and identify the gradient and y-intercept from an equation.

Key points

- A straight line has equation $y = mx + c$ where m is the gradient of the line, c is the **y-intercept** (the number where the line crosses the y-axis).
- Parallel lines have the same gradient.

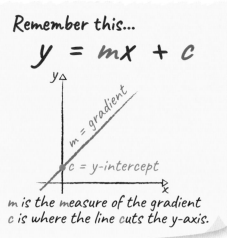

Remember this...

$$y = mx + c$$

m is the measure of the gradient
c is where the line cuts the y-axis.

Confidence bar

Sorted!

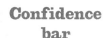

Had a look

Worked example
Grade 4

A line has equation $2y + 6 = 4x$. Work out the gradient and the y-intercept of the line. **[3 marks]**

Solution

Rearrange the equation so it's in the form $y = mx + c$:

$2y + 6 - 6 = 4x - 6$

$2y = 4x - 6$

$\frac{2y}{2} = \frac{4x - 6}{2}$

$y = 2x - 3$

The gradient is 2 and the y-intercept is -3

Worked example
Grade 5

A line passes through the points (1, 2) and (4, −7). Work out the equation of the line. **[3 marks]**

Solution

First, draw a sketch to find the gradient.

(1, 2)
−9
(4, −7)
3

Gradient = $\frac{\text{change in } y}{\text{change in } x}$

$= \frac{-9}{3} = -3$

> See page 39 for more on calculating gradients.

So far, you know the equation is $y = -3x + c$

To find the value of c, substitute the coordinate pair (1, 2) into the equation:

$2 = -3 \times 1 + c$
$2 = -3 + c$
$c = 5$

The equation is $y = -3x + 5$

> A line sloping from top left down to bottom right will have a negative gradient.

Exam corner

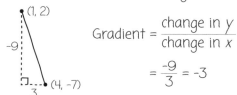

> Parallel lines have the same gradient, so rearrange each equation to find the gradient of the line.

Grade 4

1. The equations of four lines are given:

   $y = 5x + 1$ $y + 5x = 3$ $2y = 10x - 1$ $2y + 1 = 5x$

   a) Which two lines are parallel?   **[I got ___/2 marks]**

   b) Which two lines have the same y-intercept?   **[___/2 marks]**

2. Work out the equation of each of these lines.

   a) A line that passes through the point (0, −3) and has gradient 5 **[___/1 mark]**

   b) A line that passes through the points (0, 5) and (4, 7)   **[___/3 marks]**

   c) A line that passes through the points (1, 3) and (2, 1)   **[___/4 marks]**

Grade 5

Examiner's tip!

A sketch of the line will help you answer questions like these.

Kinematic graphs

You need to be able to draw and interpret graphs involving speed, distance and time.

Key points

On a **distance–time** graph,
- the gradient is the speed.

On a **speed–time** graph,
- the gradient is the acceleration.

 See page 56 for more on speed, distance and time.

Interpreting the gradient...

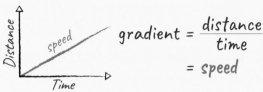

$$\text{gradient} = \frac{\text{distance}}{\text{time}}$$
$$= \text{speed}$$

$$\text{gradient} = \frac{\text{speed}}{\text{time}}$$
$$= \text{acceleration}$$

Worked example

Sophie drives a total of 14 km to work.
- She travels the first 6 km at a constant speed of 36 km/h
- She then stops for 5 minutes at roadworks.
- It takes her 15 minutes to complete the rest of the journey at a constant speed.

Draw a distance–time graph of the journey. **[4 marks]**

Solution

Work out time taken to travel first 6 km, using the formula Time = Distance ÷ Speed

Time = $6 \div 36 = \frac{1}{6}$ hr = 10 min

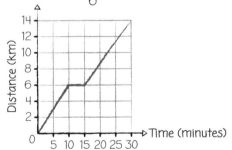

Worked example

The graph shows the speed of an object after t seconds.

a) Write down the speed of the object after 2 seconds. **[1 mark]**

b) When does the object start decelerating? **[1 mark]**

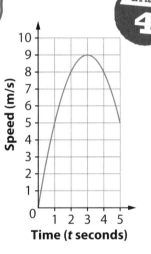

Solution

a) From the graph, you can see that after 2 seconds, speed = 8 m/s

 negative acceleration is called **deceleration**

b) The gradient of the graph is the acceleration. The gradient is negative after 3 seconds. Therefore, the object starts decelerating after 3 seconds.

Exam corner

The distance–time graph shows how a snail moved one morning.

a) How far did the snail move in total? **[I got __/1 mark]**

b) What was its speed in m/h between 09:00 and 09:30? **[__/2 marks]**

c) What was the snail doing between 09:30 and 10:15? **[__/1 mark]**

d) Draw a speed–time graph to show the same information. **[__/3 marks]**

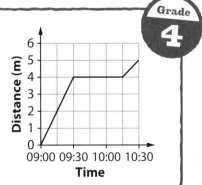

Quadratic graphs

You need to be able to draw and interpret quadratic graphs.

Key points

- A **quadratic** graph has equation
  $$y = ax^2 + bx + c$$
  where a, b and c are numbers.
- The x-intercepts give the **roots** (the solutions) of
  $$ax^2 + bx + c = 0$$
- The **turning point** of the graph is the maximum or minimum.

Quadratic graphs:

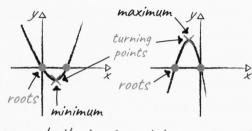

$\times$ marks the turning points

Confidence bar

Sorted!

Had a look

Worked example

Grade
5

Here is the graph of $y = x^2 + 2x - 1$

a) Write down the coordinates of the turning point of $y = x^2 + 2x - 1$ **[1 mark]**

b) Write down estimates for the roots of $x^2 + 2x - 1 = 0$ **[2 marks]**

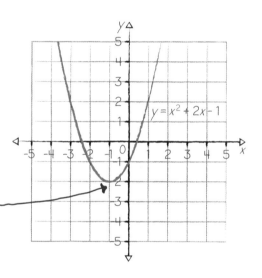

Solution

a) The turning point is the minimum point, which has coordinates (-1, -2)

b) The roots of $x^2 + 2x - 1 = 0$ are the x-intercepts of the graph.
   Approximately, $x = -2.4$ and $x = 0.4$

Exam corner

Grade
4

1. a) Complete the table of values for the equation
   $y = 2x^2 - 4$ **[I got __/2 marks]**

x	-2	-1	0	1	2
y				-2	

   b) Draw the graph of $y = 2x^2 - 4$ **[__/2 marks]**

2. Here is the graph of $y = -x^2 - 4x - 1$

   a) Write down the coordinates of the turning point of $y = -x^2 - 4x - 1$ **[__/1 mark]**

   b) Write down estimates for the roots of $-x^2 - 4x - 1 = 0$ **[__/2 marks]**

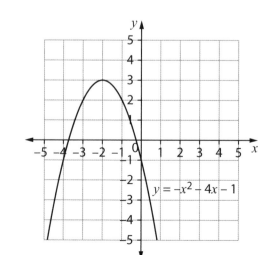

Grade
5

Solutions from graphs

Grade
4–5

You can use graphs to find or estimate the solutions of simultaneous equations.

Key points

The solution to a pair of simultaneous equations is the point of intersection of their graphs.

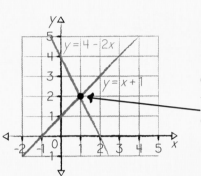

Point of intersection is (1, 2), so solution to simultaneous equations is $x = 1$, $y = 2$

 See page 40 for more on equations of straight lines.

Confidence bar

Sorted!

Had a look

Worked example

Grade
5

Use a graphical method to find the solutions of the simultaneous equations

$y = 2x + 7$ and $y = -x + 4$ **[4 marks]**

Solution

First draw both lines on the same axes.
$y = 2x + 7$ has gradient 2 and y-intercept 7
$y = -x + 4$ has gradient -1 and y-intercept 4
The lines intersect at the point (-1, 5).
The solution to the simultaneous equations is
$x = -1$, $y = 5$

Verify your answer by substituting the x-value (-1) into both equations and checking this gives y = 5

Exam corner

Grade
4

1. Use the graph on the right to estimate the solutions to the simultaneous equations $y = 4x - 1$ and $y = -3x + 8$

   Give your answers to 1 decimal place. **[I got __/2 marks]**

2. The graph of $y = 2x - 1$ is shown below.

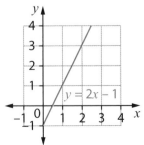

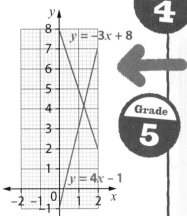

Grade
5

You can't read the exact coordinates of the point of intersection here, but you should be able to **estimate** them to 1 decimal place.

By adding another line onto the same axes, find the solutions to the simultaneous equations $y = 2x - 1$ and $y = \frac{1}{2}x + 2$ **[__/4 marks]**

Cubic and reciprocal graphs

You need to be able to draw and recognise cubic and reciprocal graphs.

Key points

- A **cubic** graph has an x^3 term in its equation. For example, $y = \boldsymbol{x^3}$

- A **reciprocal** graph has x as a denominator. For example, $y = \dfrac{1}{x}$

When $y = \dfrac{1}{x}$, the value of x cannot be 0, because $\dfrac{1}{0}$ is not a defined value. The curve will get closer and closer to the axes but will never touch them.

Confidence bar

Sorted!

☑

☑

☑

Had a look

Worked example

Grade 5

a) Complete the table of values for
$y = x^3 + 1$ **[2 marks]**

x	−2	−1	0	1	2
y				2	

b) Draw the graph of $y = x^3 + 1$ **[2 marks]**

Solution

a)

x	-2	-1	0	1	2
y	-7	0	1	2	9

b)

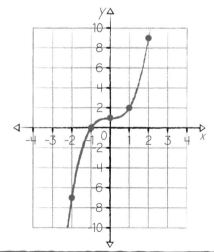

Worked example

Grade 4

Match each graph with a possible equation:
$y = 2x - 1$, $y = 2x^2 - 1$, $y = 2x^3 - 1$, $y = \dfrac{2}{x}$

[2 marks]

A   **B**

C 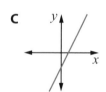 **D**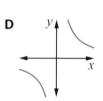

Solution

Graph A is a cubic, so $y = 2x^3 - 1$

Graph B is a quadratic, so $y = 2x^2 - 1$

Graph C is a straight line, so $y = 2x - 1$

Graph D is a reciprocal, so $y = \dfrac{2}{x}$

Exam corner

Grade 5

a) Complete the table of values for $y = 2x^3$

[I got___/2 marks]

x	−2	−1	0	1	2
y				2	

b) Draw the graph of $y = 2x^3$ **[___/2 marks]**

Rates of change

The gradient of a graph can show how a value changes over time.

Key points

- A positive gradient means the value is increasing.
- A negative gradient means the value is decreasing.
- The steeper the graph, the faster the value is changing.

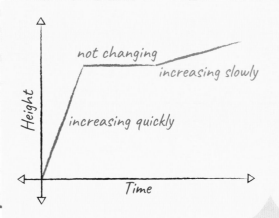

Confidence bar

Sorted!

☑
☑
☑

Had a look

Worked example

The graph shows the height of a chilli plant at the end of each week.

a) How tall was the plant after 3 weeks? **[1 mark]**

b) In which week did the plant not grow? **[1 mark]**

c) When did the plant grow the fastest and what was its speed of growth during this time? **[2 marks]**

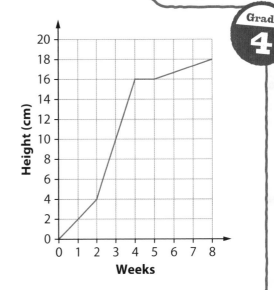

Grade
4

Solution

a) It was 10 cm tall.

b) It didn't grow during the 5th week.

c) The fastest increase was between 2 and 4 weeks.
The speed of growth was $\frac{12}{2}$ = 6 cm/week

Exam corner

1. This graph shows the cost of hiring a cement mixer.

The total cost is given by the formula:

total cost = fixed fee + cost per day × number of days

Use the graph to work out

a) the fixed fee **[I got __/1 mark]**

b) the cost per day. **[__/2 marks]**

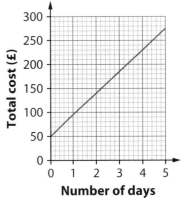

Grade
4

2. These vases are filled with water at a constant rate. Sketch a graph for each to show how the depth of water varies over time.
[__/3 marks]

a) **b)** **c)**

Grade
5

Sequences

A **sequence** is a list of numbers that follow a pattern.

Key points

- A number in a sequence is called a **term**.
- A **term-to-term rule** tells you how to work out each term in the sequence from the term before.
- In an **arithmetic sequence**, you add or subtract a number to get the next term.
- In a **geometric sequence**, you multiply or divide by a number to get the next term.

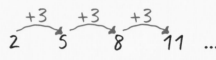

Arithmetic sequence: Add or subtract each time

$$2 \xrightarrow{+3} 5 \xrightarrow{+3} 8 \xrightarrow{+3} 11 \ldots$$

Geometric sequence: Multiply or divide each time

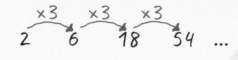

$$2 \xrightarrow{\times 3} 6 \xrightarrow{\times 3} 18 \xrightarrow{\times 3} 54 \ldots$$

Confidence bar

Sorted!

Had a look

Worked example

Grade **2**

For each of these sequences, write down

i) the term-to-term rule   **ii)** the next term   **iii)** the type of sequence.

a) 9, 5, 1, −3, …   **[3 marks]**

b) 800, 200, 50, 12.5, …   **[3 marks]**

Solution

a) I) The term-to-term rule is 'subtract 4'
   II) −3 − 4 = −7, so the next term is −7
   III) The sequence is arithmetic.

b) I) The term-to-term rule is 'divide by 4'
   II) 12.5 ÷ 4 = 3.125, so the next term is 3.125
   III) The sequence is geometric.

Exam corner

Grade **1**

1. Here are the first three terms of a sequence.

     3   6   12   24

   a) Write down the next term in the sequence.   **[I got __/1 mark]**

   b) Write down the name of this type of sequence.   **[__/1 mark]**

     Katie claims that the 10th term of the sequence is 1535

   c) Is Katie right? Give a reason for your answer.   **[__/1 mark]**

2. The first three patterns in a sequence made from ice-lolly sticks are shown.

Grade **2**

Examiner's tip!

Remembering definitions is an easy way to score marks in an exam.

Pattern 1   Pattern 2   Pattern 3

   a) Write down the term-to-term rule for this sequence.   **[__/1 mark]**

   b) How many ice-lolly sticks will there be in Pattern 6?   **[__/2 marks]**

Start by writing the number of sticks in each diagram in a list.

Using the nth term

The page before this looked at term-to-term rules. A sequence can also be described using the **position-to-term rule**, also known as the **nth term**.

Key points

- The **nth term** of a sequence is a rule that gives all the terms of a sequence when you substitute values for n.
- n must always be an integer.

If the nth term is $n^2 + 5$:

1st term = $1^2 + 5 = 6$

2nd term = $2^2 + 5 = 9$

3rd term = $3^2 + 5 = 14$

4th term = $4^2 + 5 = 21$

and so on...

Confidence bar

Sorted!

Had a look

Worked example

Grade 4

The nth term of a sequence is $11 + 3n$

a) Work out the 7th term of the sequence. **[1 mark]**

b) Is 81 a term of this sequence? Show how you get your answer. **[2 marks]**

Solution

a) To find the 7th term, substitute $n = 7$:

7th term = $11 + 3 \times 7 = 32$

b) Consider the equation $11 + 3n = 81$

giving $\qquad 3n = 70$

70 is not a multiple of 3, so the solution is not an integer.

Therefore, 81 is not in the sequence.

Worked example

Grade 4

a) Here are the first five terms of a sequence.

$$1 \quad 5 \quad 12 \quad 22 \quad 35$$

Find the next term of this sequence. **[2 marks]**

b) The nth term of a different sequence is $n^2 - 2n$

What is the 3rd term of the sequence? **[2 marks]**

Solution

a) Look for the pattern:

You need to add 16 to find the next term.

Next term = $35 + 16 = 51$

b) To find the 3rd term, substitute $n = 3$:

3rd term = $3^2 - 2 \times 3 = 3$

Exam corner

Grade 3

1. Find the term indicated from each sequence, using the nth term rule given.

a) $7n + 3$, 8th term **[I got __/1 mark]**

b) $n^2 + 7$, 6th term **[__/2 marks]**

c) $n - 2n^2$, 5th term **[__/2 marks]**

Grade 5

2. The nth term of a sequence is $100 - 7n$

a) Work out the 9th term of the sequence. **[__/1 mark]**

b) Find the first negative term of this sequence. **[__/2 marks]**

c) Show that 50 is not a term of this sequence. **[__/2 marks]**

First find the value of n by solving the inequality

$100 - 7n < 0$

Finding the nth term

You need to be able to find the rule for the nth term of an arithmetic sequence.

Key points

The nth term of an arithmetic sequence is a linear expression:
$$dn + c$$
where d and c are numbers that you have to work out.

 See page 46 for the definition of arithmetic and geometric sequences.

To find the nth term:

Work out the common difference between terms (in this case 4)
↓
Write out the multiples of the common difference: 4, 8, 12, 16
↓
Work out what to add or subtract to get the original sequence (in this case 1)
↓
Write out the nth term rule: 4n + 1

Check your answer by substituting in n = 1: (4 × 1) + 1 = 5

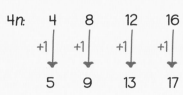

5   9   13   17
+4   +4   +4

Common difference = 4

4n: 4   8   12   16
+1   +1   +1   +1
5   9   13   17

nth term is 4n + 1

Worked example

Grade 4

Write an expression, in terms of n, for the nth term of each of these sequences.

a) 5, 14, 23, 32, 41, …   **[2 marks]**

b) 16, 6, −4, −14, −24, …   **[2 marks]**

Solution

a) 5   14   23   32   41
+9   +9   +9   +9

Common difference = 9

9n: 9   18   27   36   45
−4   −4   −4   −4   −4
5   14   23   32   41

The nth term is 9n − 4

b) 16   6   −4   −14   −24
−10   −10   −10   −10

Common difference = −10

−10n: −10   −20   −30   −40   −50
+26   +26   +26   +26   +26
16   6   −4   −14   −24

The nth term is −10n + 26 (or 26 − 10n)

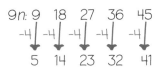
Remember: always check your answer by substituting in n = 1

Exam corner

Grade 4

1. Write an expression, in terms of n, for the nth term of each of these sequences.

a) 9, 14, 19, 24, 29, …   [I got __/2 marks]

b) 5, 3, 1, −1, −3, …   [__/2 marks]

c) $\frac{1}{2}$, 2, $3\frac{1}{2}$, 5, $6\frac{1}{2}$, …   [__/2 marks]

Remember, the common difference can be positive or negative. It can also be a decimal or a fraction.

Special sequences

You need to be able to recognise some sequences, such as square numbers, cube numbers, triangular numbers and Fibonacci-type sequences.

Key points

In a **Fibonacci**-type sequence, each term is the sum of the previous two terms.

For example, the next term of the sequence 3, 7, 10, 17, ... is 10 + 17 = 27

The 'original' Fibonacci sequence was:

$$1, 1, 2, 3, 5, 8, 13, 21, ...$$

But any sequence where you add the previous two terms to get the next term is a Fibonacci-<u>type</u> sequence.

Confidence bar

Sorted!

Had a look

Worked example

Grade 3

The first two terms of a Fibonacci-type sequence are 2 and 5. What are the next two terms? **[2 marks]**

Solution

3rd term = 1st term + 2nd term

= 2 + 5

= 7

4th term = 2nd term + 3rd term

= 5 + 7

= 12

Worked example

Grade 3

The first three terms of a sequence are shown.

Pattern 1   Pattern 2   Pattern 3

How many cubes are in the 6th term of the sequence?

[2 marks]

Solution

The sequence of numbers of cubes is 1, 8, 27, ...

which are the cube numbers.

6th term = 6^3 = 216

There are 216 cubes in the 6th pattern.

Exam corner

1. Here are the first five terms of a Fibonacci-type sequence.

Grade 3

    1   3   4   7   11

a) Find the 8th term of this sequence.   **[I got ___/2 marks]**

The first and second terms of another Fibonacci sequence are a and b

b) Write an expression for the third term, in terms of a and b **[___/1 mark]**

2. The first three terms of a sequence are shown.

Pattern 1   Pattern 2   Pattern 3

a) Draw the next pattern in the sequence.   **[___/1 mark]**

Grade 3

b) Work out the number of circles in the 7th pattern. **[___/2 marks]**

The number of circles in each pattern form a sequence called the **triangular numbers**. That's because the patterns look like triangles with increasing size.

Proportion

You can describe a proportion of a whole as a fraction or as a percentage. If you want to compare two proportions then a good method is to convert both to percentages.

Grade 2–3

Key points

- Percent means 'out of 100'
- To write a proportion as a percentage, first write as a fraction then multiply by 100%
- To compare proportions, convert them all to percentages.

What is 28 as a percentage of 70?

 First write as a fraction

28 out of $70 = \dfrac{28}{70}$

 × 100% to get a percentage

$\dfrac{28}{70} \times 100\% = \dfrac{2800}{70}\% = 40\%$

Confidence bar

Sorted!

☑
☑
☑

Had a look

Worked example

Grade 2

 Thomas has £60 and he wants to buy a T-shirt that costs £18

What proportion of his money is the cost of the T-shirt? Give your answer as a percentage.

[2 marks]

Solution

18 out of $60 = \dfrac{18}{60}$ Express as a fraction

$= \dfrac{18}{60} \times 100\%$

$= \dfrac{1800}{60}\%$

$= 30\%$ Convert to a percentage

 See page 13 for more on converting between fractions, decimals and percentages.

Worked example

Grade 3

At the start of a year, a small company has 10 employees. Two more employees join the company. Give the number of employees now, as a percentage of the number of employees at the start of the year. **[2 marks]**

Solution

There are now 12 employees.

12 out of $10 = \dfrac{12}{10}$

$= \dfrac{12}{10} \times 100\%$

$= 120\%$

Remember this...
Remember, percentages can be bigger than 100%

Exam corner

1. Ava has reached page 80 of a 400-page book.

What proportion of the book has she read?

Give your answer as a percentage. **[I got ___ /2 marks]**

Grade 2

Grade 3

2. Jake scored 35 out of 40 in his History test and 21 out of 25 in his Geography test. In which test did he score the higher percentage? Justify your answer.

[___ /2 marks]

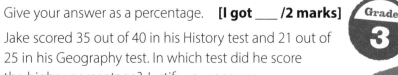

To compare proportions, write them both as percentages.

50

Ratio

A **ratio** is a neat way of comparing two or more quantities.

Key points

- A ratio can be simplified fully by dividing both sides by their highest common factor (HCF).
- Ratio problems can sometimes be solved by 'scaling up' a ratio. You do this by multiplying both sides by the same number.
- A ratio can be expressed as a fraction, e.g. if the ratio of adults to children is $1 : 2$ then $\frac{1}{3}$ of the total are adults and $\frac{2}{3}$ are children.
- Ratios can also have three or more parts, *for example a : b : c*

To simplify ratios, divide by the HCF...

For example, simplify the ratio $49 : 28$

The HCF of 49 and 28 is 7, so divide both by 7

$$\div 7 \left(\begin{array}{c} 49 : 28 \\ 7 : 4 \end{array} \right) \div 7$$

So $49 : 28$ simplifies to $7 : 4$

Confidence bar

Sorted!

☑
☑
☑

Had a look

Worked example

 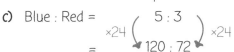

A shade of purple paint is made by mixing 300 ml of blue paint with 180 ml of red paint.

a) Write the ratio of blue paint to red paint in its simplest form.

b) What fraction of the purple paint was originally red paint?

c) How much red paint would you need to add to 120 ml of blue paint to make the same shade of purple?

Solution

> See page 18 for more on HCF.

a) The HCF of 300 and 180 is 60

$$\text{Blue : Red} = \div 60 \left(\begin{array}{c} 300 : 180 \\ 5 : 3 \end{array} \right) \div 60$$

b) The total amount of paint = $300 + 180 = 480\,\text{ml}$, so fraction of red $= \frac{180}{480} = \frac{3}{8}$

c) $$\text{Blue : Red} = \times 24 \left(\begin{array}{c} 5 : 3 \\ 120 : 72 \end{array} \right) \times 24$$

Multiply 5 by 24 to give 120 ml of blue paint.

So 72 ml of red paint is needed.

You can use a bar model to solve a ratio problem. For the Worked example:

blue = 120 ml   red = 72 ml

Exam corner

1. There are 24 white sheep and 30 grey sheep in a field. Write the ratio of white sheep to grey sheep in its simplest form.

[I got ___ /2 marks]

2. Mortar can be made by mixing water, cement and sand in the ratio $1 : 2 : 3$
How much water and sand will need to be mixed with 5 kg of cement?

[___ /3 marks]

STRIVE FOR 5 See pages 116-117 for more practice.

Using ratio

You can divide an amount in a ratio using some simple steps, or by drawing a bar model.

Key points

To divide in a ratio:

STEP 1: add up the parts of the ratio.

STEP 2: divide the total by the number of parts to see what each part is worth.

STEP 3: multiply to see how much each portion of the ratio is worth.

For other types of ratio problem, try using a bar model.

Worked example

35 people work in a design studio. The ratio of admin staff to designers is 3 : 4 How many designers are there? **[2 marks]**

Grade 4

Solution

3 + 4 = 7
There are 7 parts in total.   (STEP 1)
35 ÷ 7 = 5
Each part represents 5 people.   (STEP 2)
4 × 5 = 20
There are 20 designers.   (STEP 3)

Using bar models to answer ratio problems

To share £90 in the ratio 1 : 5 : 3, draw a bar model split in the ratio 1 : 5 : 3

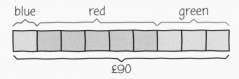
blue   red   green

£90

There are 9 boxes, so each will be worth £10 to make a total of £90. Now you can see by counting squares that the amounts of each share are £10, £50 and £30

Worked example

The ratio of pigs to chickens on a farm is 2 : 5 There are 24 more chickens than pigs. Find the total number of each animal.   **[3 marks]**

Grade 5

Solution

There are 24 more chickens than pigs so these three blocks must add up to 24. Each block is worth 8

There are 2 × 8 = 16 pigs and 5 × 8 = 40 chickens.

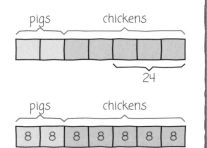
pigs   chickens

24

pigs   chickens

| 8 | 8 | 8 | 8 | 8 | 8 | 8 |

Exam corner

1. Alice and Benji share £180 in the ratio 5 : 3. Work out how much each will receive.   **[I got ___ /3 marks]**

2. A recipe for shortbread biscuits needs sugar, flour and butter. The ratio of sugar to butter is 2 : 5 and there is three times as much flour as sugar.

   a) Work out the ratio of sugar : flour : butter.   **[___ /2 marks]**
   A single shortbread biscuit weighs 26 g.

   b) Calculate how much butter is needed to make 12 shortbread biscuits.   **[___ /3 marks]**

Grade 4

Grade 5

Examiner's tip!   STRIVE FOR 5

Add your answers together to check that your total is the same as in the original question.

STRIVE FOR 5 See pages 116–117 for more practice.

Percentage change

Without using a calculator, you need to be able to find the new value after a percentage change. You also need to be able to work out the percentage change that has taken place based on the before and after values.

Key points

Confidence bar

Sorted!

☑
☑
☑

Had a look

There are three kinds of calculation with percentage change:

1) To find the value after a percentage increase, calculate the increase then add it onto the original amount.

2) To find the value after a percentage decrease, calculate the decrease then subtract it from the original amount.

3) To calculate the percentage change that has taken place, divide the change in the amount by the **original amount**.

To find the **percentage increase**: $\dfrac{\text{actual increase}}{\text{original amount}}$ ⎤

⎦ → × 100%

To find the **percentage decrease**: $\dfrac{\text{actual decrease}}{\text{original amount}}$

> See page 54 for calculator methods for percentage change.

Worked example

Grade 3

Calculate the total of this restaurant bill, including the service charge of 12%.   **[2 marks]**

Food + drinks £70
Plus service charge of 12%

Solution

10% of £70 is £7
1% of £70 is £0.70, so 2% is £1.40
Then 12% of £70 is £7 + £1.40 = £8.40
The bill will increase by 12% so add this amount:
Total = £70 + £8.40 = £78.40

Worked example

Grade 4

A car's value decreases from £12 000 to £9000 over the first year after it is produced.
Calculate the percentage decrease.   **[2 marks]**

Solution

The actual decrease in value is

$$£12\,000 - £9000 = £3000$$

The percentage decrease is

$$\frac{3\cancel{000}}{12\cancel{000}} \times 100\% = 25\%$$

> See page 50 for more on writing a percentage.

Exam corner

Grade 3

1. The cost for a child to use a climbing wall is 40% less than the cost for an adult. The cost for an adult is £25. Find the cost for a child.   **[I got ___ /2 marks]**

2. The cost of school dinner increased over the summer holiday from £2 to £2.20 Calculate the percentage increase in cost.   **[___ /2 marks]**

Grade 4

Examiner's tip! **STRIVE FOR 5**

You can check by increasing £2 by your answer. If you get £2.20 you found the right percentage increase.

Multipliers

With a calculator, you can use a **multiplier** to solve percentage problems.

Grade
4–5

Key points

- To find the **multiplier** for a problem, write the percentage as a decimal.
- **Simple interest** is where you only earn interest on the initial sum.
- **Compound interest** is where the interest is left in the account and earns interest itself.

To **increase** by a percentage (e.g. 8%), add the percentage to 100 (e.g. 108)

To **decrease** by a percentage, (e.g. 8%) **subtract** the percentage from 100, e.g. 92

Calculating a percentage change to an amount, e.g. 75

Divide this number by 100 to find the **multiplier**. E.g. 1.08 or 0.92

Multiply this number by the original amount. E.g. 8% increase on 75 = 75 × 1.08 = 81

Confidence bar

Sorted!

☑
☑
☑

Had a look

Worked example

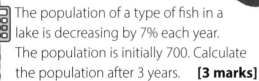

The population of a type of fish in a lake is decreasing by 7% each year. The population is initially 700. Calculate the population after 3 years. **[3 marks]**

Solution

100% – 7% = 93%

⇒ 0.93 is the multiplier

After 1 year: 700 × 0.93 = 651 fish

After 2 years: 651 × 0.93 = 605 fish

After 3 years: 605 × 0.93 = 563 fish

Instead of multiplying the answer by the multiplier each time, you can do this in one calculation:

700 × 0.93 × 0.93 × 0.93

= 700 × 0.93³ = 563 fish

Worked example

Grade 5

Natalie keeps £3500 in a savings account for 2 years. The account pays 4% interest each year. Calculate the amount of interest earned if

a) Natalie takes the interest out of the account each year **[2 marks]**

b) she leaves the interest in the account each year. **[3 marks]**

Solution

a) This is **simple interest**.

4% of £3500 = £140

Total interest for 2 years = £140 × 2 = £280

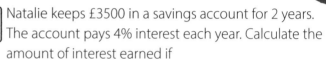

You can use the [%] button to find 4% of 3500:

4% × 3500
140

b) This is **compound interest**.

100% + 4% = 104% ⇒ 1.04 is the multiplier

Total in account after 1 year = £3500 × 1.04 = £3640

Total after 2 years = £3640 × 1.04 = £3785.60

So interest = £3785.60 – £3500 = £285.60

Exam corner

Grade 5

1. A flat is initially worth £250 000. Its value increases by 8% each year. Calculate its value after 2 years.
   [I got ___ /3 marks]

2. At the beginning of the school year, the Art department has 500 pencils. The number of pencils decreases by 13% each term. Find the number remaining after 3 terms. **[___ /3 marks]**

See pages 118–119 for more practice
STRIVE FOR 5

Original value problems

It's important to read percentage questions carefully. Sometimes you will be given the amount after a percentage increase or decrease and must calculate the original amount.

Key points

To find the original amount:

STEP 1: work out what percentage of the original you now have.

STEP 2: divide by this number to find 1%.

STEP 3: multiply by 100 to find original value.

STEP 4: check your answer by multiplying it by the percentage change.

Or, with a calculator, you can convert your percentage in step 1 to a multiplier and divide by this amount.

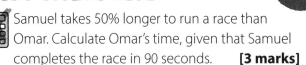

If value has been **Increased** by 10% ...

now have 110%

original 100% | 10%

If value has been **decreased** by 10% ...

original 100%

now have 90% | 10%

Confidence bar

Sorted!

☑
☑
☑

Had a look

Worked example

A TV is reduced by 20% in a sale and now costs £360. Calculate the original price of the TV. **[3 marks]**

Solution

This is a **percentage decrease**.

100% − 20% = 80%   (STEP 1)

80% is £360

1% is £360 ÷ 80 = $\frac{£360}{80}$ = £4.50   (STEP 2)

100% is £4.50 × 100 = £450   (STEP 3)

The original price of the TV was £450

With a calculator you can use **the multiplier method:**

80% = 0.8

So original price = £360 ÷ 0.8 = £450

Worked example

Samuel takes 50% longer to run a race than Omar. Calculate Omar's time, given that Samuel completes the race in 90 seconds. **[3 marks]**

Solution

This is a **percentage increase**.

100% + 50% = 150%   (STEP 1)

150% is 90 seconds

1% is 90 ÷ 150 = $\frac{90}{150}$ = 0.6 seconds   (STEP 2)

100% is 0.6 × 100 = 60 seconds   (STEP 3)

Omar's time was 60 seconds

Check the answer: 50% of 60 is 30 (STEP 4)

60 + 30 = 90 seconds, which is Samuel's time ✓

With a calculator you can use **the multiplier method:**

150% = 1.5

Omar's time = 90 ÷ 1.5 = 60 s

Exam corner

1. The length of a zebra is 15% longer than the length of a horse. Calculate the length of the horse, given that the zebra is 230 cm long.   **[I got ___ /3 marks]**

2. Leah sells her old laptop for £390, which is 40% less than the price she paid for it. Calculate the price Leah paid for the laptop.   **[___ /3 marks]**

See pages 118–119 for more practice.

STRIVE FOR 5

Compound measures

A compound measure links two measurements. For example, a rate of pay could be £11 per hour and a rate of flow of water could be 3 litres per minute.

Formula box

Speed, **density** and **pressure** are three compound measures you need to be familiar with.

You can use the triangles here to remember how to calculate these.

Cover up the measurement you want to calculate and then either multiply or divide.

$$Speed = \frac{Distance}{Time}$$

$$Density = \frac{Mass}{Volume}$$
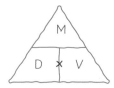

$$Pressure = \frac{Force}{Area}$$
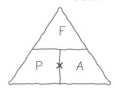

Remember these...

*Speed is in **miles** (distance) per hour (time).*
Per means divide, so speed = distance ÷ time.

I ♥ Density!
$D = \dfrac{\heartsuit}{\triangledown}$

Fly
Pilots   Aeroplanes

See page 41 for more on speed, distance and time.

Worked example
Grade 5

What is the size of force required to exert a pressure of 7 N/cm² on an area of 54 cm²?   **[2 marks]**

Solution

Draw the triangle and cover up F
Force = Pressure × Area
= 7 × 54
= 378 N

Worked example
Grade 5

The density of a piece of wood is 2.4 g/cm³ and its mass is 1.8 kg.
Calculate the volume of the wood.   **[3 marks]**

Solution

1.8 kg = 1800 g

Draw the triangle and cover up V
$$Volume = \frac{Mass}{Density} = \frac{1800}{2.4}$$
$$= 750 \, cm^3$$

Exam corner
Grade 4

1. **a)** Calculate the time taken to travel 9 m at a speed of 0.3 m/s.   **[I got ___ /2 marks]**

   b) A car is driving at 54 km/h. Calculate the distance in metres covered by the car in 10 s.   **[___ /3 marks]**

2. A force of 24 N is applied to an area of 40 m². What is the pressure? State the units of your answer.   **[___ /3 marks]**
   Grade 4

Examiner's tip!
STRIVE FOR 5

Always check the units. You may need to convert one of the measures before you can complete the calculation.

STRIVE FOR 5 See pages 120–121 for more practice.

Direct proportion

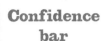
Two values in **direct proportion** will increase and decrease at the same rate. For example, if one doubles, the other doubles; if one halves, the other halves.

Key points

To solve direct proportion problems, you can use the unitary method:

STEP 1: Divide to calculate the value of 1 unit.

STEP 2: Multiply if necessary to find the value required.

Alternatively, you can use ratios to solve the problem.

A graph showing **direct proportion** is a straight line through the origin.

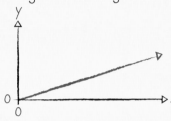

The equation is $y = kx$, where k is any number.

Worked example

Grade 3

 A pack of 20 biscuits costs £1.50 and a pack of 35 of the same biscuits cost £2.80

a) Which is better value? **[3 marks]**

A recipe for 12 portions of cheesecake requires 30 biscuits.

b) How many biscuits are required for 32 portions of cheesecake? **[2 marks]**

Solution

a) Smaller pack price per biscuit:

£1.50 ÷ 20 = £0.075 (7.5p)   (STEP 1)

Larger pack price per biscuit:

£2.80 ÷ 35 = £0.08 (8p)   (STEP 1)

The smaller pack is better value.

b) 1 portion requires 30 ÷ 12 = 2.5 biscuits

32 portions require 2.5 × 32 = 80 biscuits
      (STEP 2)

See page 51 for more on ratios.

Worked example

Grade 4

a) The graph below shows the exchange rate between pounds (£) and dollars ($) on a given day. How much is $15 worth in pounds? **[2 marks]**

b) If the exchange rate between pounds, P, and euros, E, is given by the equation $P = 0.9E$, what is 15 euros worth in pounds? **[2 marks]**

Solution

a) Draw a line straight up from $15 to the diagonal line. Then draw a line straight across to the £ axis and read the value.

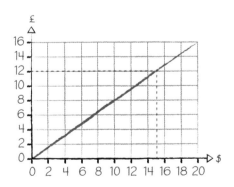

$15 ≈ £12

b) $P = 0.9 \times 15 = £13.50$

Exam corner

Grade 3

1. Which is better value: 1 litre of milk for 90p or 650 ml of milk for 65p? **[I got __ /3 marks]**

2. On a particular day, 100 Indian rupees were worth 150 Japanese yen.

   a) Draw an exchange rate graph, with values of rupees from 0 to 200 **[__ /3 marks]**

   b) How much was 120 yen worth in rupees? **[__ /2 marks]**

Grade 4

Inverse proportion

If two values are in **inverse proportion**, then one will increase while the other decreases at the same rate. For example, if one doubles, the other halves.

Key points

- To solve inverse proportion problems, start by multiplying together the given values of the two variables.

  For example, if it takes 3 people 4 hours to build a wall, then do $3 \times 4 = 12$

  So, number of 'worker-hours' needed for the task is people × hours = 12

- The product of the two variables must always equal this amount. So if you're asked how long it would take 6 people to build the same wall, the answer will be 2, because $6 \times 2 = 12$ worker-hours as before.

Remember this...

A graph showing **inverse proportion** will curve in near the origin.

The equation is $y = \dfrac{k}{x}$, where k is any number.

Inverse proportion

Worked example

Grade 4

It takes 8 cleaners 3 hours to clean a block of offices.

a) How long does it take 6 cleaners to clean the offices? **[2 marks]**

b) How many cleaners are needed to clean to the offices in 1.5 hours? **[2 marks]**

Solution

a) Total 'worker-hours' = $8 \times 3 = 24$

  It will take 6 cleaners $24 \div 6 = 4$ hours.

b) To clean the offices in 1.5 hours,

  $24 \div 1.5 = 16$ cleaners are needed

Worked example

Grade 5

The time, t hours, taken to complete a journey at speed v km/h is given by the equation $t = \dfrac{75}{v}$

a) Find the missing values for t and v

v (km/h)	1	3	5	
t (hours)		25		7.5

[3 marks]

b) Plot a graph of t against v **[3 marks]**

Solution

a) $v = 1 \Rightarrow t = \dfrac{75}{1} = 75 \qquad v = 5 \Rightarrow t = \dfrac{75}{5} = 15$

  $t = 7.5 \Rightarrow v = 10$ since $t = \dfrac{75}{10} = 7.5$

b)

Exam corner

Grade 4

1. It takes 12 gardeners 5 hours to plant the trees alongside a new stretch of motorway.

   a) How long would it take 15 gardeners to plant the trees? **[I got __ /2 marks]**

   b) How many gardeners would be needed to plant the trees in 2 hours? **[__ /2 marks]**

2. You are given that y is inversely proportional to x

   Grade 5

   a) What happens to the value of y when the value of x is doubled? **[__ /1 mark]**

   b) Which of these could be an equation for y?

   $y = 3x \qquad y = x^2 \qquad y = \dfrac{3}{x}$

   [__ /1 mark]

Time and timetables

Working with time and reading timetables are important everyday skills.

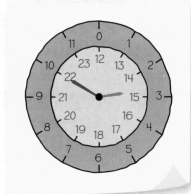

Key points

- There are 60 seconds in a minute and 60 minutes in an hour.
- When using the 12-hour clock you need to write **am** or **pm**.
- To change times after 1 pm from 12-hour to 24-hour clock, add 12 hours.

Worked example

Grade 3

Part of a train timetable between Birmingham and Bristol is shown here.

Birmingham	19:12	19:33	19:42
Cheltenham	19:53	-	20:26
Gloucester	20:15	-	-
Bristol	20:50	21:07	21:13

a) What time should you catch a train from Birmingham in order to be in Cheltenham by 8pm? **[1 mark]**

b) How long does the 19:12 train from Birmingham take to get to Bristol? **[2 marks]**

Solution

a) You would need to catch the train that arrives at 19:53, because the next train arrives after 8pm. Catch the train from Birmingham at 19:12

b) The 19:12 train arrives in Bristol at 20:50

$$19:12 \xrightarrow{\text{+48 mins}} 20:00 \xrightarrow{\text{+50 mins}} 20:50$$

Total time is 48 mins + 50 mins = 98 minutes = 1 hour and 38 minutes

> *Add or subtract time by working in steps.*
> *Show all your working.*

Exam corner

Grade 1

1. a) A swimming competition started at 10:35 and ended at 13:10. What was its duration? **[I got ___ /2 marks]**

b) The winning time for the 100 m freestyle was 1.15 minutes. Express this time in seconds. **[___ /1 mark]**

> *× 60 to change from hours to minutes*
> *× 60 to change from minutes to seconds*

Grade 3

2. Part of a bus timetable is shown here.

Ahmad lives in Camberley. It takes him 23 minutes to walk to the bus stop from his house.

a) What is the latest time Ahmad must leave home in order to catch a bus and arrive at Farnborough before 2 pm? **[___/2 marks]**

b) What is his total journey time from home to Farnborough? **[___/2 marks]**

Old Dean	12:25	12:55	13:16
Camberley	12:41	13:10	13:32
Yorktown	12:52	13:17	13:41
Frimley	13:02	13:25	13:54
Farnborough	13:12	13:34	14:03

STRIVE FOR 5 See pages 120-121 for more practice.

Measures

Different units can be used to measure length, mass and capacity. You need to be able to convert between metric units and some imperial units.

To convert (change) between metric units:

| Length | Mass | Volume |

Confidence bar

Sorted!

 ✓

 ✓

 ✓

Had a look

Worked example

Grade **3**

A large package is 1950 mm high and has a mass of 13.5 kg.

a) What is the height of the package in centimetres?　**[1 mark]**

b) What is the mass of the package in grams?　**[1 mark]**

c) The package must be less than 75 inches high to fit through a doorway.

Will the package fit through the doorway? Explain your answer. Use the conversion 1 inch ≈ 2.54 cm.　**[2 marks]**

Solution

a) $1950 \div 10 = 195\,cm$

b) $13.5 \times 1000 = 13\,500\,g$

c) First convert the height of the doorway into centimetres:
$75 \times 2.54 = 190.5\,cm$
So the package won't fit, since 195 > 190.5

Key points

- Learn how to convert between these common **metric units** for length, mass and capacity.

- Measurements can also be given in **imperial units**.

- You don't need to remember the conversions between metric and imperial.

- You can also measure capacity as a volume:
$1000\,ml = 1\,litre = 1000\,cm^3$

Exam corner

Grade **2**

1. The volume of a cup is calculated to be 230 cm³. What is the capacity of the cup in litres?　**[I got ___/1 mark]**

2. One lap of a school field is 960 m. Calculate the length of 3 laps. Give your answer in

Grade **3**

a) kilometres　**[___/2 marks]**

b) miles. Use the conversion 1 mile ≈ 1.6 km.　**[___/1 mark]**

Examiner's tip!

Check that your answer seems sensible - you should have an approximate idea of the size of metric measurements.

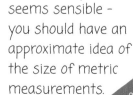
STRIVE FOR **5** See pages 122-123 for more practice

Scale drawing

Maps and scale drawings are used to represent real-life lengths on paper or on screen, while keeping everything in proportion.

Key points

- A scale can be written as a **ratio**,
  e.g. 1 : 400
  or as a sentence,
  e.g. 1 cm represents 4 m.

- If the ratio is 1 : 400,
  multiply lengths on the drawing by 400
  to get the real-life length, and
  divide lengths in real life by 400
  to get the length on the scale drawing.

- Convert to a sensible unit, e.g. cm on
  a scale drawing or map, but use m or
  km in real life.

📄 See page 51 for more on ratio.

Remember this...
If the scale is 1 : 400

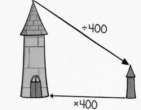

÷400

×400

- You MULTIPLY
  the length on the drawing
  to get the real-life length

- And you DIVIDE
  the real-life length to get
  the length on the drawing.

Confidence bar

Sorted!

☑
☐
☐

Had a look

Worked example

On a map, 2 cm represents 3 km.
Write the scale of the map as a ratio in
the form 1 : n **[2 marks]**

Solution

3 km = 3000 m = 300 000 cm

The ratio is 2 : 300 000

which simplifies to 1 : 150 000

Worked example

In this scale drawing of a
vegetable plot, 1 cm
represents 2 m.
Calculate the total area of
the vegetable plot. **[3 marks]**

| carrots |
| potatoes |

Solution

Width on scale drawing is 2.5 cm.
Width of real plot is 2.5 × 200 = 500 cm = 5 m
Total length on scale drawing is 3 cm.
Total length of real plot is 3 × 200 = 600 cm = 6 m
Area of vegetable plot = 5 × 6 = 30 m^2

Exam corner

1. A rectangular field is 65 m by 40 m.

   Draw the field using a scale of 1 cm = 20 m. **[I got __/2 marks]**

2. A road is 1.5 km long. On Lola's map the road is 6 cm long.

   a) Write the scale of the map as a ratio in the form 1 : n.
   [__/2 marks]

   A football pitch is 100 m by 60 m.

   b) What are the dimensions of the football pitch on Lola's map?
   [__/3 marks]

Examiner's tip! STRIVE FOR 5

Always look carefully
at the units: you may
need to convert.

STRIVE FOR 5 See pages 122–123 for more practice.

Angles

An angle is the measure of turn between two lines. You measure angles in degrees, and use the symbol ° to write a degree.

Grade 1-2

Key points

- A 90° angle is a **right angle**.

- A **full turn** is 360°

- An angle less than 90° is **acute**.

- An angle between 90° and 180° is **obtuse**.

- An angle more than 180° is **reflex**.

Remember these...

Acute — Acute angle is small...

Obtuse — Obtuse angles are blunt...

Reflex — A gymnast who can bend all the way back is Really flexible...

The angles increase in size in alphabetical order:

Acute Obtuse Reflex

Confidence bar

Sorted!

☑
☑
☑

Had a look

Worked example

Grade 1

a) Measure angle *CAB* **[1 mark]**
b) What type of angle is *CAB*? **[1 mark]**

The middle letter tells you where the angle is.

You can also write it as ∠CAB.

Solution

a) Line up the protractor along the line *AC*.

Ensure the vertex *A* is exactly at the centre mark of the protractor.

Count round from 0 on the scale.

Angle *CAB* = 126°

b) Angle *CAB* is obtuse (it's between 90° and 180°).

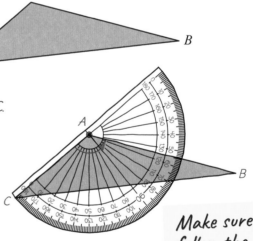

Make sure you follow the correct scale!

Exam corner

Grade 1

1. What type of angle is

   a) angle *YZX* **[I got __ /1 mark]**

   b) angle *YXZ*? **[__/1 mark]**

2. Draw and label line segments *PQ*, *QR* and ∠*PQR*, where *PQ* = 5 cm, *QR* = 3 cm and ∠*PQR* = 312° **[__ /3 marks]**

Grade 2

Examiner's tip!

It's easier to draw (or measure) an acute or obtuse angle than a reflex angle.

Here you could draw 48° since 360 − 312 = 48

Then remember to label the reflex angle 312°

Angle rules

There are rules you can use to calculate unknown angles in different situations.

Key points

- Angles on a straight line add up to 180°

- Angles around a point add up to 360°

- **Vertically opposite** angles are equal.

- **Corresponding** angles are equal.

- **Alternate** angles are equal.

Remember the names of the parallel line angles.

Corresponding angles are the same (corresponding) side of the transversal line (the line that cuts through the parallel line).

Alternate angles are the alternate sides of the transversal line.

Worked example

Find the values of x, y and z in the diagram.

Give reasons for your answers. **[5 marks]**

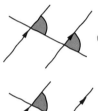

not drawn to scale

Grade 3

Solution

$x = 75°$ (vertically opposite angles are equal)

$y = 180 - 75 = 105°$

(angles on a straight line add up to 180°)

$z = y = 105°$ (corresponding angles are equal)

Exam corner

Grade 2

1. Calculate the value of angle a

   [I got ___/2 marks]

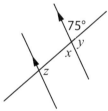

2. Find the values of x and y in this diagram.

   Give reasons for your answers.

   [___/3 marks]

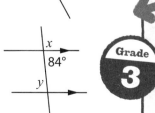

Grade 3

diagrams not drawn to scale

Examiner's tip!

If you're asked to 'Give reasons', make sure you do so. And always use the proper names of angles.

Bearings

Bearings are used in navigation to describe the direction between objects.

Key points

- Bearings are measured CLOCKWISE, starting from NORTH.

- They always have THREE figures, e.g. a bearing of 3° is written as 003°

Remember this...

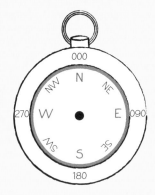

Remember the main compass points:

Never Eat Slimy Worms

Worked example

A boat sails south-east from a rock.

a) What is the bearing of the boat from the rock?　　　**[1 mark]**

b) What is the bearing of the rock from the boat?　　　**[1 mark]**

Solution

a) South-east is half-way between east (bearing of 090°) and south (bearing of 180°).

The bearing of the boat from the rock is 90 + 45 = 135°

b) The boat must turn 180° to sail back to the rock.

The bearing of the rock from the boat is 135 + 180 = 315°

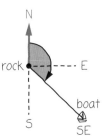

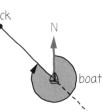

> Draw a sketch of the situation to help you understand it. Always remember to draw a line north through the starting point. That's the point from which you want to measure the bearing.

Exam corner

1. The positions of a boat and a lighthouse at 10 am are shown in the diagram.

   a) Find the bearing of the boat from the lighthouse at 10 am.　**[I got ___/2 marks]**

   b) At 2 pm the boat is due west of the lighthouse. State the bearing of the boat from the lighthouse at 2 pm.　　**[___/1 mark]**

lighthouse　　boat

2. Sofia starts at point *A* and walks for 10 m on a bearing of 220° to point *B*. She then walks due north for 5 m to point *C*.

   a) Write down the bearing of *A* from *B*.　　**[___/2 marks]**

   b) Make a scale drawing showing points *A*, *B* and *C*. Use the scale 1 cm to 1 m.　**[___/3 marks]**

> Remember: the bearing of point A from point B will always be 180° different from the bearing of Point B from Point A.

Triangles & quadrilaterals

Grade
2-4

There are lots of rules you'll need to know when working with triangles and quadrilaterals.

Key points

Remember this...
three sides the same Equilateral
two sides the same Isosceles

- Angles in a **triangle** add up to 180°.

Equilateral	**Isosceles**	**Scalene**	**Right-angled**
all sides equal	two sides equal	no sides equal	has a 90° angle
all angles equal	two angles equal	no angles equal	

- Angles in a **quadrilateral** add up to 360°.

Square	Rectangle	Kite	Rhombus	Parallelogram	Trapezium

Worked example

Grade **3**

ABCD is a parallelogram. Calculate the size of ∠*BCD*   **[2 marks]**

Solution

∠*CDA* = 80° (opposite angles in parallelogram are equal)

2 × ∠*BCD* = 360 − 160 = 200 (angles in quadrilateral add up to 360°)

∠*BCD* = 200 ÷ 2 = 100°

Examiner's tip!

You need to know and use the angle properties of all the quadrilaterals on this page.

Exam corner

Grade **2**

Grade **3**

1. a) What type of triangle is Δ*ABC*?
[I got ___ /1 mark]

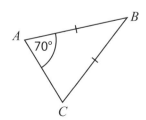

b) Calculate the size of ∠*ABC*   **[___ /2 marks]**

2. a) An unknown quadrilateral has exactly two lines of symmetry. State two possible names for the quadrilateral.   **[___ /2 marks]**

b) A kite is shown below.

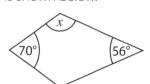

Calculate the value of *x*   **[___ /3 marks]**

Polygons

Polygons are 2D shapes with straight edges only. In addition to triangles and quadrilaterals, you need to know some of the more common polygons.

Remember these...

A pentagon has 5 sides - you hold a pen in your 5-fingered hand.

A hexagon has 6 sides - think of the x: hex ⇒ six.

A heptagon has 7 sides - a heptathlon has 7 events.

An octagon has 8 sides - think of an octopus with 8 legs.

A decagon has 10 sides - think of a decade (10 years).

Confidence bar

Sorted!

Had a look

Key points

- A polygon can be **regular** or **irregular**.
- A **regular polygon** has all sides equal and all angles equal.
- The exterior angles of any polygon add up to 360°

- To work out what the **interior angles** of any polygon add up to, use the rule:

  sum of interior angles = $(n - 2) \times 180$

  where n is the number of sides on the polygon.
- For any polygon, interior angle + exterior angle = 180°
- A regular polygon with n sides will have n **lines of symmetry** and **order of rotational symmetry** n.

E.g. for a pentagon:
sum of interior angles
= $(5 - 2) \times 180$
= 540°

The order of rotational symmetry is how many times an object fits perfectly into itself when going through a full rotation.

Exam corner

Grade 3

1. **a)** Calculate the size of an interior angle of a regular decagon. **[I got ___ /3 marks]**

   b) Write down the name of a regular polygon with 7 lines of symmetry. **[___ /1 mark]**

2. A heptagon has interior angles as shown.

   Calculate the size of the angle marked x **[___ /3 marks]**

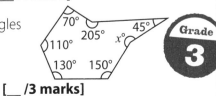

70°
205°
45°
110°
$x°$
130°
150°

Grade 3

Worked example

Grade 3

Calculate the size of an interior angle of a regular octagon.

[3 marks]

Solution

An octagon has 8 sides, so

sum of interior angles

= $(8 - 2) \times 180 = 1080°$

A regular octagon has 8 equal angles, so

interior angle = $1080 \div 8 = 135°$

Reflection

Reflection is one of the four transformations you need to know about.

Key points

- When a point is reflected in a mirror line, the original point and the reflected point are the same distance from the mirror line.
- When you reflect a shape, the object and the image are **congruent** (exactly the same shape and size).

Remember this...

With all transformations, the original shape is the **object** and the result of the transformation is the **image**.

object   image

You look at your image in a mirror.

Confidence bar

Sorted!

Had a look

Worked example

a) Describe the single transformation that maps *ABCD* to *A′B′C′D′* **[2 marks]**

b) Draw the reflection of the trapezium *ABCD* in the mirror line $y = x$ **[2 marks]**

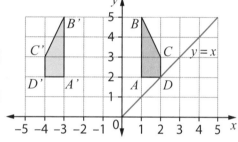

Solution

a) *A′B′C′D′* is the reflection of *ABCD* in this vertical line

The equation of this line is $x = -1$

The transformation is a reflection in the line $x = -1$

b)

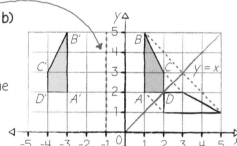

 See pages 38 and 40 for more on equations of lines.

To reflect a shape, carefully reflect all the **vertices** separately, then join up.

Vertices are the corners of a shape (one of them is called a vertex).

Exam corner

1. Reflect the shape shown in the *y*-axis.

[I got ___/2 marks]

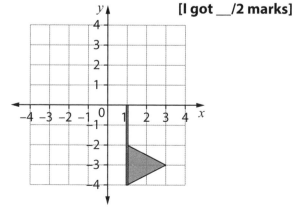

2. Describe the single transformation that maps triangle *ABC* to *A′B′C′* **[___/2 marks]**

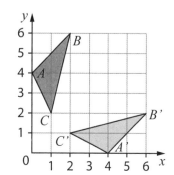

Rotation

To rotate a shape, you need to turn the object through an angle.

Key points

A rotation is described by giving:
1) the angle, e.g. 90°
2) the direction, e.g. clockwise
3) the centre of rotation, e.g. the origin or another point

When you rotate a shape, the object and the image are **congruent** (exactly the same shape and size).

Remember this...

Clockwise follows the direction that the numbers go around the clock.

Confidence bar

Sorted!

☑

☑

☑

Had a look

When rotating a shape...

- Any shape rotated by 360° ends up exactly where it started.
- When rotating by 180°, count the number of spaces up or down, and left or right, from each vertex to the centre of rotation. Then count along the exact amount again, and that's the new vertex position.
- When rotating a shape by 90° clockwise, swap the coordinates and then multiply the y-coordinate by -1
  E.g. the point (1, 2) becomes (2, -1)
- When rotating a shape by 90° anticlockwise, swap the coordinates and then multiply the x-coordinate by -1
  E.g. the point (1, 2) becomes (-2, 1)
- A rotation of 270° is the same as a rotation of 90° in the other direction.

Worked example

Describe the transformation that maps *ABC* to *DEF*
[3 marks]

Solution

This is a rotation.

The transformation is a rotation of 90° anticlockwise about the origin.

Remember to give
(1) the angle,
(2) the direction and
(3) the centre of rotation.

Exam corner

1. Rotate the triangle *ABC* 90° clockwise about the point shown. Label the image *A´B´C´*
[I got ___/3 marks]

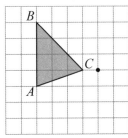

2. Describe the transformation that maps shape A to shape B.
[___/3 marks]

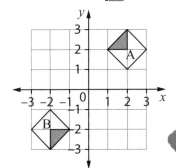

Examiner's tip!

Ask in your exam if you'd like tracing paper to do this kind of question.

Translation

Moving an object without changing its orientation is called translation.

Key points

A translation can be described using a **column vector**:

$\binom{2}{3}$ tells you to move 2 right and 3 up.

Negative values tell you to move left or down:

$\binom{-2}{-3}$ tells you to move 2 left and 3 down.

When you translate a shape, the object and image are **congruent**. They also have **the same orientation** (unlike rotations and reflections).

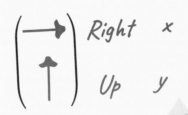

Worked example

Grade 3

a) Describe the transformation that maps shape A to shape B. **[2 marks]**

b) Translate shape A by vector $\binom{-4}{-5}$ and label the image C. **[2 marks]**

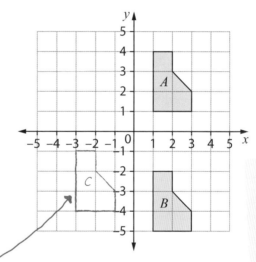

See page 92 for more on column vectors.

Solution

a) Shape A has been moved down 6, so this transformation is a translation by the vector $\binom{0}{-6}$

b) The vector $\binom{-4}{-5}$ tells you to move shape A left 4 and down 5

Work out where just one vertex will move to, then copy the rest of the shape in the same orientation.

Exam corner

Grade 3

1. Draw the image of T after translation by the vector $\binom{1}{2}$ **[I got ___/2 marks]**

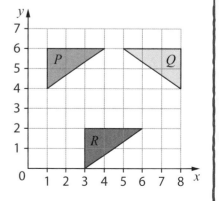

2. The shape P has been transformed in two different ways to shape Q and shape R.

   a) Which shape is a translation of P? Explain how you know. **[___/1 mark]**

   b) Describe this translation using a column vector. **[___/1 mark]**

Grade 3

Enlargement

When you enlarge a shape, all the side lengths are multiplied by the same number. This is the last of the four transformations you need to learn.

Key points

- To enlarge a shape, multiply the distance of each vertex from the **centre of enlargement** by the **scale factor**.
- The dotted lines start at the centre of enlargement and go through the corresponding vertices of the object and the image.
- When a shape is enlarged, its image is **similar** to the object.
- If the scale factor is a fraction between 0 and 1 then the 'enlarged' shape will be smaller than the original.
- To describe an enlargement, you need to write:
  1) the scale factor
  2) the centre of enlargement.

See page 72 for more on similar shapes.

Worked example

Grade 4

Enlarge the shape by scale factor 3 using the centre of enlargement shown. **[2 marks]**

Solution

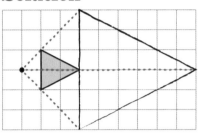

Worked example

Grade 5

Enlarge the shape by scale factor $\frac{1}{2}$ from centre of enlargement (1, 1) **[3 marks]**

Solution

The distance from (1, 1) to each vertex of the image will be $\frac{1}{2}$ the distance to the original vertex.

Confidence bar

Sorted!

Had a look

To find the centre of enlargement, draw lines through the corresponding vertices of the object and see where they meet.

Exam corner

Grade 4

Grade 5

1. **a)** Describe the transformation that maps triangle *A* to triangle *B*. **[I got __/2 marks]**
   b) Explain why triangle *C* is not an enlargement of triangle *A*. **[__/2 marks]**

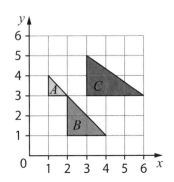

2. Enlarge this shape by a scale factor $\frac{1}{4}$ from the centre of enlargement shown. **[__/2 marks]**

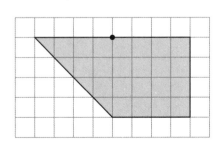

Congruent shapes

Congruent shapes are **exactly** the same shape and size.

Key points

Congruent shapes have all corresponding sides equal and all angles equal.

Triangles are congruent if they meet one of these conditions:

SSS: All three sides match.

SAS: Two sides and the angle between them match.

ASA: Two angles and any side match.

RHS: Both are right-angled triangles, hypotenuse and one other side match.

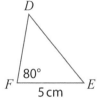

Remember this...
Congruent triangles must meet one of these conditions: SSS, SAS, ASA, RHS.

Not an ASS!

Nor AAA!

Sorted!

☑
☑
☑

Had a look

Worked example

Give a reason why these two triangles are congruent. **[1 mark]**

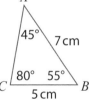

Solution

They are congruent because they satisfy the condition SAS.

Worked example

Given that the triangles are congruent,
a) state the length of *DE* **[1 mark]**
b) state the size of ∠*DEF* **[1 mark]**

Solution

a) *DE* corresponds to *AB* since it is opposite the 80° angle.

$DE = 7\,cm$

b) ∠*DEF* = ∠*ABC* = 55°

Exam corner

1. A rectangle is transformed in different ways.

   State whether the image is congruent to the object in each case:

   a) Reflected in the line $y = x$ **[I got __/1 mark]**
   b) Rotated 90° clockwise about the origin. **[__/1 mark]**
   c) Enlarged by a scale factor 2 from the point (2, 2) **[__/1 mark]**
   d) Translated by the vector $\begin{pmatrix} -1 \\ 5 \end{pmatrix}$ **[__/1 mark]**

2. a) Give a reason why triangles *PQR* and *PRS* are congruent. **[__/1 mark]**
   b) Given that ∠*PRS* = 37°, find the size of ∠*PQR* **[__/2 marks]**

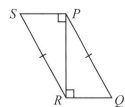

Work out how the vertices and edges match up.

Similar shapes

In maths, if we say shapes are **similar**, we mean they are the same shape, but not the same size.

Key points

- **Similar** shapes have corresponding angles the same.
- They have corresponding side lengths in proportion, i.e. in the same ratio. The ratio is called the **scale factor**.

    $$\text{scale factor (SF)} = \frac{\text{new length}}{\text{original length}}$$

Find corresponding sides on the two shapes to calculate the scale factor (SF).

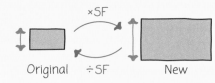

Original   ÷SF   New

Worked example

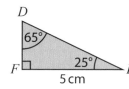

Grade 5

Triangles *ABC* and *DEF* are similar.

a) Calculate the length of *DE*   **[2 marks]**

b) State the size of ∠*CAB*   **[1 mark]**

Solution

a) Scale factor = $\frac{5}{2}$

Length of *DE* = $3 \times \frac{5}{2}$ = 7.5 cm

b) ∠*CAB* = ∠*FDE* since similar shapes have corresponding angles equal
= 65°

> **Remember this...**
>
> $$\text{scale factor} = \frac{\text{new length}}{\text{original length}}$$
>
> *Choose new over old!*

> See page 70 for more on scale factors.

Exam corner

1. The ratio of the side lengths of square *A* to square *B* is 1 : 4. The side length of square *B* is 12 cm.

     Grade 5

a) What is the side length of square *A*?   **[I got ___/2 marks]**

b) What is the ratio of the area of square *A* to the area of square *B*? Write your answer in the form 1 : *n*   **[___/2 marks]**

> *Work out the area of both squares then write as a ratio.*
>
> *Can you spot what has happened to the ratio?*

2. Triangles *VWX* and *VYZ* are similar. Calculate the length *WY*   **[___/3 marks]**

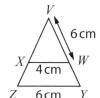

Grade 5

> See pages 51 and 61 for more on ratio.

Area and perimeter

Perimeter is calculated by adding all the lengths around the outside of a shape.

Area is found by multiplying lengths together using a formula.

Formula box

Area of rectangle = base × height

= bh

Area of triangle = (base × height) ÷ 2

= $\frac{1}{2}bh$

Area of parallelogram = base × height

= bh

Area of trapezium = $\frac{1}{2}(a + b)h$

Remember this...

Perimeter is the complete distance around the outside of the shape.

AREA IS THE SPACE INSIDE

Confidence bar

Sorted!

☑
☑
☐

Had a look

Worked example

Grade 3

a) Find the area of the trapezium shown. **[2 marks]**

b) The perimeter of the trapezium is 46 cm.
   Work out the length x **[2 marks]**

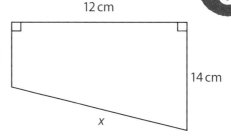

12 cm

5 cm

14 cm

x

Solution

a) Area = $\frac{1}{2}(a + b)h$

= $\frac{1}{2}(5 + 14) \times 12$

= 114 cm^2

b) Perimeter = 5 + 12 + 14 + x

= 31 + x

31 + x = 46

x = 15 cm

Always write down any formula you use and remember to include the units in your final answer.

Exam corner

1. A parallelogram is shown. Calculate its

   a) area   **b)** perimeter.
   State the unit with each of your answers. **[I got __/4 marks]**

   Grade 2

   5 cm

   4 cm

   8 cm

2. A triangle has an area of 26 cm^2. The base of the triangle has a length of 8 cm.

   Find the height of the triangle. **[__/3 marks]**

   Grade 3

STRIVE FOR 5 See pages 122-123 for more practice

Compound shapes

Compound shapes are made up of two or more simpler shapes.

 Grade 3-4

Key points

- To calculate the area of a compound shape, split it into simpler shapes and add up the area of each.
- To calculate the perimeter of a compound shape, add up the lengths of all the outside edges.

To find area of a compound shape:

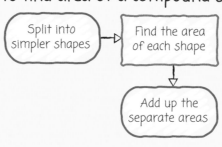

Split into simpler shapes ▷ Find the area of each shape → Add up the separate areas

Confidence bar

Sorted!

☑
☑
☑

Had a look

Worked example

 Grade 4

Calculate the area of the shape shown. **[3 marks]**

8 cm
7 cm
3 cm
12 cm

Solution

You can split the shape into a rectangle and a trapezium.

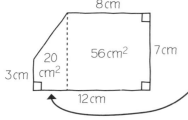

8 cm
20 cm²
56 cm²   7 cm
3 cm
12 cm

Area of rectangle = 7 × 8 = 56 cm²

Height of trapezium = 12 − 8 = 4 cm

Area of trapezium = $\frac{1}{2}(a + b)h$

$= \frac{1}{2} \times (7 + 3) \times 4 = 20$ cm²

Total area = 20 + 56 = 76 cm²

> See page 73 for all the area formulae you will need here.

> Start by splitting the shape into two then finding any missing side lengths.

Exam corner

1. For the shape shown, find
   a) the perimeter   **[I got __/2 marks]**
   b) the area.   **[__/3 marks]**

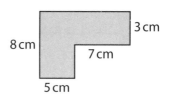

3 cm
8 cm
7 cm
5 cm

 Grade 3

2. The shape of a field is formed by a parallelogram and a rectangle as shown. The field is fully enclosed by a fence.
   a) Calculate the length of fence required.
   b) 40 g of grass seed will cover 1 m² of soil.   **[__/2 marks]**
      Calculate the amount of grass seed required to cover the field.   **[__/4 marks]**

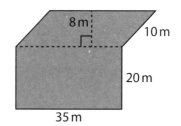

8 m
10 m
20 m
35 m

Grade 4

Circles

The circumference of a circle is its perimeter: the distance around the outside. The area is the space inside. All circle formulae use the value π

Grade 3-4

Formula box

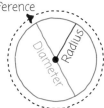

Circumference

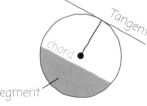
Diameter
Radius

Tangent
chord
Segment

For a circle with radius r (diameter d):

area $= \pi r^2 (= \pi \times r \times r)$

circumference $= \pi d$ (or $2\pi r$)

Remember this...

The formulae for circumference and area of a circle:

$C = \pi d$

<u>C</u>herry <u>p</u>ie is <u>d</u>elicious

$A = \pi r^2$

<u>A</u>pple <u>p</u>ies a<u>r</u>e <u>2</u>

Confidence bar

Sorted!

☑
☑
☑

Had a look

Worked example

Grade 3

A circle has a diameter of 15 cm. Calculate
a) the circumference of the circle **[2 marks]**
b) the area of the circle. **[2 marks]**

Give your answers to 1 decimal place.

Solution

a) Use $C = \pi d$
   Circumference $= \pi \times 15$
   $= 47.1$ cm (to 1 decimal place)

b) The radius of a circle is half of the diameter.
   So here $r = 15 \div 2 = 7.5$ cm
   Use $A = \pi r^2$
   Area $= \pi \times 7.5^2 = 176.7$ cm^2 (to 1 decimal place)

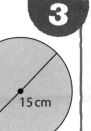

15 cm

See page 3 for more on rounding.

Calculator tips

You will need to use the button for π on your calculator:

π

To convert your answer to a decimal, use this button:

$S \Leftrightarrow D$

Check you know how to round your answer.

Exam corner

6 mm

Grade 3

1. A circular button has radius 6 mm. Calculate, to 1 decimal place:

   a) the circumference of the button **[I got __/2 marks]**
   b) the area of the button. **[__/2 marks]**

2. A circle has circumference 8π cm. Find the area of the circle. Leave your answer in terms of π **[__/3 marks]**

Grade 4

Examiner's tip! STRIVE FOR 5

If the question says 'leave your answer in terms of π', you don't need to put π into your calculator – just write the answer as a multiple of π, e.g. 2π or $\frac{1}{3}\pi$

STRIVE FOR 5 See pages 122-123 for more practice.

75

Semicircles

You need to be able to find the area and perimeter of semicircles and of compound shapes that contain them.

Grade 4–5

Formula box

Area of semicircle = area of circle ÷ 2

Perimeter of semicircle = circumference of circle ÷ 2 + diameter

 See page 75 for more on area and circumference of a circle.

Confidence bar

Sorted!

Had a look

Worked example

Grade 4

The semicircle has radius 4 cm.

Calculate

a) the area **[2 marks]**

b) the perimeter. **[3 marks]**

4 cm

Give your answers correct to 1 decimal place.

 Use $A = \pi r^2$ and $C = \pi d$ (or $2\pi r$) to find the area and the circumference of the whole circle.

Solution

a) Area of circle = $\pi \times 4^2$
$= 16\pi \, cm^2$

Area of semicircle = $16\pi \div 2$
$= 25.1 \, cm^2$ (to 1 decimal place)

b) Circumference of circle = $2 \times \pi \times 4$
$= 8\pi \, cm$

Diameter = 8 cm

Perimeter of semicircle = $8\pi \div 2 + 8$
$= 20.6 \, cm$ (to 1 decimal place)

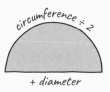 To find the perimeter of...
a semicircle: a quarter circle:

circumference ÷ 2 circumference ÷ 4 + radius

+ diameter + radius
(and remember, radius × 2 = diameter)

Worked example

Grade 5

The compound shape is formed by a rectangle and a semicircle.

Calculate its area correct to 1 decimal place. **[4 marks]**

20 cm

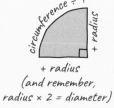

6 cm

Solution

Area of rectangle = 20×6
$= 120 \, cm^2$

Radius of semicircle = 3 cm

Area of semicircle = $\pi \times 3^2 \div 2$
$= 14.1 \, cm^2$

Total area = $120 + 14.1 = 134.1 \, cm^2$

Exam corner

Grade 4

1. A semicircle has a diameter of 12 mm. Calculate

a) the perimeter **b)** the area.

Give your answers correct to 1 decimal place.
[I got __/6 marks]

2. The shape of a playground is formed by a rectangle and part of a circle, as shown.

Grade 5

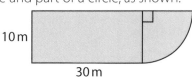

10 m

30 m

Work out the area of the playground.

Give your answer to the nearest integer. **[__/4 marks]**

Notice the right angle. This means it is quarter of a circle.

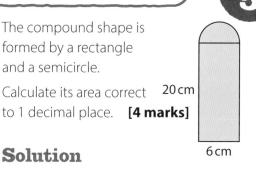 STRIVE FOR 5 See pages 122-123 for more practice.

Arcs and sectors

A **sector** is a fraction of a circle. An **arc** is a fraction of the circumference of a circle.

Formula box

If you have a sector of angle θ and radius r:

Area of sector = $\dfrac{\theta}{360}$ × area of whole circle

$\qquad\qquad = \dfrac{\theta}{360} \times \pi r^2$

Arc length = $\dfrac{\theta}{360}$ × circumference of circle

$\qquad\qquad = \dfrac{\theta}{360} \times 2\pi r$

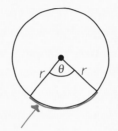

A sector is the shape of a slice of cake.

An arc is the curved edge of the slice

Confidence bar

Sorted!

☑

☑

☑

Had a look

Worked example

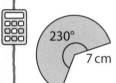

230°

7 cm

A sector can be bigger than a semicircle.

a) Calculate the arc length of the sector.

[2 marks]

b) Calculate the area of the sector. **[2 marks]**
Give your answers to 1 decimal place.

Solution

a) Arc length of sector = $\dfrac{230}{360} \times 2 \times \pi \times 7$

$\qquad\qquad = 28.1\,\text{cm}$ (to 1 decimal place)

b) Area of sector = $\dfrac{230}{360} \times \pi \times 7^2$

$\qquad\qquad = 98.3\,\text{cm}^2$ (to 1 decimal place)

Worked example

Part of a circle of radius 6 cm is shown.
Work out the area of the circle in terms of π

[2 marks]

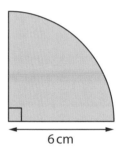

6 cm

Solution

The sector is $\frac{1}{4}$ of a circle

Area of sector = $\dfrac{1}{4} \times \pi \times 6^2$

$\qquad\qquad = 9\pi\,\text{cm}^2$

Exam corner

1. A circle of radius 9 cm has a
sector of angle 35° cut from it.
Find, to 1 decimal place,

9 cm

35°

    a) the area   **b)** the arc length

    c) the perimeter of the sector.   **[I got __/6 marks]**

2. The diagram shows a circle of diameter 21 cm.

Calculate the area of the shaded sector.
Give your answer correct to 1 decimal place.

[__/4 marks]

200°

12 cm

Take care – you are given the diameter here, so what is the radius?

3D shapes

A 3D shape is a solid object with three dimensions, for example a cuboid has length, width and height.

Key points

Prisms have a **polygon** as a base and a constant cross section. A polygon is any 2D shape with straight sides.

cube

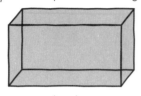

cuboid

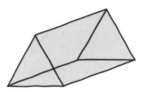

triangular prism

Note that a cylinder is **not** a prism, because a circle is not a polygon.

cylinder

Confidence bar

Sorted!

☑

☑

☑

Had a look

Pyramids have a polygon as the base and all the other faces meet at a point.

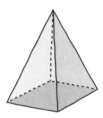

Edge

Face

Vertex

square-based pyramid

triangular-based pyramid

A **face** is a flat surface.

An **edge** is a line where two faces meet.

A **vertex** (plural **vertices**) is a point where three or more edges meet.

A triangular pyramid has 4 faces, 6 edges and 4 vertices.

It's sometimes also called a **tetrahedron**.

Worked example

Grade

1

How many faces, edges and vertices does this prism have? **[3 marks]**

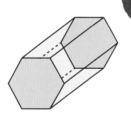

Solution

This is a hexagonal-based prism.

It has 8 faces (6 around the length and one at each end).

It has 18 edges (6 around the length and 6 at each end).

It has 12 vertices (6 at each end).

Note, a cone isn't a pyramid, for the same reason that a cylinder isn't a prism – the base isn't a polygon.

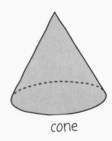

cone

Exam corner

Grade

1

1. **a)** What is this 3D shape called? **[I got __/1 mark]**

   b) Shade the face *EABF*. **[__/1 mark]**

   c) How many faces, edges and vertices does the shape have? **[__/3 marks]**

2. How many faces, edges and vertices does a hexagonal-based pyramid have?

   [__/3 marks]

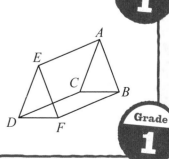

Grade

1

Plans and elevations

You can represent a 3D shape in different ways. Instead of sketching the shape in 3D you can draw a 2D view from a particular direction.

Key points

- A **plan** is the view from directly above.
- An **elevation** is the view from the side or front.
- There may be parts you can't see in a 3D sketch of a shape, because they're behind other parts.

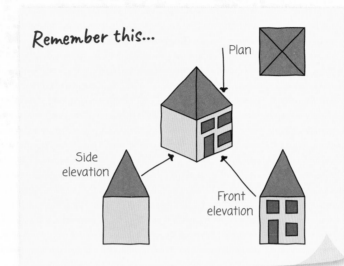

Remember this...

Plan

Side elevation

Front elevation

Worked example

The 3D solid shown is made using eight centimetre cubes. Draw a plan of the solid on the grid. **[2 marks]**

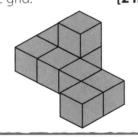

The plan can be drawn in any orientation, as long as it's from above.

Solution

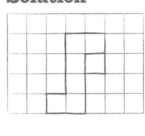

Grade 3

Worked example

The plan view and the front and side elevations of a shape are shown. The shape is made up of identical cubes. Draw a 3D sketch of the shape.

Plan

Grade 3

Front elevation

Side elevation

Solution

The plan shows the base of the shape is 3 by 2 cubes. The front and side elevation both show that the top left part of the plan view is raised by a height of 1 cube.

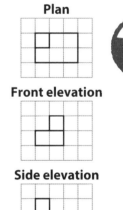

Exam corner

Grade 3

1. The 3D solid is made using six centimetre cubes. Sketch

   a) the plan   **b)** the side elevation

   c) the front elevation.   **[I got ___ /3 marks]**

Side

Front

2. The plan view and front and side elevations of a prism are shown on the grid.

   Grade 4

Plan	Front elevation	Side elevation

   Draw a 3D sketch of the prism.   **[___/2 marks]**

Nets and surface area

You need to be able to accurately draw nets and to visualise how nets will fit together.

Key points

- A **net** is a 2D shape that is folded up to make a 3D shape.
- The area of a net is the **surface area** of the 3D shape. Work out the area of all the faces and add them up.

On a dice, the opposite faces have dots that add up to 7. Try to visualise how this net will fold into a dice.

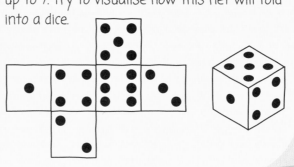

Confidence bar

Sorted!

☑

☑

☑

Had a look

Worked example

Grade 3

A triangular prism is shown.

a) Draw a net of the prism. **[2 marks]**

b) Calculate the surface area of the prism. **[4 marks]**

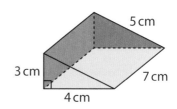
5 cm

3 cm

4 cm

7 cm

Solution

a)

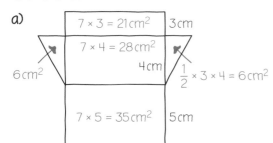

$7 \times 3 = 21\,cm^2$ 3 cm

$7 \times 4 = 28\,cm^2$

$6\,cm^2$ 4 cm $\frac{1}{2} \times 3 \times 4 = 6\,cm^2$

$7 \times 5 = 35\,cm^2$ 5 cm

7 cm

b) The net has two triangles and three rectangles.

Work out the area of each and write it on the net to make sure you don't miss any out.

Surface area = 21 + 28 + 35 + 6 + 6

= 96 cm²

You could have used a bigger rectangle here instead of the three smaller ones:

7 × 12 = 84 cm²

Exam corner

Grade 2

1. A sketch of a cuboid is shown.

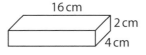
16 cm

2 cm

4 cm

Draw a net of the cuboid. **[I got __/2 marks]**

2. The net of a solid is shown.

Grade 3

a) What is this solid called? **[__/1 mark]**

b) Calculate its surface area. **[__/3 marks]**

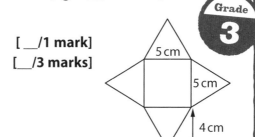
5 cm

5 cm

4 cm

The faces of a cuboid come in opposite pairs, so you can find three areas then double.

STRIVE FOR 5 — See pages 122–123 for more practice.

Prisms and cylinders

You'll need to be able to recall and use formulae for the volume and surface area of prisms.

Formula box

Volume of a cuboid = length × width × height
= *lwh*

Volume of a prism = area of base × height

Volume of a cylinder = π × radius^2 × height
= $\pi r^2 h$

Curved surface area of cylinder = 2 × π × radius × height
= $2\pi rh$

Total surface area of a closed cylinder = $2\pi rh + 2\pi r^2$

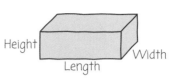
Height, Width, Length

Base, Height

Radius, Height

Confidence bar

Sorted!

☑
☐
☐

Had a look

Worked example

Grade 4

Calculate the volume of this prism. **[2 marks]**

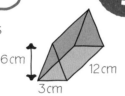
6 cm, 12 cm, 3 cm

Solution

Area of triangular base = $\frac{1}{2}$ × 3 × 6
= 9 cm^2

Volume = 9 × 12 = 108 cm^3

To understand the curved surface area of a cylinder, think of the net of a cylinder:

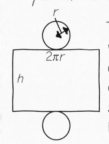
r, $2\pi r$, *h*

The rectangle will wrap around the circumference, so its width is $C = 2\pi r$

See page 80 for how to use a net to calculate surface area.

Recall the formula for the volume of a prism (Volume = area of base × height) and then re-arrange it to make area of base the subject.

Worked example

Grade 5

Calculate the surface area of this closed cylinder. **[3 marks]**

3 cm, 8 cm

Solution

Curved surface area = 2 × π × 3 × 8 = 48π

Area of circular base = π × 3^2 = 9π

Total surface area = $48\pi + 9\pi + 9\pi = 207.3$ cm^2

Exam corner

1. A prism has a volume of 350 cm^3 and a height of 14 cm.
Work out the area of the base of the prism. Give the units. **[I got __/2 marks]**

Grade 3

2. A cylindrical tube for sweets is open at one end.
The diameter of the tube is 6 cm and the length is 20 cm. Calculate, in terms of π,
a) the volume of the tube
[__/2 marks]
b) the surface area of the outside of the tube. **[__/3 marks]**

Grade 5

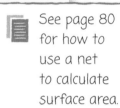
20 cm, 6 cm

Examiner's tip!

STRIVE FOR 5

Take care to avoid a common mistake when finding the surface area – this is not a solid cylinder: it is only closed at one end.

Spheres

A sphere is a curved, 'ball-shaped' 3D shape. You don't need to memorise the formulae on this page, but you need to be able to use them.

Formula box

For a sphere with radius r:

Volume of sphere $= \frac{4}{3}\pi r^3$

Surface area of sphere $= 4\pi r^2$

You need to be careful converting units of area and volume.
For example:

| To convert cm to m $\div 100$ | To convert cm^2 to m^2 $\div 100^2$ | To convert cm^3 to m^3 $\div 100^3$ |

Confidence bar

Sorted!

☑

☑

☑

Had a look

Worked example

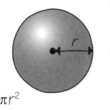

A sphere has a surface area of $36\pi\,cm^2$.
Calculate the volume of the sphere in terms of π **[4 marks]**

Solution

Surface area is given by $4\pi r^2$, which means that, for this sphere,

$4\pi r^2 = 36\pi$

$\dfrac{4\pi r^2}{4\pi} = \dfrac{36\pi}{4\pi}$ Divide both sides by 4π

$r^2 = 9$

$r = 3\,cm$

Now use the formula for volume:

Volume $= \dfrac{4}{3} \times \pi \times 3^3$

$= \dfrac{4}{3} \times \pi \times 27$

$= 36\pi\,cm^3$ Leave the answer in terms of π

Worked example

A sphere has a volume of $20\,cm^3$ and a surface area of $36\,cm^2$.
a) Write the surface area in mm^2. **[2 marks]**
b) Write the volume in mm^3. **[2 marks]**

Solution

To convert from cm to mm, you multiply by 10. So,

a) to convert from cm^2 to mm^2, multiply by 10^2:
surface area $= 36 \times 10^2 = 3600\,mm^2$

b) to convert from cm^3 to mm^3, multiply by 10^3:
volume $= 20 \times 10^3 = 20\,000\,mm^3$

Exam corner

1. A sphere has a radius of 12 cm.

   a) Work out the volume of the sphere. **[I got ___/2 marks]**

   b) Work out the surface area of the sphere. **[___/2 marks]**

     Give your answers to 3 significant figures.

2. A ball is a sphere with a diameter of 80 mm.

   Work out the surface area of the ball in cm^3.
   Leave your answer in terms of π **[___/3 marks]**

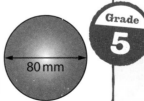

80 mm

Examiner's tip!

Always write down formulae before you use them.

Pyramids and cones

You will be given the formulae for the volume and surface area of a cone, but will need to learn the formula for the volume of a pyramid.

Formula box

$$\text{Volume of pyramid} = \frac{1}{3} \times \text{area of base} \times \text{height}$$

Volume of cone = $\frac{1}{3}$ x area of base x height

$= \frac{1}{3}\pi r^2 h$

Curved surface area of cone = $\pi r l$

Area of base of cone = πr^2

Total surface area of cone = $\pi r l + \pi r^2$

Learn this!
It works for **any** kind of pyramid.

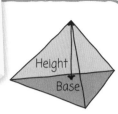
Height
Base

r is the radius of the base
h is the height
l is the slant height

Worked example

Grade 5

See page 80 for how to use a net to find the surface area of a pyramid.

The dimensions of a cone are shown.
a) Calculate the volume of the cone. **[2 marks]**
b) Calculate the total surface area of the cone. **[3 marks]**
Give your answers in terms of π

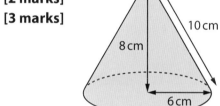
10 cm
8 cm
6 cm

Solution

a) Volume = $\frac{1}{3} \times \pi \times 6^2 \times 8$

$= 96\pi \, \text{cm}^3$

b) Curved surface area = $\pi \times 6 \times 10 = 60\pi \, \text{cm}^2$

Area of circular base = $\pi \times 6^2 = 36\pi \, \text{cm}^2$

Total surface area = $60\pi + 36\pi$

$= 96\pi \, \text{cm}^2$

The total surface area of a cone is the area of the circular base plus the curved surface area:
total surface area = $\pi r l + \pi r^2$

Exam corner

Grade 5

1. A square-based pyramid has a volume of 100 cm³.

The height of the pyramid is 12 cm.

What is the value of x, the side-length of the base? **[I got ___/3 marks]**

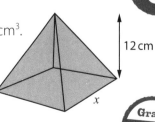
12 cm
x

2. A cone for chips has dimensions as shown.

a) Calculate the volume of the cone in terms of π **[___/2 marks]**

b) Find the area of card needed to make the cone, in terms of π **[___/2 marks]**

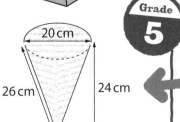
20 cm
26 cm
24 cm

Grade 5

Examiner's tip!

Take care for this classic trick question – this cone is open at the 'base' so you only need the curved surface area.

Constructing triangles

You can construct triangles with given side lengths using a ruler and a pair of compasses. 'Construct' means draw accurately.

Key points

You can use a ruler and a protractor to accurately draw a triangle when you know:

- angle-side-angle (ASA) or
- side-angle-side (SAS) or
- hypotenuse and one other side of a right-angled triangle (RHS).

To construct a triangle when you know all three side lengths (SSS), you need a pair of compasses:

STEP 1: Use a ruler to draw the first side.

STEP 2: Set your compasses to the next side length and draw an arc from one vertex.

STEP 3: Set your compasses to the final side length and draw an arc.

STEP 4: Draw lines to complete the triangle.

> 📄 See page 71 for more on congruent triangles.

Worked example

Construct a triangle with side lengths 7 cm, 4 cm and 5 cm.   **[3 marks]**

Solution

(Step 2) (Step 3)

Step 2: Set compass to 5 cm and draw an arc. Put point of compass here.

Step 3: Set compass to 4 cm and draw an arc. Put compass point here.

(Step 4) (Step 4)

Step 4: Draw lines from the ends of the horizontal line to where the arcs cross, to complete the triangle.

Step 1: Use a ruler to draw a horizontal 7 cm line.

(Step 1)

Exam corner

1. Use a ruler and a protractor to accurately draw these triangles:

a)
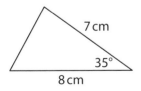

7 cm
35°
8 cm

[I got __/2 marks]

b)
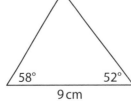

58°   52°
9 cm

[__/2 marks]

2. a) Draw a triangle with side lengths 9 cm, 5 cm and 8 cm.

[__/3 marks]

b) Construct a 60° angle.

[__/2 marks]

Examiner's tip!

Do not rub out the arcs. These are called your **construction lines**.

NO ARCS = NO MARKS!

An equilateral triangle has three 60° angles, so here you can draw two sides of an equilateral triangle of any side length.

Perpendiculars and bisectors

You need a compass to construct perpendicular lines and bisectors.

Key points

- **Perpendicular** lines are at 90°
- The shortest distance from a point to a line is the perpendicular distance.
- A **bisector** cuts a line or an angle exactly in half.
- The **perpendicular bisector** of a line segment cuts the line in half at right angles.

To draw the perpendicular bisector of *AB*:

STEP 1: Put the point of the compasses at *A* and draw arcs above and below the line.

STEP 2: Repeat at *B*.

STEP 3: Join up the points where the arcs meet.

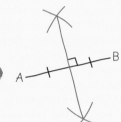

If your arcs don't cross, then your compasses aren't wide enough - ensure they are open wider than halfway.

Worked example

Grade 4

Draw the perpendicular from the dot to the line. **[2 marks]**

Solution

STEP 1: Put point of compasses on the dot and draw two arcs on the line.

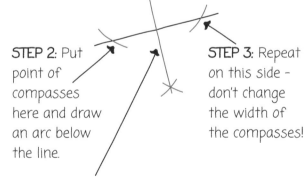

STEP 2: Put point of compasses here and draw an arc below the line.

STEP 3: Repeat on this side – don't change the width of the compasses!

STEP 4: Draw the line from the dot through where the arcs meet.

Worked example

Grade 4

Use compasses to bisect the angle. **[2 marks]**

Solution

STEP 1: Put point of compasses on the vertex and draw an arc on each line.

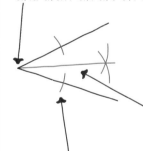

STEP 3: Repeat on the other line, so you have two arcs crossing.

STEP 2: Put point of compasses at this point and draw another arc.

STEP 4: To bisect the angle, draw the line from the vertex to where the arcs meet.

Exam corner

Grade 4

Remember to leave all your construction lines visible.

Grade 4

1. Draw the perpendicular of the line *AB* through *P*
[I got __/2 marks]

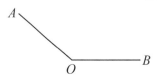

A ——————•—————— B
          P

2. Draw the angle bisector of angle *AOB*
[__/2 marks]

A
  \
   \
    _____ B
    O

Loci

A **locus** (plural **loci**) is a set of points that follow a certain rule.

Key points

- The locus of points a fixed distance from a point is a circle.
- The locus of points a fixed distance from a line is a parallel line.
- The locus of points **equidistant** from two points is a perpendicular bisector of those two points.
- The locus of points **equidistant** from two lines is an angle bisector of the angle formed where the two lines join (assuming they're not parallel).

Remember this...
Equidistant means the same distance.

Looks like equal

Confidence bar

Sorted!

Had a look

Worked example

a) Draw the locus of points that are 5 cm from the line AB. **[3 marks]**

b) Shade the region where the points are:
- less than 5 cm from the line AB <u>and</u>
- closer to point B than point A.

A ——————— B **[3 marks]**

Solution

a) Draw semicircles of radius 5 cm at each end of the line AB.

Extend the arcs a little beyond the top and bottom points so you know you've definitely drawn enough.

Then draw parallel lines 5 cm either side of the line.

See page 85 for how to construct bisectors.

b) First draw the perpendicular bisector of the line AB

Then shade the part that is closer to B

Exam corner

1. Draw the locus of points that are 8 cm from a fixed point.
[I got __/2 marks]

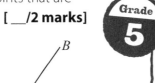

2. a) Use compasses to draw the locus of points that are equidistant from lines AB and AC. **[__/2 marks]**

b) Shade the region that is
- less than 3 cm from point A <u>and</u>
- closer to line AB than to line AC.
[__/3 marks]

Examiner's tip!

If an exam question tells you to 'draw' then you need to make an accurate representation (not just a sketch).

Pythagoras' theorem

Use Pythagoras' theorem to find missing sides in right-angled triangles.

Formula box

Pythagoras' theorem is:

$$a^2 + b^2 = c^2$$

where c is the **hypotenuse** (longest side) of the triangle and a and b are the other two sides.

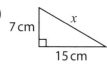

Remember this...

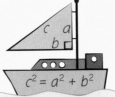

$$c^2 = a^2 + b^2$$

and it's plain-sailing!

Confidence bar

Sorted!

Had a look

Worked example

Grade 4

Calculate the missing side lengths in these triangles. **[4 marks]**

a)

7 cm
15 cm
x

b)
3.5 cm
y
9.8 cm

Use your calculator to work these out.

Solution

a) $x^2 = 7^2 + 15^2$

$x = \sqrt{7^2 + 15^2} = 16.6$ cm (to 1 d.p.)

b) $9.8^2 = 3.5^2 + y^2$

$y^2 = 9.8^2 - 3.5^2$

$y = \sqrt{9.8^2 - 3.5^2} = 9.2$ cm (to 1 d.p.)

Worked example

The points A and B have coordinates $(1, 2)$ and $(4, -2)$. Calculate the length of AB **[3 marks]**

Grade 5

Solution

Plot the points A and B on a coordinate grid.

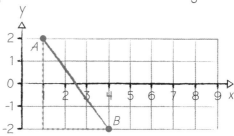

The right-angled triangle has a base of 3 and a height of 4, so $(AB)^2 = 3^2 + 4^2 = 25$

$$AB = \sqrt{25} = 5$$

Exam corner

Grade 4

1. Find the missing side lengths in these triangles.

Give your answers correct to 1 decimal place. **[I got ___/4 marks]**

a)
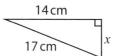
14 cm
17 cm
x

b)
y
4.2 cm
7.6 cm

2. Show that one of these triangles is right-angled and the other is not. **[___/4 marks]**

Grade 4

Examiner's tip!

If you get a question like this, you need work out $a^2 + b^2$ and see whether it equals c^2 (where c is the longest side).

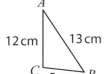
A
12 cm
13 cm
C 5 cm B

D
4 cm
6 cm
F 3 cm E

Not drawn to scale

Trigonometry 1

You can use trigonometry to find the lengths of sides in right-angled triangles.

Formula box

You need to learn these ratios for right-angled triangles:

$$\sin\theta = \frac{opposite}{hypotenuse}$$

$$\cos\theta = \frac{adjacent}{hypotenuse}$$

$$\tan\theta = \frac{opposite}{adjacent}$$

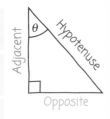

The **hypotenuse** is the longest side.

The opposite is opposite the angle θ.

The adjacent is next to the angle θ.

Remember this...

You can use a mnemonic such as...

Silly **O**ld **H**arry **C**hased **A** **H**orse **T**hrough **O**ur **A**ttic

Or simply:

SOH-CAH-TOA

People normally pronounce this 'sock-ah-toe-ah'.

Confidence bar

Sorted!

Had a look

Worked example

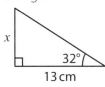

Find the value of x in this triangle.

[2 marks]

Solution

You know the <u>adjacent</u> side is 13 cm, you want to find the <u>opposite</u> side,

so use $\tan\theta = \frac{opposite}{adjacent}$

Cover up the O to get T × A:

$x = \tan 32° × 13$

$= 8.1$ cm (1 decimal place)

Calculator tip

Find these buttons on your calculator.

| sin | cos | tan |

Exam corner

1. Find the value of x in each of these triangles to 1 decimal place.

   a)

   22 cm, x, 40°

   b)

   6 cm, 52°, x **[I got___/4 marks]**

2. A plank of wood is propped up against a wall. The plank rests 0.5 m from the base of the wall and makes an angle of 70° with the floor. Work out the length of the plank to the nearest centimetre.   **[___/2 marks]**

Examiner's tip!

Draw a diagram to show the situation.

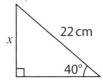

x, 70°, 0.5 m

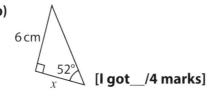

Trigonometry 2

You can use trigonometry to calculate angles in right-angled triangles.

Grade 5

Key points

To find an angle in a right-angled triangle when you know two side lengths:

STEP 1: Identify which two sides you know out of **Hypotenuse**, **Adjacent**, or Opposite.

STEP 2: Then identify which trigonometric ratio you need, for example you'll need sin θ if you know the Hypotenuse and the Opposite sides.

STEP 3: Set up your equation, $\sin\theta = \dfrac{Opposite}{Hypotenuse}$

STEP 4: Rearrange the equation to make θ the subject: $\theta = \sin^{-1}\dfrac{Opposite}{Hypotenuse}$

STEP 5: Use your calculator to find out the inverse sin of this number. That gives you the angle θ.

Remember this...
SOH-CAH-TOA

Calculator tip

To work out the inverse of cos, sin or tan, you will probably have to press shift or inv first.

$\sin^{-1}$

 sin

Confidence bar

Sorted!

☑
☑
☑

Had a look

Grade 5

Worked example

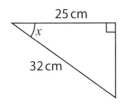

Calculate the size of the angle marked x in this triangle.

25 cm
x
32 cm

[2 marks]

Solution

You know the <u>adjacent</u> side is 25 cm, and the <u>hypotenuse</u> is 32 cm,

so use $\cos x = \dfrac{adjacent}{hypotenuse}$

Cover up the C to leave A ÷ H:

$\cos x = \dfrac{25}{32}$

$x = \cos^{-1}\left(\dfrac{25}{32}\right)$

Take the inverse cos of both sides to find x

= 38.6° (1 decimal place)

Examiner's tip!

Get to know your calculator really well before the exam. A lot of students lose marks because they don't know how to use their calculator properly.

Exam corner

Grade 5

1. Calculate the size of the angle marked x in each of these triangles. Give your answers to 1 decimal place.

   a)
   27 cm
   8 cm
   x

   b)
   6.4 cm
   x 12.9 cm

   [I got__/4 marks]

2. A tower block is 80 m tall. A camera is placed on the floor 20 m from the base of the tower block.

   Find the angle of elevation of the top of the tower block from the camera, to the nearest degree. **[__/2 marks]**

Grade 5

The angle of **elevation** or **depression** is the angle above or below a horizontal line.

80 m

Angle of elevation

20 m

Camera   Horizontal line

89

Exact values

You need to remember the exact values of sin, cos and tan for certain angles.

Key points — You should learn these exact values:

θ	$0°$	$30°$	$45°$	$60°$	$90°$
$\sin\theta$	0	$\dfrac{1}{2}$	$\dfrac{\sqrt{2}}{2}$	$\dfrac{\sqrt{3}}{2}$	1
$\cos\theta$	1	$\dfrac{\sqrt{3}}{2}$	$\dfrac{\sqrt{2}}{2}$	$\dfrac{1}{2}$	0
$\tan\theta$	0	$\dfrac{1}{\sqrt{3}}$	1	$\sqrt{3}$	(undefined)

To remember some of these values, use your left hand. Imagine your fingers labelled like shown. To find the value of sin, cos or tan for a certain angle, first bend down the finger relating to that angle. Then:

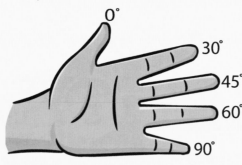

For example:

To find sin 60°, bend down the 60° finger; there are 3 fingers above, so $\sin 60° = \dfrac{\sqrt{3}}{2}$

To find cos 45°, bend down the 45° finger; there are 2 fingers below, so $\cos 45° = \dfrac{\sqrt{2}}{2}$

To find tan 60°, bend down the 60° finger; there are 3 fingers above and 1 below, so $\tan 60° = \dfrac{\sqrt{3}}{\sqrt{1}} = \sqrt{3}$

Remember this...

$\sin\theta$
Count the number of fingers <u>above</u> it.
Then take the square-root and divide by 2

$\cos\theta$
Count the number of fingers <u>below</u> it.
Then take the square-root and divide by 2

$\tan\theta$ (this is a bit different!)
Find the square root of the number of fingers <u>above</u> divided by the square root of the number of fingers <u>below</u>

Exam corner

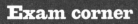

1. Write down the value of

    a) tan 30°   **b)** sin 90°
    [I got ___/2 marks]

2. Work out the value of x in this triangle. **[___/3 marks]**

2 cm, 60°, x

Worked example

Work out the value of x in this triangle. **[3 marks]**

30°, 10 cm, x

Solution

You have the <u>opposite</u> side and want to know the <u>hypotenuse</u>, so use $\sin\theta = \dfrac{opposite}{hypotenuse}$

$x = \dfrac{10}{\sin 30°}$

$= \dfrac{10}{\left(\frac{1}{2}\right)}$ since $\sin 30° = \dfrac{1}{2}$

$= 20\,cm$

Vectors

A vector has a size and a direction. There are different ways of writing vectors that you need to know about.

Key points

- The top vector can be written $\overrightarrow{AB}$ as it starts at point A and ends at point B
- It can also be printed in bold type, **a**. In handwriting you would write it with an underline, <u>a</u>
- The **size and direction** of a vector matter, but **not** the position. So the vector $\overrightarrow{CD}$ is also **a**, as it has the same size and direction as the vector $\overrightarrow{AB}$
- The vector **-a** is the same size as **a** and parallel to **a** but in the opposite direction.
- A vector that is parallel to **a** but a different length will be a multiple of **a** such as 2**a**

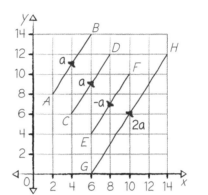

Worked example

OABC is a parallelogram. $\overrightarrow{OA}$ = **a** and $\overrightarrow{OC}$ = **c**

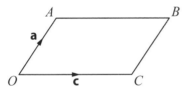

Write down these vectors in terms of **a** and **c**

a) $\overrightarrow{CO}$ b) $\overrightarrow{OB}$ c) $\overrightarrow{AC}$ **[3 marks]**

Solution

a) $\overrightarrow{CO}$ = -<u>c</u>   It's parallel to $\overrightarrow{OC}$ but in the opposite direction.

b) $\overrightarrow{OB}$ = $\overrightarrow{OA}$ + $\overrightarrow{AB}$ = <u>a</u> + <u>c</u>

When you write the vectors nose to tail, these letters will always match.

c) $\overrightarrow{AC}$ = $\overrightarrow{AO}$ + $\overrightarrow{OC}$ = -<u>a</u> + <u>c</u>

You could write <u>c</u> – <u>a</u>; the order doesn't matter.

Remember to underline the letter when you write a vector by hand.

Remember this...

Like dogs, vectors have a nose and a tail. They can be added by putting them nose to tail.

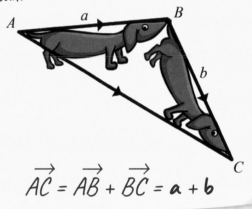

$$\overrightarrow{AC} = \overrightarrow{AB} + \overrightarrow{BC} = \mathbf{a} + \mathbf{b}$$

Exam corner

1. Trapezium *OABC* is formed from three equilateral triangles as shown.
   $\overrightarrow{OA}$ = **a** and $\overrightarrow{OD}$ = **d**

Write each of these vectors in terms of **a** and **d**

a) $\overrightarrow{DO}$ b) $\overrightarrow{OB}$ c) $\overrightarrow{OC}$ d) $\overrightarrow{AC}$

[I got ___/4 marks]

Column vectors

Column vectors are an easy way to describe the size and direction of a vector. They also make it easy to add vectors.

Key points

- To add column vectors, add the top values then add the bottom values.
- To multiply a column vector by a number, multiply both the top and bottom values by the number.

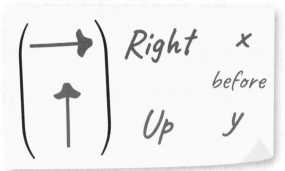

Worked example

Given that $\mathbf{a} = \begin{pmatrix} 4 \\ -2 \end{pmatrix}$ and $\mathbf{b} = \begin{pmatrix} -5 \\ 0 \end{pmatrix}$,

a) work out these column vectors:

    i) $3\mathbf{a}$ ii) $\mathbf{a} + \mathbf{b}$ iii) $2\mathbf{b} - \mathbf{a}$ **[3 marks]**

b) show the vectors $\mathbf{a}$, $\mathbf{b}$ and $\mathbf{a} + \mathbf{b}$ on a square grid.   **[3 marks]**

See page 69 for how to use column vectors to describe translations.

Solution

a) i) $3a = 3\begin{pmatrix} 4 \\ -2 \end{pmatrix} = \begin{pmatrix} 3 \times 4 \\ 3 \times -2 \end{pmatrix}$

        $= \begin{pmatrix} 12 \\ -6 \end{pmatrix}$

ii) $a + b = \begin{pmatrix} 4 \\ -2 \end{pmatrix} + \begin{pmatrix} -5 \\ 0 \end{pmatrix} = \begin{pmatrix} 4 - 5 \\ -2 + 0 \end{pmatrix}$

              $= \begin{pmatrix} -1 \\ -2 \end{pmatrix}$

iii) $2b - a = 2\begin{pmatrix} -5 \\ 0 \end{pmatrix} - \begin{pmatrix} 4 \\ -2 \end{pmatrix}$

         $= \begin{pmatrix} -10 \\ 0 \end{pmatrix} - \begin{pmatrix} 4 \\ -2 \end{pmatrix}$

         $= \begin{pmatrix} -10 - 4 \\ 0 - (-2) \end{pmatrix}$

         $= \begin{pmatrix} -14 \\ 2 \end{pmatrix}$

b)

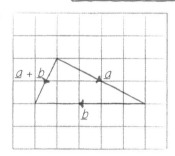

Exam corner

1. Vectors $\mathbf{a}$, $\mathbf{b}$ and $\mathbf{a} + \mathbf{b}$ are shown on the grid.

    Write them as column vectors.

                     [I got ___/3 marks]

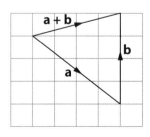

2. Given that $\mathbf{p} = \begin{pmatrix} 2 \\ 7 \end{pmatrix}$, $\mathbf{q} = \begin{pmatrix} -3 \\ 5 \end{pmatrix}$ and $\mathbf{r} = \begin{pmatrix} 1 \\ -4 \end{pmatrix}$

a) work out these column vectors:

    i) $4\mathbf{q}$ ii) $\mathbf{p} + \mathbf{q} + \mathbf{r}$ iii) $2\mathbf{p} - \mathbf{r}$ **[___/3 marks]**

b) work out which **two** of these vectors are parallel to $\mathbf{r}$:   **[___/2 marks]**

        $\begin{pmatrix} 2 \\ 8 \end{pmatrix}$ $\begin{pmatrix} -1 \\ 4 \end{pmatrix}$

        $\begin{pmatrix} 3 \\ -12 \end{pmatrix}$ $\begin{pmatrix} 4 \\ -20 \end{pmatrix}$

If two vectors are parallel, one is a multiple of the other.

Sampling

Instead of gathering information from every member of a population, it's sometimes better to use a smaller set of members, called a **sample**.

Key points

- Data from a sample can be used to estimate properties of the whole population.
- The larger the sample, the more accurate the estimates.
- Each member of the population should have an equal chance of being in the sample, otherwise the sample will be **biased**.
- A biased sample will not represent the population well.

Types of data you need to know about:

Quantitative = numerical

↖ like quantity (a number or amount)

Qualitative = non-numerical

↖ like quality (a characteristic, such as colour)

Primary = data you collect yourself (you are the **first** person to see it)

Secondary = data someone else has collected (you are at least the **second** person to see it)

Exam corner

Grade 5

Aston is researching a holiday location and wants to find out about the amount of rain there. He randomly selects 20 of the 48 days of the previous summer holiday and looks online at the weather on those days. The data is in the table.

Type of rain	Number of days
Heavy rain	2
Light rain	5
No rain	13

a) Is this primary or secondary data? Explain your answer.

[I got __/1 mark]

b) Estimate how many of the 48 days of the summer holiday had light rain.

[__/2 marks]

Worked example

Grade 5

Jessica wants to know how many books students in her school read per month. There are 1000 students in her school, so she wants to use a sample. She decides to go to the library and ask students how many books they have read that month.

a) What type of data will Jessica have? **[2 marks]**

b) Jessica asks 10 students in total, and finds that 2 of them have read more than 5 books that month.
Use this data to estimate how many students in the entire school have read more than 5 books that month. **[2 marks]**

c) Explain why the sample might be biased and your estimate in part **b)** may not be accurate. **[2 marks]**

Solution

a) This is quantitative primary data (it is numerical and Jessica has collected it herself).

b) $\frac{2}{10} = \frac{1}{5}$ of the students have read more than 5 books — Find the proportion in the sample who have read more than 5 books.

$\frac{1}{5} \times 1000 = 200$ students — Multiply the proportion in the sample by the total number of students.

c) Not all students in the school have an equal chance of being in the sample, and students in the library are likely to have read more books than average.

Organising data

You should know how to organise data using frequency tables, two-way tables and stem-and-leaf diagrams.

Key points

- A **frequency table** shows the frequency (number of items) in each category.
- A **two-way table** links two types of data.
- A **stem-and-leaf diagram** displays data in numerical order.

Confidence bar

Sorted!

☑

☑

☑

Had a look

Worked example

Grade 2

The two-way table shows the main course and dessert options chosen by a group of people.

How many people chose

a) chicken and mousse
b) fruit?   **[2 marks]**

	chicken	vegetarian
fruit	5	2
mousse	9	4

Solution

a) Look in the column for chicken and the row for mousse. 9 people chose both.

b) Add up all the values in the fruit row: 5 + 2 = 7, so 7 people chose fruit.

Stem-and-leaf diagram:

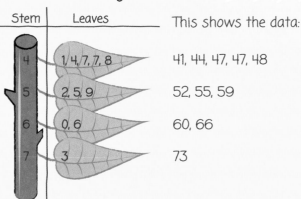

Stem	Leaves
4	1, 4, 7, 7, 8
5	2, 5, 9
6	0, 6
7	3

This shows the data:

41, 44, 47, 47, 48

52, 55, 59

60, 66

73

Key: 4 | 1 means 41

Here, the stem is the tens digits and the leaves are the units digits, but that's not always the case. The **key** explains what they represent, so it **must** be included.

Exam corner

Grade 2

1. The two-way table shows the numbers of students who study different combinations of subjects.

	French	German	Spanish
History	24	44	17
Geography	36	15	14

How many students study

a) French and Geography
b) German?   **[I got __/2 marks]**

Grade 3

2. The numbers of minutes spent on homework per day by 10 students are:

12, 8, 14, 25, 27, 9, 3, 33, 49, 33

a) Represent the data in a stem-and-leaf diagram.   **[__/3 marks]**

b) Complete the grouped frequency table.   **[__/2 marks]**

Time (minutes)	Frequency
0–9	
10–19	
20–29	
30–39	
40–49	

To complete the table, count the number of values in the list that fit in each category. For example, in the top right cell, you write 2, because there are 2 values in the list (8 and 9) which fit into the 0–9 category.

Simple charts

Pictograms, bar charts and vertical line charts can be used to represent qualitative (non-numerical) and ungrouped quantitative (numerical) data.

Grade
1–2

Key points

A **pictogram**:
- is only used for qualitative data
- uses symbols and part-symbols to represent the size of each category
- has a key

A **bar chart**:
- has labels on both axes
- has a scale on the vertical axis
- has bars of the same width
- has equal gaps between the bars

A **vertical line chart** is the same as a bar chart but uses lines instead of bars.

 See page 96 for an example of a vertical line chart.

These two charts show the same information about some people's favourite type of book

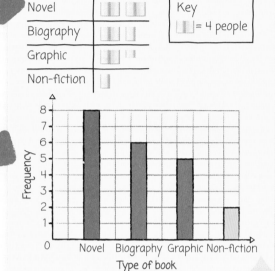

Key
|▯| = 4 people

Confidence bar

Sorted!

Had a look

A **dual bar chart** is a bar chart representing two sets of data. The bars for each category are shown side by side.

Grade 2

Worked example

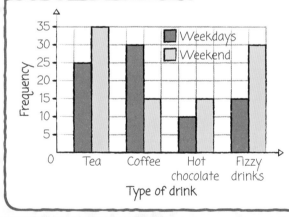

The dual bar chart shows the average number of different drinks sold per day at a café.

What is the most popular drink on weekdays?   **[1 mark]**

Solution

Look at the key on the chart. Weekdays are represented by the green bars. The tallest green bar is for coffee so this is the most popular drink on weekdays.

Exam corner

1. Jayden makes a tally of the ages of people going into a swimming pool.

   a) Complete the frequency column in the table.
      [I got ___/1 mark]

   b) Represent this information in a pictogram.
      [___/3 marks]

Age group	Tally	Frequency
Pre-school	卌 IIII	
School age	卌 II	
Adults under 65	卌 卌	
Adults age 65+	IIII	

Grade 1

2. Look at the dual bar chart in the worked example.

   a) What is the average number of cups of tea sold on a weekend day?   **[___/1 mark]**

   b) How many drinks in total are sold on average on a weekday?   **[___/2 marks]**

Grade 2

Pie charts

A **pie chart** shows you the proportion of the total in each category.
The angles in a pie chart add up to 360°

To work out how many items in a category...

size of angle → ÷ 360 → × total → number of items

For example, for apples in the pie chart shown:

160 → 160 ÷ 360 = $\frac{4}{9}$ → $\frac{4}{9}$ × 81 → 36 apples

Work backwards to find the size of an angle...

size of angle ← × 360 ← ÷ total ← number of items

160 ← $\frac{4}{9}$ × 360 ← $\frac{4}{9}$ = 36 ÷ 81 ← 36 apples

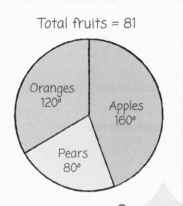

Total fruits = 81

Oranges 120°
Apples 160°
Pears 80°

Confidence bar

Sorted!
☑
☑
☑

Had a look

Worked example

The pie chart shows the proportion of people using different equipment in a gym at a given time.

There are 18 people in the gym. How many are using rowing machines?

Use of gym equipment

Cross trainer
Weights
Treadmill
Rowing machine

Solution

Use a protractor to measure the 'rowing machine' sector. You should get 60°.

Proportion = 60 ÷ 360 = $\frac{1}{6}$

Number of people = $\frac{1}{6}$ × 18 = 3

Exam corner

1. 24 people were asked their favourite snack. A pie chart was drawn. The sector for crisps was 135°. Calculate the number who preferred crisps. **[I got __/2 marks]**

2. Draw a pie chart to show the information from the table.

Favourite pet	Frequency
Dog	15
Cat	20
Other	25

[__/3 marks]

Worked example

The vertical line chart shows the reasons for staff absence at a school.

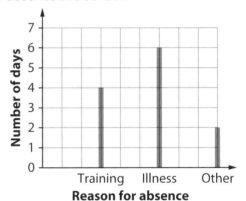

Number of days (y-axis): 0 1 2 3 4 5 6 7

Training, Illness, Other
Reason for absence

Isla wants to draw a pie chart to show this data. Calculate the angle of the sector to represent training.

Solution

First find the total number of days of absence:

Total = 4 + 6 + 2 = 12

Now find the proportion of absence days caused by training:

Proportion = 4 ÷ 12 = $\frac{1}{3}$

Angle of sector = $\frac{1}{3}$ × 360 = 120°

Check that your angles add up to 360°.

Averages and spread

There are three types of average you need to be able to work out: **mean**, **median** and **mode**. The spread of data can be measured using the **range**.

Key points

Mean: Add up all the values and divide by the total number of values.

Median: List the data in order and select the middle value. If there are two middle values, find the number half-way between them.

Mode: The most commonly occurring value. There may be more than one mode, or no mode at all.

Range: The difference between the largest and smallest values.

I'm the median height!

Arrange in order before finding median.

Mean, median or mode?

- If you have non-numerical data, use **the mode**

- If the data has an **outlier** (an unusually large or small value), it might be better to use **the median** than the mean. The mean is affected by outliers but the median isn't.

If the mean of 8 numbers is 2.5 then the total of the numbers must be 8×2.5=20

Worked example

Grade **2**

The scores of the 12 teams in a quiz are recorded as

3, 10, 1, 11, 4, 4, 7, 9, 10, 9, 9, 4

Calculate the median, mode, mean and range of the scores.

[5 marks]

Solution

Write the scores in order: 1, 3, 4, 4, 4, 7, 9, 9, 9, 10, 10, 11.

There are 12 values, so the median is the value halfway between the 6th and the 7th values. These are 7 and 9, so median = $\frac{7+9}{2}$ = 8

mode = 4 and 9 (they both occur 3 times)

mean = $\frac{3+10+1+11+4+4+7+9+10+9+9+4}{12}$ = $\frac{81}{12}$ = 6.75

range = 11 - 1 = 10

Exam corner

1. The numbers of bikes per household in a sample of 17 households are:

   1, 3, 3, 4, 2, 1, 0, 3, 5, 0, 7, 4, 2, 4, 1, 0, 4

   Calculate

   a) the median   **[I got ___/1 mark]**   **b)** the mode   **[___ /1 mark]**

   c) the mean   **[___/2 marks]**   **d)** the range   **[___ /1 mark]**

   Grade **2**

2. The mean of these eight positive integers is 2.5 and the median is 1.5

   1, 2, 2, 1, 9, 1, ?, ?

   a) Work out the values of the unknown numbers.   **[___ /3 marks]**

   b) Explain why you might choose the median instead of the mean to represent the average value of these numbers.   **[___ /1 mark]**

   Grade **4**

Averages from tables

Sometimes data is summarised in a frequency table. You need to be able to calculate the averages and range directly from the table.

To calculate the mean from a frequency table...
1. Multiply each value by its frequency.
2. Add up these values.
3. Divide by the total number of values.

It's... MAD!

 See page 97 for more on the mean, median, mode and range.

Worked example

 Grade 4

The table shows the number of sunny days per week over 21 weeks.

No. of sunny days	0	1	2	3	4	5	6	7
Frequency	3	8	4	2	1	1	0	2

Calculate
a) the median **[2 marks]**
b) the mode **[1 mark]**
c) the mean **[3 marks]**
d) the range **[1 mark]**

Note, you don't necessarily have to write out the whole list. Here there are 21 values, so the median is the 11th value. You could just stop writing there.

Solution

a) Write out the data in a list:
   0, 0, 0, 1, 1, 1, 1, 1, 1, 1, 1, 2, 2, 2, 2, 3, 3, 4, 5, 7, 7
   Median = 1
b) Mode = 1 (it has the highest frequency)
c) Add a row to the frequency table for number of days × frequency:

No. of sunny days	0	1	2	3	4	5	6	7	Total
Frequency	3	8	4	2	1	1	0	2	21
Number of days × frequency	0	8	8	6	4	5	0	14	45

   Mean = 45 ÷ 21 = 2.1 (1 d.p.)
d) Range = 7 − 0 = 7

For the mean, you could add up all the sunny days:
$$1 + 1 + 1 + 1 + 1 + 1 + 1 + 1 + 2 + 2 + 2 + 2 + 3 + 3 + 4 + 5 + 7 + 7 = 45$$
But it's quicker to use multiplication!

Exam corner

1. The number of items in a basket is recorded at a self-service checkout. Calculate or write down these values:

No. of items	3	4	5	6	7	8
Frequency	1	5	4	7	2	1

   a) median **[I got __/2 marks]**
   b) mode **[__/1 mark]**
   c) mean **[__/3 marks]**
   d) range **[__/1 mark]**

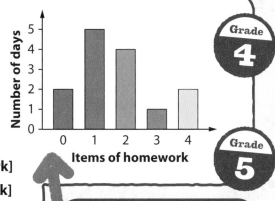 Grade 4 / Grade 5

2. A student records the number of items of homework they complete each day for two weeks, and displays the information in a bar chart. Calculate the mean. **[__/3 marks]**

Examiner's tip!

First summarise the data in a frequency table.

Grouped data

If you have data that has been grouped, you can still estimate the mean and find the **median class** and **modal class**.

Key points

Median class: The group that the middle value lies in.

Modal class: The group with the highest frequency.

To estimate the mean from a grouped frequency table...

Multiply the midpoint of each class by its frequency.

Add up these values.

Divide by the total number of values.

To estimate .... remember MAD...

Worked example

Grade 5

The lengths of 25 pieces of string are recorded in the table.

Length of string (s cm)	Number of pieces of string
$0 < s \le 8$	12
$8 < s \le 12$	6
$12 < s \le 20$	7

a) Write down the modal class. **[1 mark]**
b) Work out which class the median lies in. **[2 marks]**
c) Calculate an estimate for the mean. **[3 marks]**

This column, although it's got a different heading, shows the frequencies for each class. You could change the heading to 'Frequency'.

Solution

a) $0 < s \le 8$ is the modal class (it has the highest frequency, 12).

b) There are 25 pieces of string so the median will be the 13th.

You could add a running total column to the table:

Length of string (s cm)	Frequency	Running total
$0 < s \le 8$	12	12
$8 < s \le 12$	6	18
$12 < s \le 20$	7	25

13 lies between 12 and 18, so the 13th value lies in the

$8 < s \le 12$ class.

c) Add columns for the midpoint and midpoint × frequency:

Length of string (s cm)	Midpoint	Frequency	Midpoint × frequency
$0 < s \le 8$	4	12	48
$8 < s \le 12$	10	6	60
$12 < s \le 20$	16	7	112
Totals		25	220

Estimate for mean = 220 ÷ 25 = 8.8 cm

Remember MAD

Exam corner

Grade 5

The grouped frequency table shows the time per day spent playing computer games by a group of children.

Time (t mins)	Frequency
$0 \le t < 20$	35
$20 \le t < 40$	20
$40 \le t < 60$	16
$60 \le t < 80$	9

a) Write down the modal class. **[I got __/1 mark]**
b) Which is the median class? **[__/2 marks]**
c) Calculate an estimate for the mean. **[__/3 marks]**

Scatter graphs

A scatter graph can be used to see the relationship between two sets of data.

Key point

If the points on a scatter graph lie close to a straight line, then there is a **correlation** between the two sets of data.

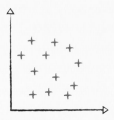

Positive correlation

Points lie close to a line with **positive** gradient.

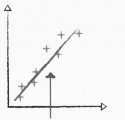

No correlation

Points are randomly scattered.

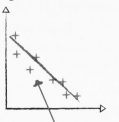

Negative correlation

Points lie close to a line with **negative** gradient.

See page 39 for more on gradients of straight lines.

Worked example

Grade 3

The table shows the number of rainy days per week and the number of road traffic accidents per week in a town over a 9-week period.

No. of rainy days	2	4	1	2	5	7	3	5	4
No. of accidents	4	6	3	6	9	10	13	6	7

a) Draw a scatter diagram to show this data. **[3 marks]**

b) Which of the points is an outlier? **[1 mark]**

c) Write down the correlation shown by the other points. **[1 mark]**

Remember, an **outlier** is a point that doesn't follow the same trend as most of the data.

Solution

a) Plot all the points on a graph.

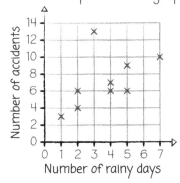

b) The point (3, 13) is an outlier.

c) Positive correlation

Exam corner

1. The scatter diagram shows the relationship between the outside temperature and the cost of heating a house.

   a) Describe the correlation shown. **[I got __/1 mark]**

   b) One of the points is an outlier. What was the temperature on this day? **[__/1 mark]**

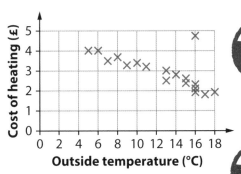

Grade 3

2. Research has found that older cars have higher CO_2 emissions. Write down the correlation between age of car and CO_2 emissions. **[__/1 mark]**

Grade 3

Lines of best fit

If two sets of data are correlated, you can draw a line of best fit on the scatter graph and use it to make estimations.

Key points

- A **line of best fit** should follow the trend of the data, ignoring any outliers.
- **Interpolating** means using a line of best fit to estimate a value within the range of the data. This will be a reliable estimate.
- **Extrapolating** means extending the line of best fit to estimate a value outside the range of the data. This estimate might be unreliable.

Confidence bar

Sorted!

Had a look

Correlation does not always indicate causation!

If two sets of data appear to be correlated, it doesn't necessarily mean that a change in one <u>causes</u> a change in the other.

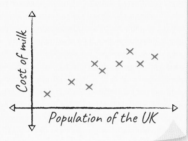

Exam corner

Grade
4

The scatter graph shows the relationship between the age of free-range hens and the number of eggs they produce in a month.

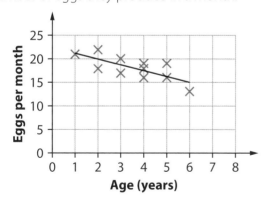

a) Use the line of best fit to estimate the number of eggs a 2-year-old hen lays per month. **[I got __/1 mark]**

b) Nur has used the line of best fit to estimate that an 8-year-old hen will lay 13 eggs in a month. Comment on Nur's estimate. **[__/2 marks]**

Worked example

Grade
4

The scatter graph shows the relationship between age of a person and speed of texting.

a) Draw a line of best fit. **[1 mark]**

b) Use the line of best fit to estimate the speed of texting for a 40-year-old. **[1 mark]**

c) Explain why you shouldn't use the line of best fit to estimate the speed of texting of a 5-year-old. **[2 marks]**

Solution

a) Ignore the outlier and draw a line through the other points.

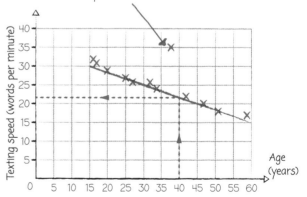

b) Draw a line from 40 to the line of best fit. This gives an estimate of 22 words per min.

c) We don't have any data for people under 16, so this would be extrapolation and any estimate found would be unreliable.

Time series

A **time series graph** is a line graph that shows how data changes over time.

Worked example

Confidence bar

Prisha is revising for her Maths GCSE. She does a practice paper every month and records her score in the table.

Month	Sept	Oct	Nov	Dec	Jan	Feb	Mar	Apr
Score (%)	44	48	42	50	55	62	65	70

a) Draw a time series graph for this data. **[3 marks]**

b) Describe the trend of the data and identify any outliers. **[2 marks]**

Sorted!

☑
☑
☑

Had a look

Solution

a) Plot each of the points then use a ruler to join with straight lines.

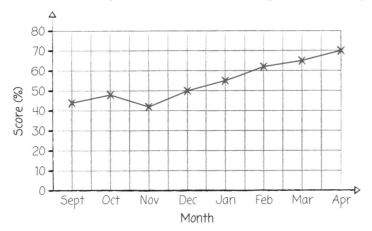

To draw a time series graph …

● put time on the x-axis
● put the thing being measured on the y-axis
● plot the points then join them with straight lines.

b) The general trend of score is increasing, apart from a dip in March (that score is an outlier).

Exam corner

The average cost of British strawberries over a 3-year period, during Spring, Summer and Autumn, is shown in the time series graph.

a) Describe the general trend.
[I got __/1 mark]

b) In which season are British strawberries cheapest? **[__/1 mark]**

c) What was the mean price of 1 kg of British strawberries over the three seasons shown for 2019?
[__/2 marks]

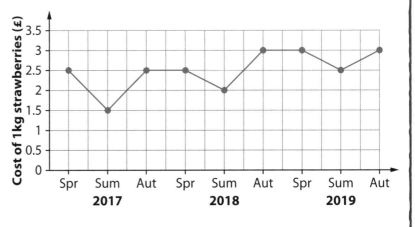

Theoretical probability

A **probability** tells you how likely an event is to happen.

Key points

- A probability is always **between 0 and 1**
- If all possible outcomes are **equally likely**, then:

  Probability of an event happening = $\dfrac{\text{number of ways it can happen}}{\text{total number of possible outcomes}}$

- This value is called the **theoretical probability**. You can write it as P(event).
- A probability can be written as a fraction, a decimal or a percentage.

The probability scale

0	$\frac{1}{4}$	$\frac{1}{2}$	$\frac{3}{4}$	1
impossible	unlikely	even chance	likely	certain

Worked example

Grade 2

Sean has a pack of 10 cards showing the numbers 1 to 10. He selects one at random. Write down the probability it is

a) a 5   **[1 mark]**
b) an odd number   **[1 mark]**
c) less than 8   **[1 mark]**

> *Note that 'less than' or 'more than' do not include the number itself.*

Solution

a) There are 10 cards and one of them is a 5.
   Probability of a 5 = $\frac{1}{10}$, or P(5) = $\frac{1}{10}$

b) Five of the cards have an odd number.
   P(odd) = $\frac{5}{10}$
   = $\frac{1}{2}$

c) Seven of the numbers are less than 8.
   P(less than 8) = $\frac{7}{10}$

Exam corner

Grade 2

1. Elijah rolls a fair, six-sided dice.

Write down the probability the dice lands on

a) 2   **[I got __/1 mark]**
b) a multiple of 3   **[__/1 mark]**
c) a number greater than 2
                   [__/1 mark]
d) 7   **[__/1 mark]**

Grade 3

2. The table shows the snack and drink choices of some students at break time.

	Fruit	Crisps
Water	15	13
Juice	7	5

Work out the probability that a randomly chosen student chooses

a) water and fruit   **[__/2 marks]**
b) crisps   **[__/2 marks]**

Write your answers as fractions in their simplest form.

> *Start by calculating the total number of students.*

> 📄 See page 94 for more on two-way tables.

Mutually exclusive events

Events are **mutually exclusive** if they cannot both happen at the same time.

Key point

The probabilities of all possible mutually exclusive outcomes must add up to 1

P(event happening) = 1 - P(event not happening)

Mutually exclusive events can't happen together.

Odd numbers   Even numbers

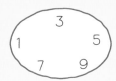   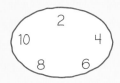

A number cannot be both odd and even.

📄 See page 109 for more on Venn diagrams.

Worked example
Grade 3

The probability that Phoebe will win a game of pool is $\frac{2}{7}$. Write down the probability that she will not win the game. **[1 mark]**

Solution

P(not winning game) = 1 - P(winning game)

$$= 1 - \frac{2}{7}$$

$$= \frac{5}{7}$$

Exam corner
Grade 3

1. A vet's waiting room contains only cats and dogs. The probability of a cat going in next is $\frac{3}{8}$. What is the probability of a dog going in next? **[I got __/1 mark]**

2. A box contains pink, blue and yellow marker pens. The probability of selecting each colour pen from the box is: **Grade 4**

Colour	Pink	Blue	Yellow
Probability	0.4	x	$2x$

a) Work out the value of x **[__/3 marks]**

b) Work out the probability of selecting a yellow pen. **[__/1 mark]**

Try writing an equation in x and remember, the probabilities must add up to 1

Worked example
Grade 4

Each card in a pack of cards shows a shape that may be a triangle, a square, a pentagon or a hexagon.

The table shows the probabilities of selecting a triangle or a square.

Shape	Triangle	Square	Pentagon	Hexagon
Probability	0.38	0.26		

The probability of selecting a pentagon is the same as the probability of selecting a hexagon.

Complete the table. **[2 marks]**

Solution

The four probabilities must add up to 1

1 - (0.38 + 0.26) = 0.36

P(pentagon) = P(hexagon) = 0.36 ÷ 2

$$= 0.18$$

Shape	Triangle	Square	Pentagon	Hexagon
Probability	0.38	0.26	0.18	0.18

Possibility spaces

A list or table showing all possible outcomes is called the **possibility space** or **sample space**.

Key points

There are different ways to show a possibility space:
- a systematic list (see first worked example)
- a grid showing the end result (see second worked example)
- a two-way table showing the combinations.

Worked example

Grade 4

a) List all the possible outcomes when three coins are flipped. **[2 marks]**

b) Write down the probability of getting three heads. **[1 mark]**

In a two-way table...

If a fair coin is flipped and a playing card is selected from a pack, the possibility space is:

Card

Coin	Black	Red
Head	HB	HR
Tail	TB	TR

Solution

a) Be systematic:

HHH	All heads
HHT, HTH, THH	2 heads, 1 tails
HTT, THT, TTH	2 tails, 1 heads
TTT	All tails

b) There are eight equally likely outcomes, so P(HHH) = $\frac{1}{8}$

Worked example

Grade 4

As part of a board game, players must select a card from a pack and roll an ordinary dice.

Half of the cards have a number 2 on them and the rest have a number 3. The player must multiply the numbers on the card and the dice together.

a) Draw a table to show the possibility space. **[2 marks]**

b) Work out the probability of scoring more than 10 **[1 mark]**

Solution

a) Multiply the two numbers together:

Dice

Card	1	2	3	4	5	6
2	2	4	6	8	10	12
3	3	6	9	12	15	18

b) There are 12 equally likely outcomes.

There are four outcomes which are more than 10.

P(more than 10) = $\frac{4}{12} = \frac{1}{3}$

Exam corner

Grade 4

1. Two dice are rolled, and the numbers are added together.

   a) Draw a table to show the possibility space. **[I got ___/2 marks]**

   b) Find the probability of getting a total of 8 **[___/1 mark]**

   Grade 4

2. A pot contains an equal number of green, blue and red counters. A counter is taken then returned, and a second counter is taken.

   a) List all the possible outcomes. **[___/2 marks]**

   b) Find the probability that both counters are the same colour. **[___/1 mark]**

Probability experiments

You can estimate the probability of an event from an experiment or from data.

Grade 3-4

The more trials in the experiment, the more accurate the estimate of the probability.

Confidence bar

Sorted!

Had a look

Worked example

Grade 3

Daisy flips a coin 60 times and gets 45 heads. Estimate the probability of heads.

Solution

Use relative frequency to estimate the probability:

Estimate of probability = $\dfrac{45}{60}$ = 0.75

Estimates for probability are usually given as decimals.

Worked example

Grade 4

The frequency tree shows the numbers of dogs and cats in a sample that have been microchipped.

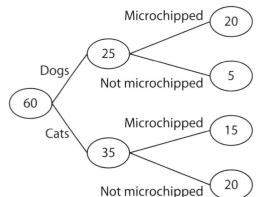

Notice how each column of numbers in this frequency tree adds up to the original total (60).

a) A cat or dog is chosen at random. What is the probability it has been microchipped? **[2 marks]**

b) A dog is chosen at random. What is the probability it has not been microchipped? **[2 marks]**

Solution

a) Total of microchipped cats and dogs = 20 + 15
   = 35

Probability = $\dfrac{35}{60}$ = $\dfrac{7}{12}$

b) You only need to consider the 25 dogs. 5 of them have not been microchipped, so

Probability = $\dfrac{5}{25}$ = $\dfrac{1}{5}$

Exam corner

1. A spinner with coloured sectors is spun 200 times. The results are: **Grade 3**

	Pink	Blue	Yellow
Frequency	40	90	70

Estimate the probability of getting blue. Give your answer as a decimal.

[I got __/1 mark]

2. At a children's farmyard, one day there were 120 children and 80 adults. 30 children and 9 adults had a ride on the tractor and the rest had a ride in the trailer. **Grade 4**

   a) Draw a frequency tree to show this information. **[__/3 marks]**

   b) If a person is chosen at random, what is the probability that they rode on the trailer? **[__/2 marks]**

Examiner's tip!

When you draw a frequency tree, check that the numbers on the final branches add up to the total at the start.

Expected results

You can use probability to work out the number of times you expect a certain outcome.

Grade 4

Key points

- The **expected frequency** of an event is the number of times you expect it to happen.

  Expected frequency = probability × number of trials

- An unfair coin or spinner or dice is said to be **biased**.

This spinner is unfair – it is biased towards red.

Worked example

Grade 4

The probability that a person is left-handed is estimated to be 9%. There are 780 students in a school. Estimate how many are left-handed.

Solution

Expected frequency = 0.09 × 780
$$= 70.2$$

About 70 students are left-handed.

(Round the final answer, as the number of students must be a whole number.)

See page 13 for converting between percentages and decimals.

See page 3 for a reminder on rounding.

Confidence bar

Sorted!

☑
☑
☑

Had a look

Worked example

Grade 4

Miles rolls a dice 200 times and gets a 6 on 30 rolls. He claims this means the dice is biased. Explain whether or not you think Miles is correct. **[2 marks]**

Solution

With a fair dice, the probability of a 6 is $\frac{1}{6}$

Expected frequency = $\frac{1}{6}$ × 200
$$= 33.333...$$

This is close to the actual result of 30, so Miles is wrong, the dice appears to be fair.

Exam corner

1. In a computer game, when you open a box you receive a positive, a negative or a neutral result. The probability of each outcome is shown in the table.

Grade 4

Result	Positive	Negative	Neutral
Probability	0.2	0.3	0.5

How many negative results would you expect to get if you open 40 boxes? **[I got __/2 marks]**

2. In each case, explain whether or not the results suggest that the coin is biased.

Grade 4

a) A coin is tossed six times and lands on heads only once. **[__/1 mark]**

b) A coin is tossed 100 times and lands on heads 25 times. **[__/1 mark]**

Remember, the more trials in the experiment, the more accurate the estimate of the probability.

The expected frequency won't always match the actual outcome, as it's just the most likely of many possible outcomes. If it's really far off, though, the dice (or coin, spinner, etc.) is probably unfair.

Tree diagrams

A tree diagram helps you to calculate the probability of two or more events.

Key points

- You multiply along the branches to find the probability of two events occurring together.
- Each time the diagram splits into branches, the probabilities of all the branches must add up to 1

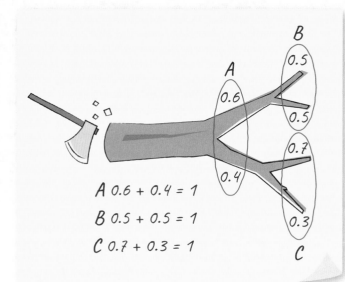

A $0.6 + 0.4 = 1$

B $0.5 + 0.5 = 1$

C $0.7 + 0.3 = 1$

Confidence bar

Sorted!

☑

☑

☐

Had a look

Worked example

In a board game, you pick a dice randomly from a bag and roll it. The tree diagram shows the probabilities.

a) What is the value of x? **[1 mark]**

b) Work out the probability of picking a black dice and rolling a 6 **[2 marks]**

Colour of dice   Number rolled

$\frac{1}{3}$ — Black

$\frac{1}{4}$ — A six

$\frac{3}{4}$ — Not a six

$\frac{2}{3}$ — Red

$\frac{1}{6}$ — A six

x — Not a six

Solution

a) Probabilities on each set of branches must add up to 1. So $x = 1 - \frac{1}{6} = \frac{5}{6}$

b) P(black and six) $= \frac{1}{3} \times \frac{1}{4} = \frac{1}{12}$ Multiply along the branches.

Exam corner

Hana has a bag of sweets and a box of chocolates. She randomly selects one sweet and one chocolate. The tree diagram shows the probability of getting each type of sweet and chocolate.

a) Fill in the missing values on the diagram.

[I got ___/2 marks]

b) Work out the probability of getting a crunchy sweet and a milk chocolate.

[__/2 marks]

Type of sweet   Type of chocolate

.... — Chewy

0.8 — Milk

.... — Dark

0.75 — Crunchy

0.8 — Milk

.... — Dark

Set notation

A **set** is just a collection of numbers or objects. You need to know some special notation to describe sets.

Key points

- The symbol ξ means the **universal set**, which contains **all** the numbers.
- You can describe a set using curly brackets, e.g. {1, 2, 3, 4} or {odd numbers}.
- $x \in A$ means x is a member of the set A.
- $A \cap B$ means the **intersection** of sets A and B (numbers in **both** sets).
- $A \cup B$ means the **union** of sets A and B (numbers in **either** set).
- A' means the **complement** of set A (numbers **not** in set A).

Confidence bar

Sorted!

☑
☑
☑

Had a look

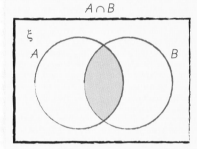

$A \cap B$

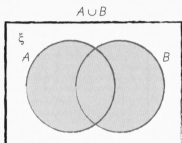

$A \cup B$

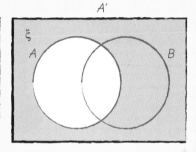

A'

Examiner's tip!

The notation might seem tricky, but if you learn what each symbol means then you'll be able to answer any exam question on this topic.

Exam corner

Grade 4

1. For the Venn diagram in the worked example, write down the numbers that are in set
   a) $A \cup B$ [I got __/1 mark]
   b) B' [__/1 mark]

2. ξ = {2, 4, 6, 8, 10, 12, 14, 16} **Grade 5**
   Set X = {multiples of 4}
   Set Y = {10, 12, 14, 16}
   Draw a Venn diagram to show this information.
   [__/4 marks]

Worked example

Grade 5

ξ = {1, 2, 3, 4, 5, 6, 7, 8, 9, 10}

A = {odd numbers} B = {prime numbers}

a) Draw a Venn diagram to show this information. **[4 marks]**
b) Write down the numbers that are in set $A \cap B$ **[1 mark]**

Solution

a)

The numbers in this section are in set A but not set B; they are odd but not prime.

The numbers in this section are in set A and set B; they are odd and prime.

2 is the only non-odd prime number.

The numbers in this section are not in set A nor in set B; they are non-prime and even.

b) $A \cap B$ means the intersection of sets A and B.

The numbers in set $A \cap B$ are 3, 5 and 7

STRIVE FOR 5 See pages 124–125 for more practice.

Probability from tables & diagrams

You can work out probabilities from Venn diagrams and two-way tables.

Key point

Remember this rule to calculate probability:

Probability of an event happening = $\dfrac{\text{number of ways it can happen}}{\text{total number of possible outcomes}}$

Confidence bar

Sorted!

Had a look

Worked example

Grade 5

60 families were asked if they went on holiday last year and, if they did, the location. The results are shown in the Venn diagram.

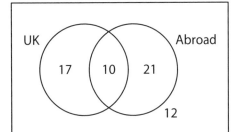

Remember the sections of a Venn diagram.

Work out the probability that a randomly chosen family
a) went abroad on holiday **[1 mark]**
b) didn't go on holiday **[1 mark]**
c) went on holiday in both the UK and abroad. **[1 mark]**

Solution

a) P(abroad) = $\dfrac{10 + 21}{60}$

= $\dfrac{31}{60}$

b) P(no holiday) = $\dfrac{12}{60}$

= $\dfrac{1}{5}$

c) P(UK and abroad) = $\dfrac{10}{60}$ = $\dfrac{1}{6}$

 See page 109 for a reminder about set notation.

Exam corner

1. A group of 40 students are surveyed to see what equipment they use to take notes in lessons.

Grade 4

	Pen	Pencil
Notebook	13	8
Sheet of paper	7	12

Work out the probability that a randomly chosen student
a) uses pen and notebook **[I got __/1 mark]**
b) uses a sheet of paper. **[__/1 mark]**

2. Some numbers are put into a Venn diagram.

Grade 5

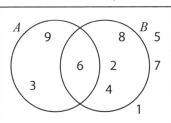

A number is selected at random from the diagram. Work out the probability the number is in set
a) A b) B c) $A \cap B$
d) $A \cup B$ e) A' **[__/5 marks]**

STRIVE FOR 5 See pages 124–125 for more practice.

Strive for 5 – Introduction

We've carefully studied past exam papers and examiner reports to identify the trickiest question types. Work through the next 14 pages to give yourself the best possible chance of reaching Grade 5.

Key Points

- You'll find a 2-page spread to help you master each of the seven question types: p112-125
- These are not just the 'hardest' topics at the highest grade. For example, questions on ratio in a real-world context are very often Grade 3 or 4 difficulty, but still catch out students who are otherwise on track for a better grade.

- We've also indicated below where the basics for these topics are covered in the main content: p1-110
- For example, ratio is covered in this section on pages 116-117, but the basics are also covered in the main content on pages 10, 51 & 52.

The 'Strive for 5' approach

Grasping a maths topic is like building a house!

On each double-page spread, you'll find these three steps to help you master each topic:

1 Laying the foundations (Fluency)

Every house needs strong foundations. Step 1: check you have secure knowledge of the basic maths. You'll find a 'Check-up box' with a handful of 1 or 2-mark questions. Try these, look up the answers, and tick the green box if you've got them right. On each spread, a 'Need more help?' box will tell you where to look for more support. ☐

2 Building the walls (Entry-level problems)

Building on the foundations, the next step is to try entry-level problems. Read through the 'Worked examples' here and then have a go at the problems in the 'Exam corner'. Take your time!

3 Completing the house (Problem solving)

You're now ready to add the roof: problem-solving questions set in context. Again, carefully go through the 'Worked example' (typically a 4 or 5-marker), read the advice, and then go to the 'Exam corner'.

Strive for 5 topic	See page...	Need more help?
Using HCF & LCM in context	112	16, 17, 18
Writing & solving equations	114	26, 27, 28, 35
Handling ratio in context	116	10, 51, 52
Tricky percentage questions	118	10, 13, 53, 54
Speed, distance & time	120	56, 59
Tackling shape calculations	122	60, 61, 73, 75
Venn diagrams & probability	124	109, 110

Examiner's tip!

When answering a problem-solving question, especially one with a lot of words, always start by underlining the key information and the key instruction. Extract the information you need **before** you start doing any maths.

Using HCF & LCM in context

Grade 3–5

This section will look at how you can use the HCF and LCM to solve more challenging questions. Look for hidden clues that tell you to use this method.

1 Laying the foundations (*Fluency*)

Make sure you have a solid and secure understanding of the questions in the check-up box before you move on.

Every house starts with strong foundations

"Grasping a topic in maths is like building a house"

Check-up box

1. Find the HCF of 24 and 32 ☐

2. Find the LCM of 24 and 32 ☐

3. Find the HCF of 12 and 80 ☐

Need more help?
Go to pages 16, 17

Grade 3–4

4. Find 240 as a product of primes. Give your answer as a product in index form. ☐

5. List the prime factors of 24 ☐

2 Building the walls (*Entry-level problems*)

Building on the foundations, we now start to add context to the questions. Look for key words and instructions. Some questions might look the same but on closer inspection they are subtly different.

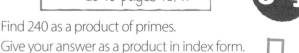

The question doesn't specifically tell you to use the HCF or LCM. Look for key words in the question that tell you which one to use.

Need more help?
Go to page 18

Worked example

Grade 3

Some Christmas bulbs are set to flash at different times. The <u>red</u> bulbs flash every <u>5</u> seconds, and the <u>green</u> bulbs flash every <u>3</u> seconds. After how many seconds will both colours flash at the same time? **[2 marks]**

Solution

Red bulbs will flash at 5, 10, 15, 20, 25.... seconds.

Green bulbs will flash at 3, 6, 9, 12, 15, 18... seconds.

The LCM of 5 and 3 is 15. They will both flash at 15 seconds.

Worked example

Grade 3

Two pieces of wood, one <u>35 cm</u> long and one <u>28 cm</u> long, are to be cut up into <u>equal length</u> pieces, with no wastage. What is the largest size that they can be cut into? **[2 marks]**

Solution

Cutting up into the same size means you need the HCF.

Factors of 35: 1, 5, 7, 35

Factors of 28: 1, 2, 4, 7, 14, 28

The HCF is 7. The wood should be cut into 7 cm pieces.

Exam corner

Grade 3

1. Two loaves of bread, one 30 cm long and one 24 cm long, need to be cut up into slices, with all slices equal. What is the largest thickness slices that they can be cut into? **[I got ___ /2 marks]**

Grade 4

2. A charity wants to give at least 50 people a badge and a poster to publicise the work they do. Badges are sold in packs of 5 and posters in packs of 7. What is the minimum of each pack they should buy, so that they have none left over? **[___ /2 marks]**

③ Complete the house (*Problem solving*)

Now we have secure foundations and solid walls, we can complete the house: problem-solving questions set in context. For these questions, you'll need to read them very carefully and then pull out the key information. Only after that, you should start applying your maths skills.

Worked example

Grade 5

A factory makes pens, rulers and protractors. By the end of one day they have made <u>360 pens, 588 rulers and 180 protractors</u>. The equipment is to be boxed up with the <u>same number of pens, rulers and protractors in each box</u>. The factory wants to put the <u>largest number of each product in every box</u>. What is the <u>minimum number of boxes</u> that can be made up, and <u>how many of each</u> piece of equipment will be in <u>every box</u>? **[5 marks]**

> Start by underlining key information AND the instruction.

Solution

Prime factor decomposition of the quantities:

$360 = 2^3 \times 3^2 \times 5$

$588 = 2^2 \times 3 \times 7^2$

$180 = 2^2 \times 3^2 \times 5$

The highest common factor is $2^2 \times 3$,

So there are 12 of each item in each box.

$\frac{180}{12} = 15$ boxes

> It must be the HCF we are looking for, because we want to group the items and we have a set number to use.

> Use 180 because that is the smallest number of items in any of the groups.

> **Need more help?** Go to page 18

Exam corner

Grade 5

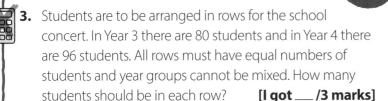

3. Students are to be arranged in rows for the school concert. In Year 3 there are 80 students and in Year 4 there are 96 students. All rows must have equal numbers of students and year groups cannot be mixed. How many students should be in each row? **[I got ___ /3 marks]**

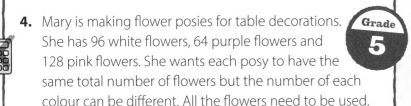

4. Mary is making flower posies for table decorations. She has 96 white flowers, 64 purple flowers and 128 pink flowers. She wants each posy to have the same total number of flowers but the number of each colour can be different. All the flowers need to be used.

Grade 5

   a) Show that the maximum number of posies is 32 **[___ /3 marks]**

   b) How many of each colour flower is in each posy? **[___ /1 mark]**

Next steps...

List what you need to revise/practise:

- ☐ ....
- ☐ ....
- ☐ ....
- ☐ ....
- ☐ ....

Tick when done

Writing & solving equations

Grade 2–5

This section will look at problems in a context and how to write equations to solve them.

① Laying the foundations (*Fluency*)

Make sure you have a solid and secure understanding of the questions in the check-up box before you move on.

Every house starts with strong foundations

"Grasping a topic in maths is like building a house"

Check-up box

Grade 2–3

1. Solve these equations.

a) $3x + 5 = 7$ ☐

b) $-12 = 2x + 8$ ☐

c) $4x + 7 = -2 + 7x$ ☐

d) $3x - 2 = 28 - 2x$ ☐

2. Claire thinks of a number, squares it and subtracts 5. Her answer is 76. What number did she start with? ☐

3. Solve these simultaneous equations.

$$y - 2x = 1$$
$$y = -4x + 19$$ ☐

> 📄 **Need more help?**
> Go to pages 26, 27, 28

② Building the walls (*Entry-level problems*)

Building on the foundations, we now start to add context to the questions. Look for key words and instructions. Some questions might look the same but on closer inspection they are subtly different.

> 📄 **Need more help?**
> Go to page 35

Grade 5

Worked example

Find the values of x and y in this isosceles triangle. **[4 marks]**

Solution

The triangle is isosceles so

$$y + 3 = x + 18$$
$$y - x = 15 \ (1)$$

> Rearrange to form equation (1)

Since it is a triangle, we also know that

$$y + 3 + x + 18 + x - 6 = 180$$
$$y + 2x + 15 = 180$$
$$y + 2x = 165 \ (2)$$

> Rearrange and simplify to form equation 2

Now we have two equations to solve using elimination.

Subtract (1) - (2): $y - x - (y + 2x) = 15 - 165$
$$-3x = -150$$
$$x = 50$$

Substitute in (1): $y - 50 = 15$
$$so \ y = 65$$

> *Remember STOP*
> *If the sign is the Same, Take away.*
> *If the signs are Opposite, Plus.*

Exam corner

Grade 5

1. Andy buys three T-shirts and four pairs of socks at a total cost of £55.30. Karim buys four T-shirts and three pairs of socks for £68.60

Find the cost of one T-shirt and the cost of one pair of socks. **[I got ___ /4 marks]**

3 Complete the house (*Problem solving*)

Now we have secure foundations and solid walls, we can complete the house: problem-solving questions set in context. For these questions, you'll need to read them very carefully and then pull out the key information. Only after that, you should start applying your maths skills.

Worked example

Grade 5

<u>Hannah</u> is <u>older</u> than her sister Rosie.

The <u>sum</u> of their ages is <u>22</u> years.

The <u>difference</u> between their ages is <u>8</u> years.

<u>Construct and solve two simultaneous equations</u> to work out the ages of Hannah and Rosie.

[4 marks]

> 1) Start by underlining key information AND the instruction.

Solution

Say Hannah is x years old and Rosie is y years old.

$x + y = 22$ (1)

$x - y = 8$ (2)

(1) + (2): $2x = 30$ so $x = 15$

$15 + y = 22$

$\qquad y = 7$

$15 - 7 = 8$ ✓

So Hannah is 15 years old and Rosie is 7

> 2) Form equations using what you are told in the question.
> We know that Hannah is older.

> 3) Solve using elimination.

> 4) Substitute the value of x into equation (1)

> 5) Check this works in equation (2)

Exam corner

Grade 5

2. Sam is Max's younger brother. The difference between their ages is 5 years. In three years' time, Max will be three times Sam's age now. Find the ages of Max and Sam. **[I got ___ /4 marks]**

3. Ezra has some 10p and 5p coins in his pocket. He has 12 coins altogether. The total of the coins is 80p. How many of each coin does Ezra have? **[___ /4 marks]**

Grade 5

Next steps...

List what you need to revise/practise:

.... ☐

.... ☐

.... ☐

.... ☐

.... ☐

Tick when done

Examiner's tip!

Sometimes the need to form simultaneous equations is 'hidden' in the question. The trick is to recognise this, then decide how best to solve the equations.

Handling ratio in context

This section will look at how to tackle the longer ratio questions, especially ones that use a real-world context.

① Laying the foundations (*Fluency*)

Make sure you have a solid and secure understanding of the questions in the check-up box before you move on.
Every house starts with strong foundations

"Grasping a topic in maths is like building a house"

Check-up box

Need more help?
Go to pages 10, 51, 52

Go to pages 10, 51, 52

Grade 2–3

1. Write the ratio 12:18 in its simplest form. ☐
2. Share £100 in the ratio 3:2 ☐
3. Find 15% of 60 ☐

4. The ratio of red to yellow balls is 4:5, what fraction of the balls are yellow? ☐
5. Write 0.4 as a fraction in its simplest form. ☐
6. Convert 12% to a decimal in its simplest form. ☐

② Building the walls (*Entry-level problems*)

Building on the foundations, we now start to add context to the questions. Look for key words and instructions. Some questions might look the same but on closer inspection they are subtly different.

Worked example

Grade 3

Ben, Sarah and Lisa share some money in the ratio 3:4:5. Lisa gets £30. How much does Sarah get? **[2 marks]**

Solution

B [ ][ ][ ]
S [ ][ ][ ][ ]
L [ ][ ][ ][ ][ ]

Start by drawing a bar to show the ratio. You could 'stack' the bars or draw them next to each other.

If Lisa has £30 then each 'box' is worth 30 ÷ 5 = £6

Sarah gets £6 × 4 = £24

Worked example

Grade 4

Ben, Sarah and Lisa share some money in the ratio 3:4:5. Lisa gets £30 more than Ben. How much does Sarah get? **[2 marks]**

Solution

B [ ][ ][ ]
S [ ][ ][ ][ ]
L [ ][ ][ ][ ][ ]

Start in the same way as the first example.

If Lisa has £30 **more** than Ben then each 'box' is worth 30 ÷ 2 = £15

So Sarah gets 4 × 15 = £60

These two questions look very similar. In the pressure of the exam, make sure you focus on the key words that help you decide what to do.

Exam corner

Grade 4

1. *A* and *B* are two weights. *B* is 4 times heavier than *A*. The difference in the weights is 12 kg. What is the weight of *B*? **[I got ___ /2 marks]**

2. Gavin, Syed and Freya share some sweets in the ratio 7:5:2. Syed has 15 more sweets than Freya. How many sweets does Gavin have?

[___ /3 marks]

3 Complete the house (*Problem solving*)

Now we have secure foundations and solid walls, we can complete the house: problem-solving questions set in context. For these questions, you'll need to read them very carefully and then pull out the key information. Only after that, you should start applying your maths skills.

Worked example

Grade 5

In a group of boys and girls, the ratio of boys to girls is 2:3.

25% of the boys are left-handed.

$\frac{1}{3}$ of the girls are left-handed.

What percentage of the overall group is right-handed? **[4 marks]**

Solution

Boys ▭

Girls ▭

Boys | L | | | |

Girls | L | | |

Boys ▭

Girls ▭

The fraction of the group that is right-handed is $\frac{7}{10}$, so the percentage is 70%

1) Start by underlining key information AND the key instruction.

2) Now draw the ratio of boys to girls as bars.

3) We need to split the boys' 2 boxes into 4 so we can show 25% are left-handed, and mark $\frac{1}{3}$ of the girls' boxes to show left-handed.

4) To answer this question, we need to make all the boxes the same size. There are 7 boxes that will represent right-handed students out of a possible 10

Exam corner

Grade 5

3. A school receives a donation of money. 10% of the money is for administration. The remaining money is split between the girls' football team and the school library in the ratio 2:7. The library receives £210. How much money was donated?

[I got ___ /4 marks]

4. Daniel inherits some money from a relative.

Grade 5

He spends 25% of the money on a new bike.

He puts $\frac{2}{3}$ of the remaining amount in a savings account.

He splits what is left in the ratio 1:3 between his two cousins James and Florence.

If Florence gets £300, how much did Daniel inherit?

[___ /4 marks]

Next steps...

List what you need to revise/practise:

.... ☐

.... ☐

.... ☐

.... ☐

.... ☐

.... ☐

Tick when done

Tricky percentage questions

This section will look at how you can break down percentage questions and use basic skills to answer trickier questions.

Grade **2–5**

1 Laying the foundations (*Fluency*)

Make sure you have a solid and secure understanding of the questions in the check-up box before you move on.

Every house starts with strong foundations

"Grasping a topic in maths is like building a house"

Check-up box

 Need more help? Go to pages 10, 13

Grade **2–4**

1. Write 45% as a fraction in its simplest form. ☐

2. Write 18% as a decimal. ☐

3. How do you find 10% of a value without a calculator? ☐

4. What is the multiplier for increasing by 2%? ☐

5. What is 12% of £2400? ☐

6. Reduce £500 by 25% ☐

2 Building the walls (*Entry-level problems*)

Building on the foundations, we now start to add context to the questions. Look for key words and instructions. Some questions might look the same but on closer inspection they are subtly different.

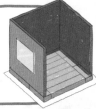

Worked example

Grade **5**

Kirsty invests £3546 in an account which pays 3% compound interest per year. How much interest will Kirsty have earned after 3 years? **[3 marks]**

Solution

The multiplier for a 3% increase is 1.03

After 1 year Kirsty will have 3546 × 1.03 = £3652.38

After 2 years 3652.38 × 1.03 = £3761.9514

After 3 years 3761.9514 × 1.03 = £3874.81

> WATCH OUT! The question asks how much interest Kirsty will have earned after 3 years, NOT how much money she will have in the account.

Interest = 3874.81 − 3536 = £338.81

Worked example

Grade **5**

A car depreciates in value at a rate of 13% per year. How much will the car be worth after 2 years if it was purchased for £3000? **[3 marks]**

Solution

The multiplier for a 13% decrease is 0.87

After 1 year 3000 × 0.87 = 2610

After 2 years 2610 × 0.87 = 2270.7

> Any answer with money needs to be to 2 d.p.

Car's value = £2270.70

 Need more help? Go to pages 53, 54

Exam corner

Grade **5**

1. Sally invests £2350 for 4 years at 2.3% compound interest. Calculate the amount invested at the end of the 4 years. **[I got __ /3 marks]**

Grade **5**

2. Gurinder invested an amount of money at 5% per annum compound interest. At the end of 2 years the value of his investment was £661.50. How much of the £661.50 was interest? **[__ /4 marks]**

③ Complete the house (*Problem solving*)

Now we have secure foundations and solid walls, we can complete the house: problem-solving questions set in context. For these questions, you'll need to read them very carefully and then pull out the key information. Only after that, you should start applying your maths skills.

Worked example

Grade 5

Helen buys 6 kg of mixed nuts to sell at the school fair. She pays £12 for the nuts.

Helen puts all of the nuts into bags of 150 g each. She sells each bag for 50 p.

At the fair Helen sells all of the bags of nuts.

Work out her percentage profit to 1 decimal place. **[4 marks]**

> 1) Start by underlining key information AND the instruction.

Solution

$6 \text{ kg} = 6000 \text{ g}$

> 2) Check and convert the units.

Number of bags $= \dfrac{6000}{150} = 40$

> 3) Work out how many 150 g bags from the 6000 g.

Amount received $= 40 \times 0.50 = £20$

> 4) Calculate how much Helen will sell them for.

Profit $= 20 - 12 = £8$

> 5) Calculate the profit.

Percentage profit $= \dfrac{\text{difference}}{\text{original}} \times 100\%$

$= \dfrac{8}{12} \times 100\% = 0.\dot{6} \times 100\%$

$= 66.7\%$ to 1 d.p.

> 6) Calculate the profit as a percentage of the original cost.

📄 **Need more help?**
Go to page 54

Exam corner

Grade 5

3. After a new organic pondweed remedy is applied to a lake, the area covered by pondweed decreases at a rate of 11% every 24 hours. At midnight on Monday, 1200 cm² was covered. What area of the lake was covered by midnight on Wednesday? Give your answer to the nearest cm². **[I got ___ /3 marks]**

Grade 5

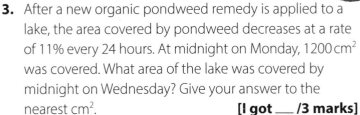

4. Henry buys 6 litres of energy drink for £18. He decides to sell the drink to friends. He shares it into 300 ml bottles and sells each bottle for £1.25. If Henry sells all the bottles, work out his percentage profit. Give your answer to 1 decimal place. **[___ /4 marks]**

Next steps...

List what you need to revise/practise:

- .... ☐
- .... ☐
- .... ☐
- .... ☐
- .... ☐
- .... ☐

Tick when done

Speed, distance & time

This section will look at how to approach those tricky questions involving speed, distance and time. You need to be careful with units.

Grade 3–5

① Laying the foundations (*Fluency*)

Make sure you have a solid and secure understanding of the questions in the check-up box before you move on.
Every house starts with strong foundations

"Grasping a topic in maths is like building a house"

Check-up box

Need more help? Go to pages 56, 59

Grade 3

1. Convert the following to minutes.

   a) 2.3 hours ☐   **b)** 1 hour 14 mins ☐   **c)** 0.6 hours ☐

2. A car travels 18 miles in 30 minutes. What is its average speed in mph? ☐

3. I leave home at 08:00 and it takes 34 minutes to walk to the bus stop. I wait 14 minutes

   for my bus. The bus arrives at my office at 09:22. How long was my bus journey? ☐

② Building the walls (*Entry-level problems*)

Building on the foundations, we now start to add context to the questions. Look for key words and instructions.

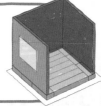

Worked example

Grade 4

Lara travels by coach from London to Bristol, a distance by road of 118 miles. The coach leaves London at 09:45. The coach has an average speed of 45 mph. Work out what time Lara should arrive in Bristol, to the nearest minute.

[3 marks]

Solution

Speed = 45mph, distance = 118 miles

$\text{Time} = \dfrac{\text{distance}}{\text{speed}} = \dfrac{118}{45} = 2.6222...$ hours

0.622... × 60 = 37.333... minutes

Add 2 hours 37 minutes on to 09:45, giving arrival time 12:22

Since this is a time question, we need the speed and the distance.

2.622... hours means 2 hours and 0.622... hours. We need to convert this to minutes.

Exam corner

Grade 3

1. Leo is taking part in a swimming competition. His race starts at 13:00. He swims for 42 minutes then rests before his next race at 14:40

   How long is his rest?   **[I got ___ /2 marks]**

Grade 4

2. Carrie walks at an average speed of 3 mph. She sets off at 9:45 and stops at 11:15. She calculates the distance she has walked like this:

   Distance = speed × time; time = 1 hour 30 min

   Distance = 3 × 1.3 = 3.9 miles

   Explain her mistake and calculate the correct distance.

   [___ /2 marks]

③ Complete the house (*Problem solving*)

Now we have secure foundations and solid walls, we can complete the house: problem-solving questions set in context. For these questions, you'll need to read them very carefully and then pull out the key information. Only after that, you should start applying your maths skills.

Grade 5

Worked example

Megan and Michaela ran the same 11-mile race. Megan took 2 hours 12 minutes. Michaela started running 10 minutes after Megan. Michaela caught up with Megan at the 6-mile point. Assuming they both ran at constant speed, calculate Michaela's speed.　　　　**[5 marks]**

Solution

2 hours 12 minutes = 2.2 hours

Megan's speed = $\frac{11}{2.2}$ = 5 mph

Time = $\frac{distance}{speed}$ = $\frac{6}{5}$ = 1.2 hours, which is 1 hour 12 min

Since Michaela set off 10 minutes after Megan, it must take Michaela 1 hour 2 mins to run 6 miles.

1 hour 2 min is $1\frac{2}{60}$ = $1\frac{1}{30}$ = 1.0333... hours

Michaela's speed = $\frac{6}{1.0333...}$ = 5.8 mph

> 1) Start by underlining key information AND the instruction.

> 2) Check the units.

> 3) We need to know how long it takes Megan to run the first 6 miles.

When there is a lot to do in a question, don't panic. Write down what you know about speed. You can start with the formula to help you get going. And always remember to check units.

Exam corner

Grade 5

3. Mark is driving on the motorway. He sees a road sign that tells him the distance to the next junction is 23 miles. The speed limit on a motorway is 70 mph.

　　He thinks he will get to the junction in less than 15 minutes if he drives at the speed limit. Is he correct? You must show your working out.　　**[I got ___ /2 marks]**

4. A train travels at an average speed of 16 m/s.

Grade 5

　　a) Express its average speed in km/h.　　**[___ /2 marks]**

　　b) The train sets off at 9.03 am on a 120 km non-stop journey.
　　　　At what time should it reach its destination?
　　　　　　　　　[___ /3 marks]

Next steps...

List what you need to revise/practise:

.... ☐

.... ☐

.... ☐

.... ☐

.... ☐

Tick when done

Tackling shape calculations

This section will look at how you can break down long questions involving shape and cost calculations.

1 Laying the foundations (*Fluency*)

Make sure you have a solid and secure understanding of the questions in the check-up box before you move on.
Every house starts with strong foundations

"Grasping a topic in maths is like building a house"

Check-up box

1. Convert

   a) 7 cm to mm ☐

   b) 1500 cm³ to m³ ☐

   c) 3 cm² to mm² ☐

2. What is the perimeter of a square with sides 12 cm? ☐

3. Find the area of a circle with radius 4 cm.
   Leave your answer in terms of π ☐

To convert units...

of length - use length conversions:

12 cm to mm $12 \times 10 = 120$ mm

of area - use length conversions SQUARED:

12 cm² to mm² $12 \times 10^2 = 1200$ mm²

of volume - use length conversions CUBED:

12 cm³ to mm³ $12 \times 10^3 = 12\,000$ mm³

📄 **Need more help?**
Go to page 60, 73, 75

---

2 Building the walls (*Entry-level problems*)

Building on the foundations, we now start to add context to the questions. Look for key words and instructions.

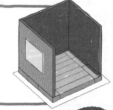

Worked example

A circle in a wall mural has radius 300 cm. Each tin of paint costs £12 and will cover an area of 15 m². How much will it cost to paint the circle? **[4 marks]**

Solution

300 cm = 3 m ◄— *Check and convert units.*

Decide if you need to calculate perimeter, area or volume. The key word is 'cover' - this is area.

Area of a circle $A = \pi r^2$ ◄—

Leave your answer on the calculator. Don't round too early.

$3^2 \times \pi = 28.27433...$

$28.27433 \div 15 = 1.88495...$

So 2 tins are needed.

Cost $12 \times 2 = £24$ ◄— *Do the cost calculation.*

Worked example

A square's side length of 20 cm is enlarged by a scale factor of 4. Find the area of the enlarged square. Give your answer in m². **[3 marks]**

Solution

Enlarged side length = $20 \times 4 = 80$ cm
New area = $80 \times 80 = 6400$ cm²
Convert cm² to m²: divide by 100²
$6400 \div 100^2 = 0.64$ m²

📄 **Need more help?**
Go to page 61

Exam corner

1. A square has area 14 400 cm². Calculate its perimeter in m. **[I got ___ /2 marks]**

2. A tin of soup has radius 5 cm and height 12 cm. How many tins would you need for 5 litres of soup? **[___ /4 marks]**

③ Complete the house (*Problem solving*)

Now we have secure foundations and solid walls, we can complete the house: problem-solving questions set in context. For these questions, you'll need to read them very carefully and then pull out the key information. Only after that, you should start applying your maths skills.

Grade 5

Worked example

A container is in the shape of a cylinder with radius 0.8 m and height 1.3 m.

The container is to be filled with oil.

Oil costs £0.45 per litre.

Aida has a budget of £1000.

Does she have enough money to fill the container with oil?   **[4 marks]**

> 1) Start by underlining key information AND the instruction.

Solution

Radius = 80 cm, height = 130 cm

> 2) Check units. The radius is in m but the cost is per litre (1000 cm³). Convert 0.8 m and 1.3 m into cm.

Cylinder volume = π × 80² × 130 = 2 613 805.088 cm³

> 3) This is a VOLUME question – a cylinder is being FILLED.

This is 2 613 805.088/1000 = 2613.805 088 litres

Cost to fill the tank = 2613.805 088 × 0.45 = £1176.21

> 4) Cost calculation

Aida does not have enough money because it will cost more than £1000.

> 5) Make sure you have answered the question.

Exam corner

Grade 5

3. A new playground is to be in the shape of a regular pentagon with sides 600 cm. Fencing will be used around the outside. Each fence panel costs £22.50 and is 1.5 m long.

The builder charges £60 per day. The job will take 4 days to complete. How much will it cost for the fence and the labour?   **[I got ___ /4 marks]**

Grade 5

4. A cube has volume 216 000 cm³. The outside of the cube is to be painted. Paint is sold in tins that cover 2 m². How many tins will need to be bought?   **[___ /4 marks]**

Examiner's tip!

Look for key words such as **around the outside, cover** or **fill.** These will help you decide if it is a perimeter, area or volume question.

Next steps...

List what you need to revise/practise:

.... ☐

.... ☐

.... ☐

.... ☐

.... ☐

Tick when done

Venn diagrams & probability

Grade 5

This section will look at how you can use Venn diagrams to solve challenging probability questions.

1 Laying the foundations (*Fluency*)

Make sure you have a solid and secure understanding of the questions in the check-up box before you move on.
Every house starts with strong foundations

"Grasping a topic in maths is like building a house"

Check-up box

Grade 5

ξ = {12, 13, 14, 15, 16, 17, 18, 19, 20}

A = {prime numbers}

B = {numbers greater than 15}

C = {multiples of 3}

📄 **Need more help?**
Go to page 109

1. Write the numbers in each of the sets A, B and C ☐
2. Write down the numbers that are in set $B \cap C$ ☐
3. Write down the numbers in set $A \cup C$ ☐

You may find it helpful to draw a Venn diagram with three circles. Build it up in the same way as you did with two circles.

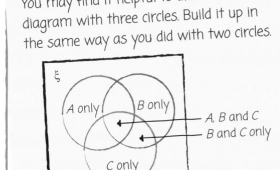

2 Building the walls (*Entry-level problems*)

Building on the foundations, we now start to add context to the questions. Look for key words and instructions.

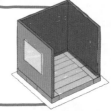

Worked example

Grade 5

Elijah asks his friends if they have a laptop (L) or a tablet (T). He displays the information on a Venn diagram.

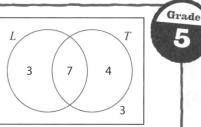

Elijah says 'the probability of having a laptop is $\frac{10}{17}$ and the probability of having a tablet is $\frac{11}{17}$, so the probability of having a laptop or a tablet is $\frac{7}{17}$'. Is he correct? Explain your answer.

[2 marks]

📄 **Need more help?**
Go to page 110

Solution

Elijah is incorrect because he has given the probability of having both a laptop and a tablet. The total number of people that have a tablet or a laptop is 3 + 7 + 4 = 14 so the probability is $\frac{14}{17}$

Exam corner

Grade 5

1. A group of 100 students is asked if they have pets. 30 own dogs, 12 own cats and dogs, 45 own cats, 9 own cats and rabbits, 40 own rabbits, 10 own dogs and rabbits, 7 own dogs, cats and rabbits.

   a) Draw a Venn diagram to represent this information. **[I got ___ /4 marks]**
   b) Find the probability that a student chosen at random owns none of these pets. **[___ /1 mark]**

③ Complete the house (*Problem solving*)

Now we have secure foundations and solid walls, we can complete the house: problem-solving questions set in context. For these questions, you'll need to read them very carefully and then pull out the key information. Only after that, you should start applying your maths skills.

Worked example

Myles draws this Venn diagram to represent the opinions of 50 people.

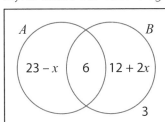

Find

a) the value of x

b) $P(A)$

c) $P(A \cap B)$

d) $P(B')$ **[7 marks]**

> Treat a question involving algebra in exactly the same way as you would all other Venn diagram questions.

Solution

a) $23 - x + 6 + 12 + 2x + 3 = 50$

$$44 + x = 50$$

$$x = 6$$

> Now we know the value of x, we can substitute this in.

b) A: $23 - 6 + 6 = 23$ so $P(A) = \dfrac{23}{50}$

c) $P(A \cap B) = \dfrac{6}{50} = \dfrac{3}{25}$

d) $P(B')$: $23 - 6 + 3 = 20$ so $P(B') = \dfrac{20}{50} = \dfrac{2}{5}$

> Start by deciding on the part of the diagram that represents the probability, then calculate the value.

Exam corner

2. There are 25 students in a sixth-form class. They are asked if they study English (E) or Maths (M). The results show that

$$P(E) = \frac{10}{25} \qquad P(E \cap M) = \frac{6}{25} \qquad P(E \cup M) = \frac{18}{25}$$

Draw a Venn diagram to display this information.

[I got ___ /4 marks]

3. On holiday with friends, Evie asks what activity they want to do – archery, cinema, both, or neither. The Venn diagram is incomplete.

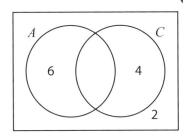

If archery costs £12, the cinema costs £6, and Evie collects £150, how many people signed up to both activities?

[___ /3 marks]

Next steps...

List what you need to revise/practise:

.... ☐

.... ☐

.... ☐

.... ☐

.... ☐

Tick when done

Answers

A correct final answer automatically scores all the marks, unless specified otherwise.

Page 1, Place value

1. **a** 0.7, 0.704, 0.74, 0.744
    1 mark for correct order.
    b 3 thousandths or $\frac{3}{1000}$
    1 mark for correct answer.
2. $336 \div 10 \div 100 = 0.336$
    1 mark for correct answer.

Page 2, Order of operations

1. $\frac{32}{11}$
    1 mark for correct value ($\frac{32}{11}$ or 2.9090… or $2\frac{10}{11}$);
    1 mark for correct answer as an improper fraction.
2. **a** $7 - 2 + 3 = 5 + 3 = 8$
    1 mark for correct answer.
    b $2 \times 3^2 + 2\sqrt{3 \times 9 - 2} = 2 \times 9 + 2\sqrt{27 - 2}$
    $$= 18 + 2\sqrt{25}$$
    $$= 18 + 2 \times 5$$
    $$= 18 + 10$$
    $$= 28$$
    1 mark for 18; 1 mark for $2\sqrt{25}$ or 10; 1 mark for correct answer. Total 3 marks. Make sure you show all your working in a question like this.

Page 3, Rounding and truncating

1. **a** 80
    1 mark for correct answer.
    b 79.5
    1 mark for correct answer.
2. $12.63 \times 3.5 = 44.205$
    $$= £44.21 \text{ to 2 decimal places}$$
    1 mark for multiplying 12.63 by 3.5 correctly; 1 mark for rounding your answer to the nearest penny. If you get the wrong answer to 12.63×3.5, you can still score 1 mark for rounding correctly.

Page 4, Significant figures

1. **a** £9600
    1 mark for correct answer.
    b £10 000
    1 mark for correct answer.
2. $1.65 \div 48 = 0.034375$
    $$= 0.034 \text{ kg to 2 significant figures}$$
    1 mark for dividing 1.65 by 48; 1 mark for rounding answer to 2 s.f.
    If you get the wrong answer to $1.65 \div 48$, you can still score 1 mark for rounding correctly.

Page 5, Estimation

1. $22.5 + 1.9 \times 4.3 \approx 20 + 2 \times 4 = 28$
    So no, Simon's answer does not seem approximately correct (he has used the wrong order of operations).
    1 mark for rounding values and estimating answer; 1 mark for correct conclusion. You can't score the mark for the conclusion unless you either attempt the estimation yourself or explain what Simon has done wrong.
2. Volume $= 96 \times 22.1 \times 19.3$
    $$\approx 100 \times 20 \times 20$$
    $$= 40\,000\,\text{cm}^3$$
    1 mark for multiplying three values to give volume, 1 mark for rounding correctly (could use 22 for 2nd value), 1 mark for correct answer (could have 44 000). Total 3 marks.

Page 6, Error intervals

1. $26.5 \le t < 27.5$
    1 mark for both values correct, even if you use < instead of ≤ (or vice-versa); 1 mark for fully correct answer with correct inequality signs.
2. **a** $229.5 \le c < 230.5$
    1 mark for both values correct, even if you use < instead of ≤ (or vice-versa); 1 mark for fully correct answer with correct inequality signs.
    b $230 \le c < 240$
    1 mark for both values correct, even if you use < instead of ≤ (or vice-versa); 1 mark for fully correct answer with correct inequality signs.

Page 7, Calculating with negative numbers

1. $3 - (-12) = 3 + 12 = 15\,°C$
    1 mark for correct answer.
2. **a** -20
    1 mark for correct answer
    b $(-6)^2 \div (-3) = 36 \div (-3) = -12$
    1 mark for positive 36; 1 mark for correct final answer. If you write $(-36) \div (-3) = 12$ then you can have 1 mark for doing this calculation correctly – but you must have written it down.
    c $-5 \times 2 - (-7) = -10 + 7 = -3$
    1 mark for either working out $-5 \times 2 = -10$ or showing that $-(-7) = +7$; 1 mark for correct final answer.

Page 8, Calculating with decimals

1. $136.46 + 52.02 = 188.48$
    $188.48 \div 8 = £23.56$
    1 mark for 188.48; 1 mark for dividing your answer to the sum by 8; 1 mark for correct answer. If you add 136.46 and 52.02 incorrectly, you can still score a mark for dividing correctly by 8. Total 3 marks.

2. $\dfrac{3.114 - 0.54}{0.18} = \dfrac{2.574}{0.18} = \dfrac{257.4}{18} = 14.3$

*1 mark for 2.574; **1 mark** for attempting to divide by 18; **1 mark** for correct answer. If you get the wrong value as the numerator you can still score a mark by recognising you need to divide by 18. Total 3 marks.*

Page 9, Introduction to fractions

1. $\dfrac{16}{40} = \dfrac{2}{5}, \dfrac{3}{18} = \dfrac{1}{6}, \dfrac{1}{3} = \dfrac{2}{6}$

Order: $\dfrac{3}{18} \left(\text{or } \dfrac{1}{6}\right), \dfrac{1}{3} \left(\text{or } \dfrac{2}{6}\right), \dfrac{16}{40} \left(\text{or } \dfrac{2}{5}\right)$

*1 mark for simplifying $\dfrac{16}{40}$ and $\dfrac{3}{18}$; **1 mark** for correct order (you can either write the original fractions or equivalent ones).*

2. $\dfrac{37}{5}$

1 mark for correct answer.

Page 10, Proportions of amounts

1. $\dfrac{1}{9}$ of £90 = 90 ÷ 9 = £10, $\dfrac{2}{9}$ of £90 = 10 × 2 = £20

$\dfrac{1}{15}$ of £90 = 90 ÷ 15 = £6, $\dfrac{7}{15}$ of £90 = 6 × 7 = £42

90 – (20 + 42) = 28

Mira has £28 left.

*1 mark for £20; **1 mark** for £42; **1 mark** for subtracting the two values (at least one correct) from £90; **1 mark** for correct answer. Total 4 marks.*

2. 10% of 60 = 6, 5% = 3, so 85% = 8 × 6 + 3 = 51

1% of 150 = 1.5, so 32% = 32 × 1.5 = 48

The plant he had the most of was basil.

*1 mark for 51; **1 mark** for 48; **1 mark** for correct conclusion (you must have scored the other 2 marks to get this mark). Total 3 marks.*

Page 11, Calculating with fractions 1

1. $2\dfrac{1}{3} \times \dfrac{5}{21} = \dfrac{7}{3} \times \dfrac{5}{21} = \dfrac{35}{63} = \dfrac{5}{9}$

*1 mark for writing $2\dfrac{1}{3}$ as improper fraction; **1 mark** for multiplying numerators and multiplying denominators; **1 mark** for correct, simplified answer. Total 3 marks.*

2. $\dfrac{3}{4} \div \dfrac{5}{14} = \dfrac{3}{4} \times \dfrac{14}{5} = \dfrac{42}{20} = 2\dfrac{2}{20} = 2\dfrac{1}{10}$

*1 mark for writing $\dfrac{3}{4} \times \dfrac{14}{5}$; **1 mark** for multiplying numerators and multiplying denominators; **1 mark** for final answer as a mixed number (can score this mark for correctly converting your answer to a mixed number). Total 3 marks.*

Page 12, Calculating with fractions 2

1. a $\dfrac{6}{7} - \dfrac{2}{7} = \dfrac{4}{7}$

1 mark for correct answer.

b $\dfrac{3}{8} + \dfrac{1}{4} = \dfrac{3}{8} + \dfrac{2}{8} = \dfrac{5}{8}$

*1 mark for writing with a common denominator (e.g. 8, 16 or 32); **1 mark** for correct answer (any fraction equivalent to $\dfrac{5}{8}$).*

2. $1\dfrac{8}{9} + \dfrac{5}{6} = \dfrac{17}{9} + \dfrac{5}{6} = \dfrac{34}{18} + \dfrac{15}{18} = \dfrac{49}{18}$

$\dfrac{49}{18} - \dfrac{1}{18} = \dfrac{48}{18} = 2\dfrac{12}{18} = 2\dfrac{2}{3}$

The tub weighs $2\dfrac{2}{3}$ kg.

*1 mark for writing $\dfrac{5}{6}$ and $\dfrac{8}{9}$ (or $\dfrac{17}{9}$) over a common denominator (e.g. 18, 36 or 54); **1 mark** for finding $\dfrac{49}{18}$ (or equivalent); **1 mark** for subtracting $\dfrac{1}{18}$ from your sum found (or from $\dfrac{5}{6}$ or $1\dfrac{8}{9}$); **1 mark** for correct answer as mixed number and in simplest form. Total 4 marks.*

Page 13, Fractions, decimals, percentages

1. a i $0.061 = \dfrac{61}{1000}$ **ii** $0.061 = 6.1\%$

1 mark for each correct answer.

b $5\% = \dfrac{5}{100} = \dfrac{1}{20}$

*1 mark for writing over 100; **1 mark** for correct, simplified answer.*

2. $\dfrac{3}{8} = 3 \div 8 = 0.375 = 37.5\%$

37.5% + 13% = 50.5%

100% – 50.5% = 49.5%

49.5% are travelling for leisure.

*1 mark for converting $\dfrac{3}{8}$ to a percentage; **1 mark** for subtracting two percentages from 100%; **1 mark** for correct answer. Total 3 marks.*

Page 14, Powers and roots

1. $\sqrt[3]{9.261} = 2.1$

Side length is 2.1 cm.

1 mark for correct answer.

2. $5 + \sqrt{100 - 4^3} = 5 + \sqrt{100 - 64}$

$\qquad\qquad = 5 + \sqrt{36}$

$\qquad\qquad = 5 + 6$

$\qquad\qquad = 11$

*1 mark for $4^3 = 64$; **1 mark** for $\sqrt{36} = 6$; **1 mark** for correct answer. Total 3 marks.*

Page 15, Calculating with indices

1. a i $8^7 \div 8^3 = 8^{7-3} = 8^4$

    ii $(8^{-5})^2 = 8^{-5 \times 2} = 8^{-10}$

1 mark for each correct answer.

b $8 \times 8^{-4} \div 8^{-5} = 8^{1 + (-4) - (-5)} = 8^2$

*1 mark for method to add –4 and subtract –5; **1 mark** for correct answer.*

2. a i $13^0 = 1$ **ii** $6^{-1} = \dfrac{1}{6}$

1 mark for each correct answer.

b $\left(\dfrac{1}{3}\right)^{-2} = \left(\left(\dfrac{1}{3}\right)^2\right)^{-1} = \left(\dfrac{1^2}{3^2}\right)^{-1} = \left(\dfrac{1}{9}\right)^{-1} = 9$

*1 mark for finding reciprocal (of $\dfrac{1}{3}$ or $\dfrac{1}{9}$) or for finding $\left(\dfrac{1}{3}\right)^2$; **1 mark** for correct answer.*

Page 16, Factors and multiples

1. a Factors of 98: 1, 2, 7, 14, 49, 98

Factors of 70: 1, 2, 5, 7, 10, 14, 35, 70

HCF is 14

*1 mark for listing some factors of 98 and 70 (at least 2 of each); **1 mark** for selecting a common factor; **1 mark** for correct answer. Total 3 marks.*

b Multiples of 80: 80, 160, 240, …
Multiples of 120: 120, 240, …
LCM is 240
1 mark for listing some multiples of 80 and 120; 1 mark for correct answer.
2 Factors of 63: 1, 3, 7, 9, 21, 63
Factors of 42: 1, 2, 3, 6, 7, 14, 21, 42
The tiles must be 21 cm × 21 cm.
1 mark for finding factors of 63 and 42; 1 mark for correct answer (units not required).

Page 17, Prime factor decomposition

1. a $54 = 2 \times 3 \times 3 \times 3 = 2 \times 3^3$
1 mark for answer not in index form; both marks for correct answer in correct form.
  b $650 = 2 \times 5 \times 5 \times 13 = 2 \times 5^2 \times 13$
1 mark for answer not in index form; both marks for correct answer in correct form.
2. $6 = 2 \times 3$, $14 = 2 \times 7$ and $50 = 2 \times 5^2$
Therefore, number is $2 \times 3 \times 7 \times 5^2$
(or $2 \times 3 \times 7 \times 5 \times 5$)
1 mark for using $6 = 2 \times 3$ or $14 = 2 \times 7$ or $50 = 2 \times 5^2$; 1 mark for correct answer.

Page 18, Finding HCF and LCM

1. a

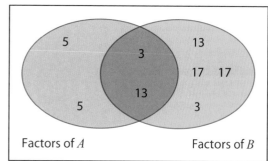

HCF = $3 \times 13 = 39$
1 mark for drawing a correct Venn diagram, or for other valid method such as writing out the factors and circling; 1 mark for recognising answer as the product of numbers in the intersection; 1 mark for answer in index form. Total 3 marks.
  b LCM $= 3 \times 3 \times 5 \times 5 \times 13 \times 13 \times 17 \times 17$
     $= 3^2 \times 5^2 \times 13^2 \times 17^2$
1 mark for writing out product of factors; 1 mark for answer in index form.
2. HCF $= 14 \Rightarrow y = 2$
First number is $2 \times 7 \times 2 = 28$
LCM $= 420 \Rightarrow 420 = 2 \times$ (second number)
Second number is $420 \div 2 = 210$
1 mark for finding correct value of y; 1 mark for finding 28; 1 mark for method to find second number (either divide LCM by 2 or find x = 5 then multiply factors together); 1 mark for finding 210. Total 4 marks.

Page 19, Standard form

1. a 0.000 002 01 m
1 mark for correct number (units not needed).
  b $2.01 \times 10^{-6} \times 100 = 2.01 \times 10^{-4}$ cm
1 mark for correct number in standard form (units not needed).

2. Saturn to Jupiter $= 6.46 \times 10^7$ km
Jupiter is closer to Saturn than Uranus is, since smaller power of 10
Alternative method:
Saturn to Uranus $= 1\,450\,000\,000$ km
Jupiter is closer to Saturn than Uranus is, since $64\,600\,000 < 1\,450\,000\,000$.
1 mark for converting one distance into standard form / ordinary number; 1 mark for correct conclusion (must have converted).

Page 20, Calculating with standard form

1. a $42\,000\,000$
     $\underline{-\,6\,100\,000}$
     $35\,900\,000$ which is 3.59×10^7
1 mark for converting both to ordinary numbers (or writing both with the same power of 10); 1 mark for correct subtraction; 1 mark for correct answer in standard form. Total 3 marks.
  b $(9 \times 10^{-7}) \times (8 \times 10^5) = (9 \times 8) \times (10^{-7} \times 10^5)$
               $= 72 \times 10^{-2}$
               $= 7.2 \times 10^{-1}$
1 mark for attempting to multiply 9 by 8 and add the powers; 1 mark for correct answer in any form; 1 mark for correct answer in standard form. Total 3 marks.
2. $(2.1 \times 10^4) \div (3 \times 10^6) = (2.1 \div 3) \times (10^4 \div 10^6)$
               $= 0.7 \times 10^{-2}$
               $= 0.007$ km²
1 mark for attempting to divide 2.1 by 3 and subtract the powers; 1 mark for correct answer in any form; 1 mark for correct answer as ordinary number including units. Total 3 marks.

Page 21, Terms and expressions

1. a $4x + 3y$
1 mark for correct answer.
  b $20 - (4x + 3y)$, or $20 - 4x - 3y$
1 mark for correct answer.
2. a $5 - s = 5 - 8 = -3$
1 mark for correct answer.
  b $4s + 5t = 4 \times 8 + 5 \times (-3)$
          $= 32 - 15 = 17$
1 mark for substituting in values (using multiplication sign or brackets); 1 mark for correct answer.
  c $3st = 3 \times 8 \times (-3) = -72$
1 mark for substituting in values (using multiplication sign or brackets); 1 mark for correct answer.

Page 22, Simplifying expressions

1. a $3m - 7m + 8m = 4m$
1 mark for correct answer.
  b $7t - s + 3 - t - 4 - 5s = 6t - 6s - 1$
1 mark for each correct term (including correct sign) in answer. Total 3 marks.
2. a $y + 3x + y + x + 5y + x + 5y + x$
     $= 12y + 6x$ (cm)
1 mark for adding up the lengths (allow mark if up to 2 missing terms); 1 mark for correct, simplified answer.

b $3xy + 5xy = 8xy$ (cm²)

1 mark for multiplying to give either term; 1 mark for correct, simplified answer.

Page 23, Formulae

1. $P = 7 + 2c$

1 mark for correct expression 7 + 2c; 1 mark for correct formula.

2. $V = \frac{9^2 \times 24}{3} = 648 \, \text{cm}^3$

1 mark for substituting into formula; 1 mark for correct answer.

Page 24, Equations and identities

1. $3x + 2 + x - 5 = 4x - 3$ is an identity (true for all values of x).

$5x - 7 = x + 5$ is an equation not an identity (only true when $x = 3$).

$2x - 4 - 3x = 5x - 4$ is an equation not an identity (only true for $x = 0$).

$6 - 2x = -2x + 6$ is an identity (true for all values of x).

2 marks for both identities found and no incorrect answers; 1 mark for only 1 identity found (or 2 found plus 1 found incorrectly).

2. a formula

b expression

c identity

1 mark for each correct answer.

Page 25, Functions

1. a $x \rightarrow \boxed{-5} \rightarrow \boxed{\times 3} \rightarrow y$

1 mark for correct answer in function machine.

b $3 - 5 = -2$

$y = -2 \times 3 = -6$

1 mark for correct answer.

c $6 \div 3 = 2$

$x = 2 + 5 = 7$

1 mark for attempting to apply the inverse of both your functions in reverse order; 1 mark for correct answer.

d $y = 3(x - 5)$ or could write $y = 3x - 15$

1 mark for correct answer.

2. a $17 \rightarrow 21 \rightarrow 7 \rightarrow -6$

Output is -6

1 mark for applying first 2 functions; 1 mark for correct answer.

b $-12 \rightarrow 1 \rightarrow 3 \rightarrow -1$

Input is -1

1 mark for attempting to apply the inverse operations in correct order; 1 mark for correct answer.

c $x \rightarrow (x + 4) \rightarrow \frac{x+4}{3} \rightarrow \frac{x+4}{3} - 13$ (or equivalent).

Output is $\frac{x+4}{3} - 13$

1 mark for writing $\frac{x+4}{3}$ or $(x + 4) \div 3$; 1 mark for correct answer.

Page 26, Solving linear equations

1. a $\frac{13x}{13} = -\frac{65}{13}$

$x = -5$

1 mark for correct answer.

b $\frac{m}{5} \times 5 = 11 \times 5$

$m = 55$

1 mark for correct answer.

c $3y + 7 - 7 = 31 - 7$

$\frac{3y}{3} = \frac{24}{3}$

$y = 8$

1 mark for subtracting 7 from both sides; 1 mark for correct answer.

d $6p + 15 = 3$

$6p + 15 - 15 = 3 - 15$

$\frac{6p}{6} = \frac{-12}{6}$

$p = -2$

1 mark for subtracting 15 from both sides; 1 mark for correct answer.

2. $9h + 18 = 58.5$

$9h + 18 - 18 = 58.5 - 18$

$\frac{9h}{9} = \frac{40.5}{9}$

$h = 4.5$

She worked for 4.5 hours.

1 mark for forming correct equation; 1 mark for attempting to subtract 18 and divide by 9; 1 mark for correct answer. Total 3 marks.

Page 27, Harder linear equations

1. a $3x + 4x + 6 = 20 - 4x + 4x$

$7x + 6 - 6 = 20 - 6$

$\frac{7x}{7} = \frac{14}{7}$

$x = 2$

1 mark for adding 4x to both sides (or subtracting 3x); 1 mark for correct answer.

b $\frac{x+6}{5} \times 5 = 8 \times 5$

$x + 6 - 6 = 40 - 6$

$x = 34$

1 mark for multiplying both sides by 5; 1 mark for correct answer.

c $\frac{3x}{4} - 3 + 3 = 9 + 3$

$\frac{3x}{4} \times 4 = 12 \times 4$

$\frac{3x}{3} = \frac{48}{3}$

$x = 16$

1 mark for multiplying both sides by 4 correctly (could have 3x − 12 = 36 instead); 1 mark for correct answer.

2. Let Lucy's number be x

$4x + 15 = 5 - x$

$4x + x + 15 = 5 - x + x$

$5x + 15 - 15 = 5 - 15$

$\frac{5x}{5} = -\frac{10}{5}$

$x = -2$

1 mark for forming correct equation; 1 mark for adding x to both sides (or subtracting 4x); 1 mark for correct answer. Total 3 marks.

Page 28, Rearranging formulae

1. a $y - 2 = 7x + 2 - 2$

$\quad y - 2 = 7x$

$\quad \frac{y-2}{7} = \frac{7x}{7}$

$\quad x = \frac{y-2}{7}$

1 mark for applying an operation to both sides of equation (e.g. subtracting 2); 1 mark for correct answer.

b $y \times 4 = \frac{3x+z}{4} \times 4$

$\quad 4y = 3x + z$

$\quad 4y - z = 3x + z - z$

$\quad 4y - z = 3x$

$\quad \frac{4y-z}{3} = \frac{3x}{3}$

$\quad x = \frac{4y-z}{3}$

1 mark each for applying two operations to both sides of equation (e.g. multiplying by 4 and subtracting z); 1 mark for correct answer. Total 3 marks.

c $\quad y + x = 4 - x + x$

$\quad y - y + x = 4 - y$

$\quad x = 4 - y$

1 mark for adding x to both sides or subtracting 4 from both sides; 1 mark for correct answer.

2. a $E \times 2 = \frac{1}{2}ms^2 \times 2$

$\quad \frac{2E}{m} = \frac{ms^2}{m}$

$\quad s^2 = \frac{2E}{m}$

$\quad s = \sqrt{\frac{2E}{m}}$

1 mark for multiplying both sides by 2; 1 mark for dividing both sides by m; 1 mark for final answer. Total 3 marks.

b $s = \sqrt{\frac{2 \times 8}{4}} = \sqrt{4} = 2$

1 mark for substituting into the rearranged formula found in part a. (or into the original formula); 1 mark for correct answer.

Page 29, Expanding single brackets

1. a $5(2x + 4) = 10x + 20$

1 mark for correct answer.

b $x(3x - 1) = 3x^2 - x$

1 mark per correct term (including sign).

2. $x(y - 1) = xy - x$

$3x(y + 7) = 3xy + 21x$

Area $= xy - x + 3xy + 21x$

$\quad = 4xy + 20x$

1 mark for correct expression for area of either rectangle; 1 mark for correct expansion of expression for either rectangle; 1 mark for attempting to add the two expanded expressions; 1 mark for correct answer. Total 4 marks.

Page 30, Factorising into single brackets

1. a $2x(3 - x)$

1 mark for correctly factorising with x or 2 outside brackets; 1 mark for fully factorised correct answer.

b $7a(2b + 3a)$

1 mark for correctly factorising with 7 or a outside brackets; 1 mark for fully factorised correct answer.

c $xy^2(z + z^2 + 1)$

1 mark for xy^2 outside bracket and at least two terms inside bracket correct; 1 mark for correct answer.

2. $12t^2 - 9t = 3t(4t - 3)$

Length $= 3t$, width $= 4t - 3$ (or vice versa)

Alternatively, can have length and width (either way around) equal to 3 and $4t^2 - 3t$, or t and $12t - 9$

1 mark for factorising; 1 mark for correct answers for length and width.

Page 31, Expanding double brackets

a $ab + 2a + b + 2$

1 mark for at least 3 correct terms; 1 mark for correct answer.

b $x^2 - 4x + 3x - 12 = x^2 - x - 12$

1 mark for at least 3 correct terms; 1 mark for correct, simplified expression.

c $6x^2 - 4x - 3x + 2 = 6x^2 - 7x + 2$

1 mark for at least 3 correct terms; 1 mark for correct, simplified expression.

d $(3x + 2)(3x + 2) = 9x^2 + 6x + 6x + 4$

$\quad = 9x^2 + 12x + 4$

1 mark for at least 3 correct terms; 1 mark for correct, simplified expression.

Page 32, Factorising into double brackets

1. a $(x + 2)(x + 7)$

1 mark for correct answer.

b $(x + 10)(x - 2)$

1 mark for brackets with x and two numbers that multiply to give –20; 1 mark for correct answer.

c $(x - 6)(x + 3)$

1 mark for brackets with x and two numbers that multiply to give –18; 1 mark for correct answer.

d $(x - 9)(x - 1)$

1 mark for brackets with x and two numbers that multiply to give +9; 1 mark for correct answer.

2. $x^2 - 10x + 25 = (x - 5)(x - 5) = (x - 5)^2$

Side length $= x - 5$

1 mark for correct factorisation, 1 mark for side length.

Page 33, Difference of two squares

a $(x + 10)(x - 10)$

1 mark for correct answer.

b $x(x + 8)$

1 mark for correct answer.

c $(7x + 1)(7x - 1)$

1 mark for correct answer.

d $(x - 3)(x - 5)$

1 mark for brackets with x and two numbers that multiply to give +15; 1 mark for correct answer.

e $12x(2 - x)$
1 mark for correct answer.

f $(x + y)(x - y)$
1 mark for correct answer.

Page 34, Solving quadratic equations

a $(x + 4)(x + 2) = 0$
$x + 4 = 0$ or $x + 2 = 0$
$x = -4$ or $x = -2$
1 mark for correctly factorising; 1 mark for each correct value of x. Total 3 marks.

b $(x + 11)(x - 11) = 0$
$x + 11 = 0$ or $x - 11 = 0$
$x = -11$ or $x = 11$
1 mark for correctly factorising (or for writing down one correct answer); 1 mark for both correct values of x

c $2x(x - 3) = 0$
$2x = 0$ or $x - 3 = 0$
$x = 0$ or $x = 3$
1 mark for correctly factorising; 1 mark for each correct value of x. Total 3 marks.

d $x^2 + x - 12 = 0$
$(x + 4)(x - 3) = 0$
$x + 4 = 0$ or $x - 3 = 0$
$x = -4$ or $x = 3$
1 mark for rearranging to get zero on one side; 1 mark for factorising; 1 mark for each correct value of x. Total 4 marks.

Page 35, Simultaneous equations 1

a $x + 4y = 48$ (1), $3x + 4y = 56$ (2)
(2) – (1): $2x = 8$
$x = 4$
Substitute into (1): $4 + 4y = 48$
$4y = 44$
$y = 11$
1 mark for subtracting the equations; 1 mark for correct value of x; 1 mark for correct value of y. Total 3 marks. Full marks also available if the same answer is achieved by a different method of substituting the equations.

b $x + 2y = 11$ (1), $-3x + 5y = 44$ (2)
Multiply (1) by 3: $3x + 6y = 33$ (3)
(3) + (2): $11y = 77$
$y = 7$
Substitute into (1): $x + 14 = 11$
$x = -3$
1 mark for correct equation in either x or y; 1 mark for correct value of y; 1 mark for correct value of x. Total 3 marks.

Page 36, Simultaneous equations 2

1. a $4x + 2y = 28$ (1) and $2x + 3y = 22$ (2)
1 mark for each correct equation.

b Multiply equation (2) by 2: $4x + 6y = 44$ (3)
(3) – (1): $4y = 16$
$y = 4$ cm
Substitute into equation (2): $2x + 12 = 22$
$2x = 10$
$x = 5$ cm
1 mark for multiplying equation (2) by 2 (or you could divide equation (1) by 2 instead); 1 mark for subtracting equations; 1 mark for correct values of y and x. Total 3 marks.

2. Using m = cost of bottle of milk, c = cost of pack of cheese:
$5m + 2c = 10.3$ (1) and $2m + 3c = 10.94$ (2)
Multiply equation (1) by 3: $15m + 6c = 30.9$ (3)
Multiply equation (2) by 2: $4m + 6c = 21.88$ (4)
(3) – (4): $11m = 9.02$
$m = 0.82$
Substitute into equation (2): $1.64 + 3c = 10.94$
$3c = 9.3$
$c = 3.1$

The cost of a bottle of milk is £0.82 (or 82p) and the cost of a pack of cheese is £3.10
1 mark for correct equations (you can use any two letters); 1 mark for multiplying equation (1) by 3 and equation (2) by 2 (or you could multiply equation (1) by 2 and equation (2) by 5 instead); 1 mark for subtracting the new equations; 1 mark for correct value of m or c; 1 mark for correct cost of milk and cheese including units. Total 5 marks.

Page 37, Solving inequalities

1. a

1 mark for hollow circle at 0; 1 mark for filled-in circle at 3

b 1, 2, 3
1 mark for all 3 correct values and no incorrect values.

2. a $x + 9 - 9 > 12 - 9$
$x > 3$
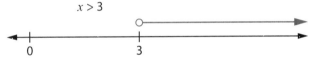
1 mark for correct solution (check you have the correct inequality sign); 1 mark for showing on number line (must have a hollow circle).

b $-3x + 3x \leq 12 + 3x$
$0 \leq 12 + 3x$
$0 - 12 \leq 12 - 12 + 3x$
$-12 \leq 3x$
$\frac{-12}{3} \leq \frac{3x}{3}$
$-4 \leq x$
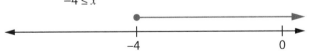
1 mark for subtracting 12 from both sides or adding $3x$ to both sides; 1 mark for correct solution (check you have the correct inequality sign); 1 mark for showing on number line (must have a filled-in circle). Total 3 marks.

c $2x + 13 - 13 \geq 25 - 13$
$2x \geq 12$
$\frac{2x}{2} \geq \frac{12}{2}$
$x \geq 6$

1 mark for rearranging correctly; 1 mark for correct solution (check you have the correct inequality sign); 1 mark for showing on number line (must have a filled-in circle). Total 3 marks.

Page 38, Drawing linear graphs

1. a

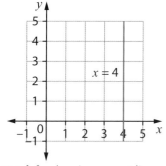

1 mark for drawing correct line.

b

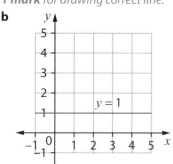

1 mark for drawing correct line.

2. a

x	−1	0	1	2
y	−2	1	4	7

1 mark for two correct values; *1 mark* for all three correct.

b

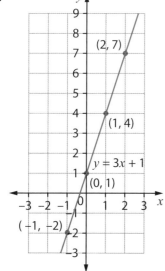

1 mark for plotting at least 2 correct points from the table; *1 mark* for drawing correct line.

Page 39, Finding gradients

1. a Gradient = 3, equation is $y = 3x$
1 mark for correct gradient; *1 mark* for correct equation.
b Gradient = −2, equation is $y = -2x$
1 mark for correct gradient; *1 mark* for correct equation.

Page 40, Equation of a straight line

1. a $2y = 10x − 1$ becomes $y = 5x − \frac{1}{2}$
which is parallel to $y = 5x + 3$
1 mark for rearranging one of the equations to make y the subject; *1 mark* for correct answer.

b $2y + 1 = 5x$ becomes $y = \frac{5}{2}x − \frac{1}{2}$
which has the same y-intercept as $2y = 10x − 1$
$\left(y = 5x − \frac{1}{2}\right)$
1 mark for rearranging another equation to make y the subject; *1 mark* for correct answer.

2. a $y = 5x − 3$
1 mark for correct answer.
b Gradient $= \frac{2}{4} = \frac{1}{2}$
$y = \frac{1}{2}x + 5$
1 mark for correct gradient; *1 mark* for writing
$y = mx + 5$ with your value of the gradient as m; *1 mark* for correct answer. Total 3 marks.
c Gradient $= \frac{-2}{1} = -2$
$y = -2x + c$
Substitute in the point (1, 3): $3 = -2 \times 1 + c$
$$3 = -2 + c$$
$$c = 5$$
$y = -2x + 5$
Or,

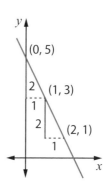

1 mark for correct gradient; *1 mark* for attempting to find value of c, by either substituting into the equation or sketching part of the graph; *1 mark* for writing $y = mx + c$ with your value of the gradient as m and your y-intercept as c; *1 mark* for correct answer. Total 4 marks.

Page 41, Kinematic graphs

a 5 m
1 mark for correct answer.
b Speed $= \frac{4}{0.5} = 8$ m/h
Or, speed $= \frac{4}{30} = \frac{2}{15}$ m/min which is 8 m/h
1 mark for using correct formula for speed; *1 mark* for correct answer in m/h.
c Resting/not moving
1 mark for correct answer.
d

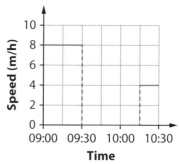

1 mark for each correct section of graph (09:00–09:30, 09:30–10:15, 10:15–10:30). Total 3 marks.

Page 42, Quadratic graphs

1. a

x	−2	−1	0	1	2
y	4	−2	−4	−2	4

1 mark for at least two correct values; 1 mark for all values correct.

b

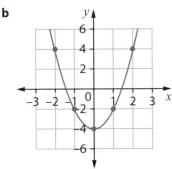

1 mark for plotting values from table; 1 mark for correct points joined with a smooth curve.

2. a Turning point is (−2, 3)

1 mark for correct answer.

b Roots are approximately $x = -3.7$ and $x = -0.3$

1 mark for each root, total 2 marks. Allow 0.1 either side (e.g. between −3.8 and −3.6, and between −0.4 and −0.2 respectively).

Page 43, Solutions from graphs

1. Solutions to 1 d.p. are $x = 1.3$ and $y = 4.1$

1 mark for x correct; 1 mark for y correct. Allow 0.1 either side (e.g. between 1.2 and 1.4, and between 4.0 and 4.2 respectively).

2.

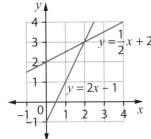

Solutions are $x = 2$, $y = 3$

1 mark for drawing a line with positive gradient and y-intercept 2; 1 mark for correct line; 1 mark for correct value of either x or y according to your graph; 1 mark for both values correct. Total 4 marks.

Page 44, Cubic and reciprocal graphs

a

x	−2	−1	0	1	2
y	−16	−2	0	2	16

1 mark for at least two correct values; 1 mark for all values correct.

b

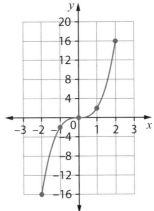

1 mark for plotting values from table; 1 mark for joining with smooth curve.

Page 45, Rates of change

1. a Fixed fee = £50

1 mark for correct answer.

b Choose two points, e.g. (0, 50) and (2, 140).

Gradient $= \frac{\text{change in } y}{\text{change in } x} = \frac{90}{2} = 45$

Cost per day = £45

1 mark for using correct rule to calculate gradient; 1 mark for correct answer.

2. a

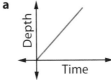

1 mark for correct graph.

b

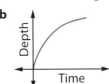

1 mark for correct graph.

c

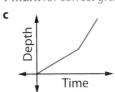

1 mark for correct graph.

Page 46, Sequences

1. a $24 \times 2 = 48$

1 mark for correct answer.

b Geometric (multiply by 2 each time)

1 mark for correct answer.

c Every term after the first term will be an even number, because you are multiplying by 2 each time. So Katie is incorrect.

1 mark for correct answer, including reason.

2. a (Start at 3 and) add 2

1 mark for correct answer.

b Sequence is 3, 5, 7, 9, 11, 13, …

Pattern 6 will have 13 ice-lolly sticks.

1 mark for continuing the sequence; 1 mark for correct answer.

Page 47, Using the nth term

1. a 8th term = $7 \times 8 + 3 = 59$
1 mark for correct answer.

b 6th term = $6^2 + 7 = 43$
1 mark for substituting $n = 6$ into rule; 1 mark for correct answer.

c 5th term = $5 - 2 \times 5^2 = 5 - 50 = -45$
1 mark for substituting $n = 5$ into rule; 1 mark for correct answer.

2. a 9th term = $100 - 7 \times 9 = 100 - 63 = 37$
1 mark for correct answer.

b $100 - 7n < 0$
$100 < 7n$
$n > \frac{100}{7} = 14\frac{2}{7}$
The first negative term is the 15th term:
15th term = $100 - 7 \times 15 = -5$
Or, write out the sequence (could start at 9th term as found in part **a**):
(93, 86, 79, 72, 65, 58, 51, 44, 37,) 30, 23, 16, 9, 2, –5
The first negative term is –5
1 mark for solving inequality or for writing out the sequence; 1 mark for correct answer.

c $100 - 7n = 50$
$7n = 50$
$n = \frac{50}{7}$ is not an integer, so 50 is not a term of this sequence.
Alternatively, write out the sequence:
93, 86, 79, 72, 65, 58, 51, 44
You can see 50 is not a term of this sequence.
1 mark for finding n or writing out the sequence; 1 mark for stating that this shows 50 is not a term.

Page 48, Finding the nth term

a Common difference = 5
5n: 5 10 15 20 25
+4 +4 +4 +4 +4
9 14 19 24 29
The nth term is $5n + 4$
1 mark for a rule involving $5n$; 1 mark for fully correct answer.

b Common difference = –2
–2n: –2 –4 –6 –8 –10
+7 +7 +7 +7 +7
5 3 1 –1 –3
The nth term is $-2n + 7$ (or $7 - 2n$)
1 mark for a rule involving $-2n$; 1 mark for fully correct answer.

c Common difference = $1\frac{1}{2}$ or 1.5
$1\frac{1}{2}n$: $1\frac{1}{2}$ 3 $4\frac{1}{2}$ 6 $7\frac{1}{2}$
–1 –1 –1 –1 –1
$\frac{1}{2}$ 2 $3\frac{1}{2}$ 5 $6\frac{1}{2}$
The nth term is $1\frac{1}{2}n - 1$ (or $1.5n - 1$)
1 mark for a rule involving $1\frac{1}{2}n$ or $1.5n$; 1 mark for fully correct answer.

Page 49, Special sequences

1. a 6th term = $7 + 11 = 18$
7th term = $11 + 18 = 29$
8th term = $18 + 29 = 47$
1 mark for adding two previous terms to find next term; 1 mark for correct answer.

b 3rd term = $a + b$
1 mark for correct answer.

2. a

1 mark for correct answer.

b Sequence is 1 3 6 10 15 21 28
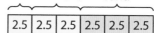
+2 +3 +4 +5 +6 +7
The 7th pattern has 28 circles.
1 mark for writing out at least two more correct terms of the sequence; 1 mark for correct answer.

Page 50, Proportion

1. 80 out of 400 = $\frac{80}{400} \times 100\% = 20\%$
1 mark for writing as a fraction; 1 for correct answer as a percentage.

2. 35 out of 40 = $\frac{35}{40} \times 100\% = \frac{350}{4}\% = 87.5\%$
21 out of 25 = $\frac{21}{25} \times 100\% = 84\%$
Jake scored highest on his History test.
1 mark for 87.5% or 84%; 1 mark for both percentages and the correct conclusion. You can also score both marks for comparing the proportions as decimals: 0.875 and 0.84

Page 51, Ratio

1. white : grey = $24 : 30 = 4 : 5$ (divide both parts by 6)
1 mark for writing 24 : 30 (must be correct way around); 1 mark for correct, fully simplified answer.

2.
water cement   sand

| 2.5 | 2.5 | 2.5 | 2.5 | 2.5 | 2.5 |

Water = 2.5 kg
Sand = $3 \times 2.5 = 7.5$ kg
1 mark for indicating that 1 part is 2.5 kg (on a bar diagram or by writing 5 ÷ 2); 1 mark for correct answer for water; 1 mark for correct answer for sand. Total 3 marks.

Page 52, Using ratio

1. $5 + 3 = 8$
$180 \div 8 = 22.5$
$5 \times 22.5 = 112.5$ so Alice receives £112.50
$3 \times 22.5 = 67.5$ so Benji receives £67.50
1 mark for finding that one part is worth 22.5; 1 mark for multiplying your value for one part (even if it's wrong) by either 5 for Alice or 3 for Benji; 1 mark for both final answers correct. Total 3 marks.

2. a sugar : flour = 1 : 3 = 2 : 6
  sugar : flour : butter = 2 : 6 : 5
  *1 mark for 1 : 3 or equivalent ratio for sugar : flour; **1 mark** for correct 3-part ratio (order must be correct). If you have correct ratio in the wrong order, then score 1 out of 2*
b $26 \times 12 = 312$ g
  $312 \div 13 = 24$ g
  Amount of butter $= 24 \times 5 = 120$ g
  *1 mark for finding total mass of 12 biscuits; **1 mark** for working out value of one part (this could be seen on a bar model); **1 mark** for correct answer. Total 3 marks.*
  Alternatively:
  $26 \div 13 = 2$ g
  $2 \times 5 = 10$ g
  $12 \times 10 = 120$ g
  *1 mark for finding value of one part for a single biscuit; **1 mark** for multiplying by 5 or 12; **1 mark** for correct answer. Total 3 marks.*

Page 53 Percentage change

1. 10% of £25 is £2.50
  40% of £25 is £2.50 $\times 4 = £10$
  Cost for child $= £25 - £10 = £15$
  *1 mark for attempting to find 40% and subtracting your answer from £25; **1 mark** for correct answer.*
2. Percentage increase $= \frac{0.2}{2} \times 100\% = 10\%$
  *1 mark for writing $\frac{change}{original}$; **1 mark** for correct answer.*

Page 54, Multipliers

1. 100% + 8% = 108% $\Rightarrow$ multiplier is 1.08
  After 1 year: £250 000 $\times 1.08 = £270 000$
  After 2 years: £270 000 $\times 1.08 = £291 600$
  *1 mark for finding multiplier of 1.08; **1 mark** for multiplying by your multiplier twice or for writing 250 000 $\times$ (your multiplier)^2; **1 mark** for correct answer. Total 3 marks.*
2. 100% − 13% = 87% $\Rightarrow$ multiplier is 0.87
  After 1 term: 500 $\times 0.87 = 435$
  After 2 terms: 435 $\times 0.87 = 378.45$
  After 3 terms: 378.45 $\times 0.87 = 329.2515$
  329 pencils are remaining after 3 terms.
  *1 mark for finding multiplier of 0.87; **1 mark** for multiplying by your multiplier three times or for writing 500 $\times$ (your multiplier)^3; **1 mark** for correct answer of 329. Total 3 marks.*

Page 55, Original value problems

1. 100% + 15% = 115%
  115% is 230 cm
  1% is 230 $\div$ 115 = 2 cm
  100% is 2 $\times$ 100 = 200 cm
  *1 mark for using 115% (or 1.15), **1 mark** for finding 1% (or dividing by 1.15), **1 mark** for correct final answer. Total 3 marks.*

2. 100% − 40% = 60%
  60% is £390
  1% is 390 $\div$ 60 = £6.50
  100% is 6.5 $\times$ 100 = £650
  *1 mark for using 60% (or 0.6), **1 mark** for finding 1% (or dividing by 0.6), **1 mark** for correct final answer. Total 3 marks.*

Page 56, Compound measures

1. a Time $= \frac{9}{0.3} = 30$ s
  *1 mark for writing or using time $= \frac{distance}{speed}$; **1 mark** for correct answer.*
b 54 km/h = 54 000 m/h = 900 m/min = 15 m/s
  Distance in 10 s = 15 $\times$ 10 = 150 m
  *1 mark for converting speed to m/s (or you could convert speed to m/h and write 10 s as $\frac{1}{360}$ hours); **1 mark** for using distance = speed $\times$ time; **1 mark** for correct answer. Total 3 marks.*
2. Pressure $= \frac{24}{40} = 0.6$ N/m^2
  *1 mark for using pressure $= \frac{force}{area}$; **1 mark** for correct value of pressure; **1 mark** for correct units (could also use Pa for units). Total 3 marks.*

Page 57, Direct proportion

1. 1 litre: cost for 1 ml = 90 $\div$ 1000 = 0.09p
  650 ml: cost for 1 ml = 65 $\div$ 650 = 0.1p
  1 litre of milk is better value.
  *1 mark for finding price for 1 ml (or, e.g., 50 ml or 100 ml) for big bottle; **1 mark** for price for 1 ml (or 50 ml or 100 ml) for smaller bottle, in order to make fair comparison; **1 mark** for correct conclusion (must have working to justify it). Total 3 marks.*
2. a

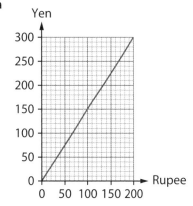

*1 mark for line through origin and through point (100, 150); **1 mark** for correct scale on both axes; **1 mark** for both axes labelled. Total 3 marks.*
Alternatively, you could have Yen on the x-axis and Rupee on the y-axis.

b Either use graph:

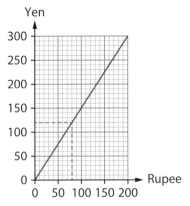

Or:

$1 \text{ yen} = \frac{100}{150} = \frac{2}{3}$ rupees

So $120 \text{ yen} = \frac{2}{3} \times 120 = 80$ rupees

1 mark for drawing lines on graph as shown; 1 mark for correct answer.

Or: 1 mark for finding value of 1 yen (or another sensible number such as 10 yen or 20 yen); 1 mark for correct answer.

Page 58, Inverse proportion

1. a Number of 'worker-hours' = $12 \times 5 = 60$

Time = $60 \div 15 = 4$ hours

1 mark for finding number of 'worker-hours'; 1 mark for correct answer.

b Number of gardeners = $60 \div 2 = 30$

1 mark for dividing your number of 'worker-hours' from part a) by 2; 1 mark for correct answer.

2. a It is halved (or divided by 2).

1 mark for correct answer.

b $y = \frac{3}{x}$

1 mark for correct answer.

Page 59, Time and timetables

1. a 25 mins + 2 hours + 10 min

= 2 hours and 35 mins

1 mark for attempting to add durations; 1 mark for correct answer.

b $1.15 \times 60 = 69$ s

1 mark for correct answer.

2. a He must catch bus at Camberley at 13.10, so at the latest he must leave home 23 minutes earlier, at 12:47

1 mark for identifying correct bus; 1 mark for correct answer.

b Total journey time = 23 mins + 24 mins

= 47 minutes

1 mark for adding durations (must have correct duration for bus); 1 mark for correct answer.

Page 60, Measures

1. $230 \div 1000 = 0.23$ litres

1 mark for correct answer.

2. a $960 \times 3 = 2880$ m

$2880 \div 1000 = 2.88$ km

1 mark for converting a length in m to km; 1 mark for correct answer.

b $2.88 \div 1.6 = 1.8$ miles

1 mark for correct answer.

Page 61, Scale drawing

1.

1 mark for rectangle drawn with length of 3.25 cm or width of 2 cm; 1 mark for both correct. Or: 1 mark for 3.25 and 2 both written down but not drawn.

2. a 1.5 km = 1500 m = 150 000 cm

Ratio is 6 : 150 000 = 1 : 25 000

1 mark for converting 1.5 km to cm; 1 mark for correct answer.

b 100 m = 10 000 cm, 60 m = 6000 cm

Length is 10 000 ÷ 25 000 = 0.4 cm

Width is 6000 ÷ 25 000 = 0.24 cm

1 mark for converting length or width to cm; 1 mark for dividing length or width by your value of n found in part a), 1 mark for both correct answers. Total 3 marks.

Page 62, Angles

1. a $\angle YZX$ is a right angle (90°).

1 mark for correct answer.

b $\angle YXZ$ is an acute angle (less than 90°).

1 mark for correct answer.

2.

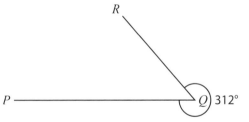

1 mark for PQ drawn 5 cm long and QR drawn 3 cm long; 1 mark for angle PQR = 312° (internal angle = 48°); 1 mark for all correct and labelled. Total 3 marks.

Page 63, Angle rules

1. $a = 360 - 90 - 52 = 218°$

(Angles around a point add up to 360°)

1 mark for subtracting 90 and 52 from 360; 1 mark for correct answer.

2. $x = 180 - 84 = 96°$

Angles on a straight line add up to 180°

$y = 84°$

Alternate angles are equal.

1 mark for subtracting 84 from 180; 1 mark for correct answer for x with reason; 1 mark for correct answer for y with reason. Total 3 marks.

Page 64, Bearings

1. **a** 073°

   1 mark for angle between 71° and 75°; 1 mark for bearing between 072° and 074°

   b 270°

   1 mark for correct answer.

2. **a** 220 – 180 = 40 so bearing is 040°

   1 mark for subtracting 180, 1 mark for correct answer written as a 3-digit bearing.

   b

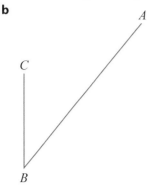

   1 mark for lines drawn to scale, with AB = 10 cm and BC = 5 cm (this diagram is half size); 1 mark for CB vertical; 1 mark for angle CBA = 40°. Total 3 marks.

Page 65, Triangles and quadrilaterals

1. **a** $\triangle ABC$ is isosceles (since $AB = CB$).

   1 mark for each correct answer.

   b $\angle BCA$ = 70° (since $\triangle ABC$ is isosceles)

   $\angle ABC$ = 180 – 2 × 70 = 40° (since angles in a triangle add up to 180°)

   1 mark for attempting to subtract (2 × 70) from 180; 1 mark for correct answer.

2. **a** Rectangle, rhombus

   1 mark for each correct answer. If you write more than two answers then you can only score at most 1 mark in total.

   b 360 – 70 – 56 = 234 (angles in a quadrilateral)

   x = 234 ÷ 2 = 117° (symmetry properties of a kite)

   1 mark for subtracting from 360; 1 mark for dividing by 2; 1 mark for correct answer. Total 3 marks.

Page 66, Polygons

1. **a** Sum of interior angles = (10 – 2) × 180

   = 1440°

   Interior angle = 1440 ÷ 10 = 144°

   1 mark for using (n – 2) × 180, or for finding 1440; 1 mark for dividing sum by 10; 1 mark for correct answer. Total 3 marks. An alternative method may also be used: 1 mark for finding the exterior angle of 36° by 360 ÷ 10; 1 mark for subtracting 36 from 180; 1 mark for the correct answer.

   b Heptagon

   1 mark for correct answer.

2 Angle sum of a heptagon = (7 – 2) × 180 = 900°.

   x = 900 – (45 + 130 + 150 + 70 + 110 + 205) = 190°

   1 mark for correct angle sum; 1 mark for subtracting other angles from angle sum; 1 mark for correct answer. Total 3 marks.

Page 67, Reflection

1.

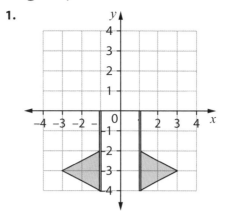

   1 mark for at least 3 points in correct place; 1 mark for all correct points, joined up.

2. Reflection in the line $y = x$

   1 mark for 'reflection'; 1 mark for completely correct including equation.

Page 68, Rotation

1.

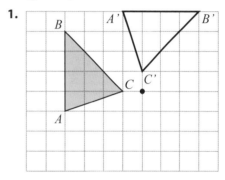

   1 mark for triangle in correct orientation; 1 mark for correct position; 1 mark for all correct including labels. Total 3 marks.

2. Rotation of 180° (clockwise or anticlockwise), centre the origin.

   1 mark for 'rotation'; 1 mark for 180° (direction not needed); 1 mark for centre at the origin. Total 3 marks.

Page 69, Translation

1.

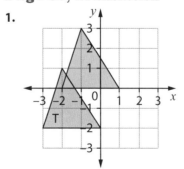

   1 mark for triangle T translated either 1 across or 2 up; 1 mark for fully correct translation.

2. **a** Shape R is a translation of P since it has the same orientation (alternatively: since shape Q is a reflection)

   1 mark for shape R and reason.

   b Translation by vector $\begin{pmatrix} 2 \\ -4 \end{pmatrix}$.

   1 mark for correct vector.

Page 70, Enlargement

1. **a** Enlargement of scale factor 2 from centre of enlargement (0, 5).
    1 mark for enlargement with correct scale factor; 1 mark for correct centre (of enlargement). Total 3 marks.
    b C is not an enlargement of A since it is not similar (or not in proportion) to A. The height has been multiplied by 2, but the width has been multiplied by 3; or, corresponding lengths are not in the same ratio.
    1 mark for stating not similar / not in proportion; 1 mark for explanation of how you know.

2.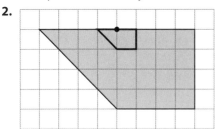

    1 mark for correct dimensions; 1 mark for correct position and dimensions.

Page 71, Congruent shapes

1. **a** congruent
    b congruent
    c not congruent
    d congruent
    1 mark for each correct answer.

2. **a** They meet the condition RHS (right-angled triangles with hypotenuses and one other side the same length, in this case PR as it is in both triangles).
    1 mark for RHS.
    b $\angle PQR = \angle RSP$
    $= 180 - 90 - 37 = 53°$
    1 mark for identifying corresponding angle and/or subtracting from 180); 1 mark for correct answer.

Page 72, Similar shapes

1. **a** $A : B = 1 : 4 = 3 : 12$
    So $A = 3$ cm
    1 mark for multiplying 1 by 3 or for dividing 12 by 4; 1 mark for final answer including unit.
    b Area $A = 3^2 = 9$; area $B = 12^2 = 144$
    So area A : area $B = 9 : 144 = 1 : 16$
    1 mark for finding areas of A and B; 1 mark for correct ratio in simplest form.
    (Notice that the ratio of lengths is 1 : 4 and the ratio of areas is $1^2 : 4^2$; alternatively, scale factor = 4 and scale factor for area = 4^2)

2. Scale factor $= \frac{6}{4} = 1.5$
    Length of $VY = 6 \times 1.5 = 9$ cm
    Length of $WY = 9 - 6 = 3$ cm
    1 mark for finding scale factor; 1 mark for finding length of VY; 1 mark for correct answer. Total 3 marks.

Page 73, Area and perimeter

1. **a** Area $= 4 \times 8 = 32$ cm^2
    1 mark for multiplying 4 and 8; 1 mark for correct answer including unit.
    b Perimeter $= 8 + 5 + 8 + 5$ or $2(8 + 5)$
    $= 26$ cm
    1 mark for adding the 4 correct lengths; 1 mark for correct answer including unit.

2. Area $= \frac{1}{2} bh$
    $\frac{1}{2} \times 8 \times h = 26$
    $4h = 26$
    $h = \frac{26}{4} = 6.5$
    Height $= 6.5$ cm
    1 mark for using correct formula; 1 mark for solving an equation involving h; 1 mark for correct answer. Total 3 marks.

Page 74, Compound shapes

1. **a** Perimeter $= 2(8 + 12)$
    $= 40$ cm
    Or, $8 + 5 + 5 + 7 + 3 + 12 = 40$ cm
    1 mark for either method; 1 mark for correct answer.
    b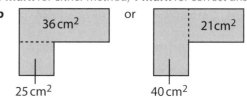
    Area $= 25 + 36$ (or $40 + 21$)
    $= 61$ cm^2
    1 mark for calculating any correct area; 1 mark for adding two correct areas; 1 mark for correct answer. Total 3 marks.

2. **a** Perimeter $= 35 + 20 + 10 + 35 + 10 + 20$
    $= 130$
    130 m of fence is required.
    1 mark for adding 6 lengths; 1 mark for correct answer.
    b Area of rectangle $= bh = 35 \times 20 = 700$ m^2
    Area of parallelogram $= bh = 35 \times 8 = 280$ m^2
    Total area $= 700 + 280 = 980$ m^2
    Grass seed required $= 980 \times 40 = 39\,200$ g
    (or 39.2 kg)
    1 mark for area of parallelogram; 1 mark for total area; 1 mark for multiplying any area by 40; 1 mark for correct answer. Total 4 marks.

Page 75, Circles

1. **a** $C = 2 \times \pi \times 6 = 37.7$ mm
    1 mark for using correct formula; 1 mark for correct answer.
    b $A = \pi \times 6^2 = 113.1$ mm^2
    1 mark for using correct formula; 1 mark for correct answer.

2. $C = \pi d = 8\pi$ so $d = 8$
    $r = \frac{8}{2} = 4$
    $A = \pi r^2 = \pi \times 4^2 = 16\pi$ cm^2
    1 mark for finding diameter or radius: 1 mark for using correct area formula; 1 mark for correct answer in terms of π. Total 3 marks.

Page 76, Semicircles

1. a Perimeter = π × 12 ÷ 2 + 12
   = 30.8 mm
   1 mark for finding half the circumference of the circle;
   1 mark for adding the diameter; 1 mark for correct
   answer to 1 decimal place. Total 3 marks.

   b Area = π × 6² ÷ 2
   = 56.5 mm²
   1 mark for using radius of 6 to find area of whole circle;
   1 mark for finding half the area of the whole circle;
   1 mark for correct answer to 1 decimal place.
   Total 3 marks.

2. Area of rectangle = 10 × 30 = 300 m²
   Area of quarter circle = π × 10² ÷ 4 = 78.5 m²
   Total area = 300 + 78.5 = 379 m² (to the nearest integer)
   1 mark for finding correct area of rectangle;
   1 mark for using radius of 10 to find area of circle;
   1 mark for dividing area of circle by 4 and adding to area
   of rectangle; 1 mark for correct answer to the nearest
   integer. Total 4 marks.

Page 77, Arcs and sectors

1. a Area = $\frac{35}{360}$ × π × 9² = 24.7 cm²
   1 mark for using correct formula; 1 mark for answer
   correct to 1 decimal place.

   b Arc length = $\frac{35}{360}$ × 2 × π × 9 = 5.5 cm
   1 mark for using correct formula; 1 mark for answer
   correct to 1 decimal place.

   c Perimeter = 5.5 + 2 × 9 = 23.5 cm
   1 mark for adding 2 × 9 to the value from b. for arc
   length; 1 mark for answer correct to 1 decimal place.

2. $\frac{200}{360}$ × π × 10.5² = 192° to the nearest degree
   1 mark for using formula for circumference of circle;
   1 mark for substituting values of r and circumference into
   formula for arc length; 1 mark for rearranging to make
   the angle the subject; 1 mark for correct answer to the
   nearest degree. Total 4 marks.

Page 78, 3D shapes

1. a triangular prism
   1 mark for correct answer.

   b

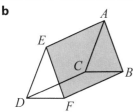

   1 mark for shading correct face.

   c 5 faces, 9 edges, 6 vertices
   1 mark for each correct answer.

2. 7 faces, 12 edges, 7 vertices
   1 mark for each correct answer.

Page 79, Plans and elevations

1. a

   1 mark for correct plan.

   b

   1 mark for correct elevation.

   c

   1 mark for correct elevation.

2.

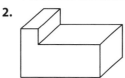

   1 mark for a 3D solid with correct shape at front,
   1 mark for fully correct prism.

Page 80, Nets and surface area

1.

   4 cm
   2 cm
   16 cm

   1 mark for net with at least 4 correct faces; 1 mark for all
   correct and dimensions written on.

2. a Square-based pyramid
   1 mark for correct answer.

   b Surface area = 5 × 5 + 4 × $\left(\frac{1}{2} × 5 × 4\right)$
   = 25 + 4 × 10
   = 65 (cm²)
   1 mark for finding area of one of the triangles; 1 mark for
   adding area of the square to 4 × the area of a triangle;
   1 mark for correct answer. Total 3 marks.

Page 81, Prisms and cylinders

1. Area of base = 350 ÷ 14 = 25 cm²
   1 mark for dividing by 14; 1 mark for correct answer
   including unit.

2. a Radius = 6 ÷ 2 = 3 cm
   Volume = π × 3² × 20 = 180π (cm³)
   1 mark for using correct formula for volume; 1 mark for
   correct answer in terms of π

   b Curved surface area = 2 × π × 3 × 20 = 120π
   Area of circular base = π × 3² = 9π
   Total surface area = 120π + 9π = 129π (cm²)
   1 mark for using correct formula for curved surface area;
   1 mark for using correct formula for area of base; 1 mark
   for correct answer in terms of π. Total 3 marks.

Page 82, Spheres

1. a Volume $= \frac{4}{3} \times \pi \times 12^3 = 7238.229\ldots$
$\qquad\qquad\quad = 7240$ (cm³) to 3 s.f.

1 mark for using correct formula for volume; *1 mark* for correct answer rounded to 3 s.f.

b Surface area $= 4 \times \pi \times 12^2 = 1809.557\ldots$
$\qquad\qquad\qquad = 1810$ (cm²) to 3 s.f.

1 mark for using correct formula for surface area; *1 mark* for correct answer rounded to 3 s.f.

2. Surface area $= 4 \times \pi \times 4^2$
$\qquad\qquad\quad = 64\pi$ cm²

1 mark for using correct formula with r in mm or cm; *1 mark* for using radius 4 cm or for finding answer in mm² then dividing by 100 to find answer in cm²; *1 mark* for correct answer. Total 3 marks

Page 83, Pyramids and cones

1. $\frac{1}{3} \times x^2 \times 12 = 100$
$\qquad\quad 4x^2 = 100$
$\qquad\quad x^2 = 25$
$\qquad\quad x = 5$ cm

1 mark for using correct formula; *1 mark* for finding area of base or value of x^2; *1 mark* for correct answer. Total 3 marks.

2. a Volume $= \frac{1}{3} \times \pi \times 10^2 \times 24$
$\qquad\qquad\quad = 800\pi$ (cm³)

1 mark for using correct formula (note that r is 10 as the diameter is 20); *1 mark* for correct answer in terms of π

b Curved surface area $= \pi \times 10 \times 26$
$\qquad\qquad\qquad\qquad = 260\pi$ (cm²)

1 mark for using correct formula; *1 mark* for correct answer in terms of π

Page 84, Constructing triangles

1. a

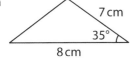

1 mark for drawing line of 8 cm (to the nearest mm) and angle of 35° (to the nearest degree); *1 mark* for completely correct triangle.

b

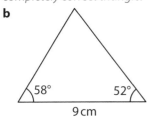

1 mark for drawing line of 9 cm (to the nearest mm) and angle of either 58° or 52° (to the nearest degree); *1 mark* for completely correct triangle.

2. a

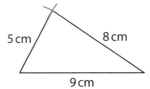

1 mark for 9 cm line and at least one correct arc; *1 mark* for both arcs correct; *1 mark* for completely correct triangle including construction lines. Total 3 marks.

b

1 mark for drawing arcs of equal radius from both ends of line; *1 mark* for fully correct answer including construction lines.

Page 85, Perpendiculars and bisectors

1.

1 mark for attempting all the arcs; *1 mark* for correct answer (to nearest degree) including all arcs. (You can use a protractor to check your line is perpendicular to AB.)

2.

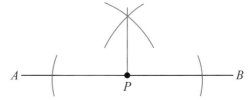

1 mark for attempting all the arcs; *1 mark* for 70° angle drawn (to nearest degree) and all arcs drawn. (You can use a protractor to check the angle.)

Page 86, Loci

1.

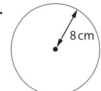

1 mark for drawing a circle; *1 mark* for accurate circle with radius 8 cm (to nearest mm).

2. a Construct angle bisector:

1 mark for all arcs attempted; *1 mark* for correct angle bisector. (You can use a protractor to check that each angle is 27°.)

b On your diagram for part **a)**, draw circle of radius 3 cm with centre at A

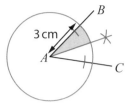

1 mark for drawing circle of radius 3 cm; *1 mark* for shading above the angle bisector; *1 mark* for shading inside the circle. Total 3 marks.

Page 87, Pythagoras' theorem

1. a $x = \sqrt{17^2 - 14^2} = 9.6$ cm

1 mark for using Pythagoras' theorem with 17 as the hypotenuse; *1 mark* for correct answer to 1 decimal place.

b $y = \sqrt{4.2^2 + 7.6^2} = 8.7$ cm

1 mark for using Pythagoras' theorem with y as the hypotenuse; *1 mark* for correct answer to 1 decimal place.

2. Triangle ABC:
$12^2 + 5^2 = 144 + 25 = 169$
$13^2 = 169$
Triangle ABC is right-angled since it satisfies Pythagoras' theorem.
Triangle DEF:
$4^2 + 3^2 = 16 + 9 = 25$
$6^2 = 36$ not 25
Triangle DEF is not right-angled since it does not satisfy Pythagoras' theorem.

1 mark for calculating $12^2 + 5^2$; *1 mark* for comparing to 13^2 and writing the correct conclusion for triangle ABC; *1 mark* for calculating $4^2 + 3^2$; *1 mark* for comparing to 6^2 and writing the correct conclusion for triangle DEF. Total 4 marks.

Page 88, Trigonometry 1

1. a $\sin 40° = \frac{x}{22}$
$x = 22 \times \sin 40° = 14.1$ cm (to 1 decimal place)

1 mark for using correct ratio with values in the correct places; *1 mark* for correct answer to 1 decimal place.

b $\tan 52° = \frac{6}{x}$
$x = \frac{6}{\tan 52°} = 4.7$ cm (to 1 decimal place)

1 mark for using correct ratio with values in the correct places; *1 mark* for correct answer to 1 decimal place.

2. $\cos 70° = \frac{0.5}{x}$
$x = \frac{0.5}{\cos 70°} = 1.46$

Length of plank = 1.46 m (to the nearest cm)

1 mark for using correct ratio with values in the correct places; *1 mark* for correct answer to nearest cm.

Page 89, Trigonometry 2

1. a $\sin x = \frac{8}{27}$

$x = \sin^{-1}\left(\frac{8}{27}\right) = 17.2°$ (to 1 decimal place)

1 mark for using correct ratio with values in the correct places; *1 mark* for correct answer to 1 decimal place.

b $\cos x = \frac{6.4}{12.9}$

$x = \cos^{-1}\left(\frac{6.4}{12.9}\right) = 60.3°$ (to 1 decimal place)

1 mark for using correct ratio with values in the correct places; *1 mark* for correct answer to 1 decimal place.

2. For angle of elevation θ, $\tan \theta = \frac{80}{20}$

$\theta = \tan^{-1}\left(\frac{80}{20}\right) = 76°$ (to the nearest degree)

1 mark for using correct ratio with values in the correct places; *1 mark* for correct answer to nearest degree.

Page 90, Exact values

1. a $\tan 30° = \frac{1}{\sqrt{3}}$ (or $\frac{\sqrt{3}}{3}$)
1 mark for correct answer.

b $\sin 90° = 1$
1 mark for correct answer.

2. $\cos 60° = \frac{x}{2}$
$\frac{1}{2} = \frac{x}{2}$
$x = 1$ cm
1 mark for using correct ratio; *1 mark* for using or writing $\cos 60° = \frac{1}{2}$; *1 mark* for correct answer. Total 3 marks.

Page 91, Vectors

1. a $\overrightarrow{DO} = -\mathbf{d}$ **b** $\overrightarrow{OB} = \mathbf{a} + \mathbf{d}$
c $\overrightarrow{OC} = 2\mathbf{d}$ **d** $\overrightarrow{AC} = 2\mathbf{d} - \mathbf{a}$
1 mark for each correct answer.

Page 92, Column vectors

1. $\mathbf{a} = \begin{pmatrix} 4 \\ -3 \end{pmatrix}$, $\mathbf{b} = \begin{pmatrix} 0 \\ 4 \end{pmatrix}$, $\mathbf{a} + \mathbf{b} = \begin{pmatrix} 4 \\ 1 \end{pmatrix}$
1 mark for each correct answer.

2. a i $4\mathbf{q} = 4\begin{pmatrix} -3 \\ 5 \end{pmatrix} = \begin{pmatrix} 4 \times -3 \\ 4 \times 5 \end{pmatrix} = \begin{pmatrix} -12 \\ 20 \end{pmatrix}$

ii $\mathbf{p} + \mathbf{q} + \mathbf{r} = \begin{pmatrix} 2 \\ 7 \end{pmatrix} + \begin{pmatrix} -3 \\ 5 \end{pmatrix} + \begin{pmatrix} 1 \\ -4 \end{pmatrix}$
$= \begin{pmatrix} 2 + (-3) + 1 \\ 7 + 5 + (-4) \end{pmatrix}$
$= \begin{pmatrix} 0 \\ 8 \end{pmatrix}$

iii $2\mathbf{p} - \mathbf{r} = 2\begin{pmatrix} 2 \\ 7 \end{pmatrix} - \begin{pmatrix} 1 \\ -4 \end{pmatrix} = \begin{pmatrix} 2 \times 2 - 1 \\ 2 \times 7 - (-4) \end{pmatrix}$
$= \begin{pmatrix} 3 \\ 18 \end{pmatrix}$

1 mark for each correct answer.

b $\begin{pmatrix} -1 \\ 4 \end{pmatrix} = -\mathbf{r}$ so parallel to $\mathbf{r}$

$\begin{pmatrix} 3 \\ -12 \end{pmatrix} = 3\mathbf{r}$ so parallel to $\mathbf{r}$

1 mark for each correct answer. (If you put more than two answers then you will lose a mark for each incorrect answer you give.)

Page 93, Sampling

a The data is secondary since Aston didn't collect it himself.
1 mark for correct answer including explanation.

b $\frac{5}{20} = \frac{1}{4}$ of the days in the sample had light rain.
Estimated number of days with light rain in the whole summer holiday = $\frac{1}{4}$ of 48 = 12
1 mark for finding the proportion of days with light rain in the sample; *1 mark* for correct answer.

Page 94, Organising data

1. a 36

1 mark for correct answer.

b 44 + 15 = 59

1 mark for correct answer.

2. a

0	3, 8, 9
1	2, 4
2	5, 7
3	3, 3
4	9

Key: 1 | 2 means 12

1 mark for a correct key; 1 mark for a stem-and-leaf diagram (allow 2 missing or incorrect values); 1 mark for fully correct answer. Total 3 marks.

b

0–9	3
10–19	2
20–29	2
30–39	2
40–49	1

1 mark for at least 4 frequencies correct; 1 mark for fully correct table.

Page 95, Simple charts

1. a

Age group	Tally	Frequency
Pre-school	卌 IIII	9
School age	卌 II	7
Adults under 65	卌 卌	10
Adults age 65+	IIII	4

1 mark for all values correct.

b Key: ▢ = 4 people

Pre-school	▢▢▫
School age	▢▫
Adults under 65	▢▢▢
Adults age 65+	▢

1 mark for pictogram with two rows correct; 1 mark for three rows correct; 1 mark for completely correct pictogram including a clear key (any suitable symbol). Total 3 marks. (You can score all the marks for using the frequencies that you wrote down in part a), even if they were wrong.)

2. a 35

1 mark for correct answer.

b Total number of drinks = 25 + 30 + 10 + 15 = 80

1 mark for adding up correct values; 1 mark for correct answer.

Page 96, Pie charts

1. Proportion = $135 \div 360 = \frac{3}{8}$

Number preferring crisps = $\frac{3}{8} \times 24 = 9$

Or: One person is represented by $360 \div 24 = 15°$

Number preferring crisps = $135 \div 15 = 9$

1 mark for finding proportion of total in category, or for finding angle that one person is represented by; 1 mark for correct answer.

2. Total = 15 + 20 + 25 = 60

Proportion for dog = $\frac{15}{60} = \frac{1}{4}$

Angle for dog = $\frac{1}{4} \times 360 = 90°$

Proportion for cat = $\frac{20}{60} = \frac{1}{3}$

Angle for cat = $\frac{1}{3} \times 360 = 120°$

Proportion for other = $\frac{25}{60} = \frac{5}{12}$

Angle for other = $\frac{5}{12} \times 360 = 150°$

Favourite pet

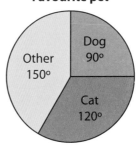

1 mark for all angles correct; 1 mark for constructing pie chart with at least one sector correct to the nearest 1°; 1 mark for fully correct and labelled pie chart. Total 4 marks.

Page 97, Averages and spread

1. a Data in order:

0, 0, 0, 1, 1, 1, 2, 2, 3, 3, 3, 4, 4, 4, 4, 5, 7

Median = 3 bikes per household

1 mark for correct answer.

b Mode = 4 bikes per household

1 mark for correct answer.

c Mean = $\frac{44}{17}$ = 2.59 bikes per household (2 d.p.)

1 mark for attempting to add up and divide by 17; 1 mark for correct answer.

d Range = 7 − 0 = 7

1 mark for correct answer.

2. a Total = 8 × 2.5 = 20

20 − (1 + 2 + 2 + 1 + 9 + 1) = 4

So, the two unknown numbers must be either 1 and 3, or 2 and 2

The ordered list is either

1, 1, 1, (1, 2) 2, 3, 9, which has a median of 1.5, or

1, 1, 1, (2, 2) 2, 2, 9, which has a median of 2

We are told the median is 1.5 so the unknown numbers must be 1 and 3

1 mark for finding total value; 1 mark for giving two values which give mean of 2.5; 1 mark for correct answer. Total 3 marks.

b The value 9 is unusually high, so might be considered an outlier. The mean is affected by the outlier but the median isn't.

1 mark for correct answer.

Page 98, Averages from tables

1. **a** The total frequency is 20, so need the average of the 10th and 11th numbers of items, which are 5 and 6.
Median = $\frac{5+6}{2}$ = 5.5 items
1 mark for considering average of 10th and 11th values;
1 mark for correct answer.

b Mode = 6 items (highest frequency)
1 mark for correct answer.

c

No. of items	3	4	5	6	7	8	Total
Frequency	1	5	4	7	2	1	20
No. of items × frequency	3	20	20	42	14	8	107

Mean = 107 ÷ 20 = 5.35 items
1 mark for multiplying each value by its frequency;
1 mark for dividing total of these values by total frequency; 1 mark for correct answer. Total 3 marks.

d Range = 8 − 3 = 5
1 mark for correct answer.

2.

Items of homework	0	1	2	3	4	Total
Frequency	2	5	4	1	2	14
Items of homework × frequency	0	5	8	3	8	24

Mean = 24 ÷ 14 = 1.7 (1 d.p.)
1 mark for multiplying each value by its frequency;
1 mark for dividing total of these values by total frequency; 1 mark for correct answer. Total 3 marks.

Page 99, Grouped data

a Modal class is $0 \leqslant t < 20$
1 mark for correct answer.

b

Time (*t* mins)	Frequency	Running total
$0 \leqslant t < 20$	35	35
$20 \leqslant t < 40$	20	55
$40 \leqslant t < 60$	16	71
$60 \leqslant t < 80$	9	80

There are 80 in total so median is around the 40th which is in the $20 \leqslant t < 40$ class.
1 mark for doing a running total or attempting to find the 40th or 41st value; 1 mark for correct answer.

c

Time (*t* mins)	Mid-point	Frequency	Midpoint × frequency
$0 \leqslant t < 20$	10	35	350
$20 \leqslant t < 40$	30	20	600
$40 \leqslant t < 60$	50	16	800
$60 \leqslant t < 80$	70	9	630
Total		80	2380

Estimate for mean = 2380 ÷ 80 = 29.75 mins
1 mark for correct midpoints; 1 mark for multiplying midpoints by frequencies and adding up; 1 mark for correct answer. Total 3 marks.

Page 100, Scatter graphs

1. **a** Negative correlation
1 mark for correct answer.

b 16 °C
1 mark for correct answer.

2. Positive correlation
1 mark for correct answer.

Page 101, Lines of best fit

a 20 eggs
1 mark for correct answer.

b This would be extrapolation as we only have data for up to 6-year-old hens, so any estimate would be unreliable.
1 mark for using term 'extrapolation', or for explaining that it's outside the range of the data; 1 mark for saying estimate will be unreliable.

Page 102, Time series

a The general trend of the cost of strawberries is increasing.
1 mark for correct answer.

b They are cheapest in summer.
1 mark for correct answer.

c Mean = $\frac{3 + 2.5 + 3}{3}$ = £2.83
1 mark for using correct 3 values from graph;
1 mark for correct answer.

Page 103, Theoretical probability

1. **a** P(2) = $\frac{1}{6}$
b P(multiple of 3) = $\frac{2}{6}$ or $\frac{1}{3}$
c P(greater than 2) = $\frac{4}{6}$ or $\frac{2}{3}$
d P(7) = 0
1 mark for each correct answer.

2. **a** P(water and fruit) = $\frac{15}{40}$ = $\frac{3}{8}$
1 mark for adding up the 4 numbers to get total 40;
1 mark for correct, simplified answer.
b P(crisps) = $\frac{18}{40}$ = $\frac{9}{20}$
1 mark for 18; 1 mark for correct, simplified answer.

Page 104, Mutually exclusive events

1. P(dog) = 1 − P(cat) = $1 - \frac{3}{8} = \frac{5}{8}$
1 mark for correct answer.

2. **a** $0.4 + x + 2x = 1$
$3x = 0.6$
$x = 0.2$
1 mark for forming correct equation; 1 mark for attempting to solve the equation; 1 for correct value of x. Total 3 marks.
b P(yellow) = 2 × 0.2 = 0.4
1 mark for correct answer.

Page 105, Possibility spaces

1. **a**

	1	2	3	4	5	6
1	2	3	4	5	6	7
2	3	4	5	6	7	8
3	4	5	6	7	8	9
4	5	6	7	8	9	10
5	6	7	8	9	10	11
6	7	8	9	10	11	12

1 mark for table drawn and at least 10 correct values inside; 1 mark for fully correct answer.
b P(total of 8) = $\frac{5}{36}$
1 mark for correct answer.

2. a GG, GB, GR, BB, BG, BR, RR, RG, RB

*1 mark for listing at least 6 correct outcomes; **1 mark** for all 9 outcomes.*

b P(same colour) = $\frac{3}{9}$ $\left(\text{or } \frac{1}{3}\right)$

1 mark for correct answer.

Page 106, Probability experiments

1. Estimated probability of blue = $\frac{90}{200}$ = 0.45

1 mark for correct answer as a decimal.

2. a

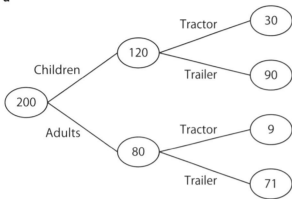

*1 mark for a frequency tree with at least one correct set of branches; **1 mark** for correct frequency tree with fewer than three labels or frequencies incorrect or missing; **1 mark** for completely correct frequency tree. Total 3 marks.*

b Probability = $\frac{71 + 90}{200}$ = $\frac{161}{200}$ = 0.805

*1 mark for adding to find total number who had trailer ride; **1 mark** for correct answer as a fraction or a decimal.*

Page 107, Expected results

1. Expected frequency = 0.3 × 40 = 12

*1 mark for multiplying probability by number of trials; **1 mark** for correct answer.*

2. a You would expect 3 heads not 1, but this is a very small number of trials so the results don't suggest the coin is biased.

1 mark for correct answer including reason.

b You would expect 50 heads not 25, so this does suggest that the coin is biased.

1 mark for correct answer including reason.

Page 108, Tree diagrams

a

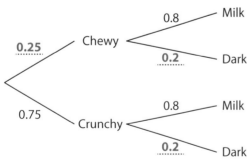

*1 mark for 0.25 in correct place; **1 mark** for both 0.2 in correct places.*

b P(crunchy and milk) = 0.75 × 0.8
= 0.6

*1 mark for attempting to multiply 0.75 by 0.8; **1 mark** for correct answer.*

Page 109, Set notation

1. a The numbers in set A ∪ B are 1, 2, 3, 5, 7, 9

1 mark for all the correct numbers and no incorrect numbers.

b The numbers in set B′ are 1, 4, 6, 8, 9, 10

1 mark for all the correct numbers and no incorrect numbers.

2.

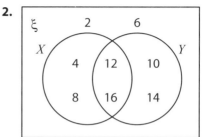

*1 mark for Venn diagram with rectangle and two overlapping circles (or ovals); **1 mark** for only 12 and 16 in the intersection; **1 mark** for only 2 and 6 outside both circles in the universal set; **1 mark** for fully correct Venn diagram. Total 4 marks.*

Page 110, Probability from tables & diagrams

1. a P(pen and notebook) = $\frac{13}{40}$

1 mark for correct answer.

b P(paper) = $\frac{7 + 12}{40}$ = $\frac{19}{40}$

1 mark for correct answer.

2. a P(A) = $\frac{3}{9}$ $\left(\text{or } \frac{1}{3}\right)$

b P(B) = $\frac{4}{9}$

c P(A ∩ B) = $\frac{1}{9}$

d P(A ∪ B) = $\frac{6}{9}$ $\left(\text{or } \frac{2}{3}\right)$

e P(A′) = $\frac{6}{9}$ $\left(\text{or } \frac{2}{3}\right)$

1 mark for each correct answer. Total 5 marks.

Pages 112–113, Using HCF & LCM in context

Check-up box

1. 8

2. Multiples of 24: 24, 48, 72, 96, 120
Multiples of 32: 32, 64, 96, 128
LCM = 96

3. Factors of 12: 1, 2, 3, 4, 6, 12
Factors of 80: 1, 2, 4, 5, 8, 10, 16, 20, 40, 80
HCF = 4

4. 240 = 2 × 2 × 2 × 2 × 3 × 5 = $2^4 × 3 × 5$

5. Factors of 24: 1, 2, 3, 4, 6, 8, 12, 24
Prime factors: 2, 3

Exam corner

1. Factors of 30: 1, 2, 3, 5, 6, 10, 15, 30
Factors of 24: 1, 2, 3, 4, 6, 8, 12, 24
HCF = 6, so loaves should be cut into 6 cm slices.

*1 mark for listing factors of 30 and 24; **1 mark** for correct answer.*

2. Multiples of 5 over 50: 50, 55, 60, 65, 70, 75
Multiples of 7 over 50: 56, 63, 70, 77
LCM (over 50) = 70

So they need $\frac{70}{5}$ = 14 packs of badges
and $\frac{70}{7}$ = 10 packs of posters.

1 mark for the LCM; 1 mark for both correct answers.

3. $80 = 2^4 \times 5$
$96 = 2^5 \times 3$
Number in each row = HCF = 2^4 = 16
1 mark for attempt at prime decomposition of either 80 or 96; 1 mark for correct decomposition of both 80 and 96; 1 mark for correct answer. Total 3 marks.

4. a $96 = 2^5 \times 3, 64 = 2^6, 128 = 2^7$
HCF = 2^5 = 32, so maximum number of posies is 32
1 mark for correct prime factor decomposition of 96, 64 or 128; 1 mark for correct prime factor decomposition of any two of 96, 64 and 128; 1 mark for HCF as 32. Total 3 marks.

b $\frac{96}{32}$ = 3 white, $\frac{64}{32}$ = 2 purple, $\frac{128}{32}$ = 4 pink
1 mark for correct number of all colours of flower.

Pages 114–115, Writing & solving equations

Check-up box

1. a $3x = 2, x = \frac{2}{3}$ or $0.\dot{6}$
b $-20 = 2x, x = -10$
c $4x + 9 = 7x$
$9 = 3x, x = 3$
d $5x = 30, x = 6$

2. $x^2 - 5 = 76$
$x^2 = 81, x = 9$

3. $y = 1 + 2x = -4x + 19$
$6x = 18, x = 3$
$y = 7$

Exam corner

1. Let t = cost of T-shirt and s = cost of pair of socks.
$3t + 4s = 55.30 \times 4 \Rightarrow 12t + 16s = 221.20$
$4t + 3s = 68.60 \times 3 \Rightarrow 12t + 9s = 205.80$
Subtract: $\qquad\qquad\quad 7s = 15.40$
$\qquad\qquad\qquad\qquad\quad s = 2.20$
Substitute into first equation:
$3t + 8.8 = 55.30$
$3t = 46.5, t = 15.50$
A T-shirt costs £15.50 and a pair of socks costs £2.20
1 mark for scaling both equations to make coefficients of t or s the same; 1 mark for subtracting the equations to eliminate s or t; 1 mark for each correct answer. Total 4 marks.

2. Let m = Max's age and s = Sam's age.
$m - s = 5$
$m + 3 = 3s \Rightarrow m - 3s = -3$
Subtract: $2s = 8, s = 4$
Substitute into first equation:
$m - 4 = 5, m = 9$
Sam is 4 years old and Max is 9 years old.
1 mark for forming each initial equation; 1 mark for subtracting the equations to eliminate m; 1 mark for each correct answer. Total 4 marks.

3. Let x = number of 10p coins and y = number of 5p coins.
$x + y = 12 \Rightarrow 5x + 5y = 60$ (multiplying by 5)
$10x + 5y = 80$
Subtract: $5x = 20, x = 4$
Substitute into first equation:
$4 + y = 12, y = 8$
He has four 10p coins and eight 5p coins.
1 mark for scaling one equation to make coefficients of x or y the same; 1 mark for subtracting the equations to eliminate x or y; 1 mark for each correct answer. Total 4 marks.

Pages 116–117, Handling ratio in context

Check-up box

1. 2 : 3

2. 3 + 2 = 5 parts
Each part = 100 ÷ 5 = 20
20 × 3 = £60 and 20 × 2 = £40

3. 10% = 6 so 5% = 3
15% = 9

4. $\frac{5}{9}$

5. $\frac{4}{10} = \frac{2}{5}$

6. 0.12

Exam corner

1.

A			12	
B				

Each box is worth 4, so B weighs 16 kg.
1 mark for any correct method for finding value of one part; 1 mark for correct answer.

2.

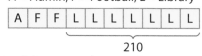

Each box is worth 5, so Gavin has 35 sweets.
1 mark for identifying the difference is 3 parts; 1 mark for any method of finding the value of one part/box; 1 mark for correct answer. Total 3 marks.

3. A = Admin, F = Football, L = Library

A	F	F	L	L	L	L	L	L	L

210

Each box is worth 30, so the total donated is
30 × 10 = £300
Alternative solution:
2 + 7 = 9
Total for library and football = $\frac{210}{7} \times 9$ = £270
Total donated = $\frac{270}{0.9} \times 100$ = £300
1 mark for realising that 9 parts remain; 1 mark for one part being £30; 1 mark for £270; 1 mark for final correct solution. Total 4 marks.

4.

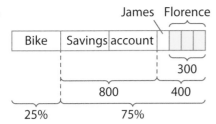

Florence gets £300 and this is 3 parts, so James gets £100.

This £400 given to James and Florence is $\frac{1}{3}$ of amount remaining after buying the bike.

So $\frac{2}{3}$ = £800 is put into savings account.

This £400 + £800 = £1200 is 75% of the amount inherited.

So total inherited is £1600

1 mark for £400 given to cousins; 1 mark for £800 into savings account; 1 mark for £1200 as 75% of total; 1 mark for correct answer. Total 4 marks.

Pages 118–119, Tricky percentage questions

Check-up box

1. $\frac{45}{100} = \frac{9}{20}$
2. 0.18
3. Divide by 10
4. 1.02
5. 10% is 240, 1% is 24 so 12% is 240 + 24 + 24 = £288
6. 50% = 250 so 25% = 125
   Reduced amount = 500 – 125 = £375

Exam corner

1. Multiplier = 1.023
   After 1 year amount invested = 1.023 × 2350 = 2404.05
   After 2 years amount invested = 1.023 × 2404.05
   $\qquad$ = 2459.3415
   After 3 years amount invested = 1.023 × 2459.3415
   $\qquad$ = 2515.908042
   After 4 years amount invested = 1.023 × 2515.908042
   $\qquad$ = 2573.773927
   Or, using power of multiplier, after 4 years amount invested = 1.023^4 × 2350 = 2573.773927
   Rounding to 2 d.p. gives £2573.77
   1 mark for correct multiplier; 1 mark for calculation using repeated multiplication (or power of 4); 1 mark for correct final answer. Total 3 marks.

2. Multiplier = 1.05
   After 2 years: initial investment × 1.05 × 1.05 = 661.50
   Rearrange to give: investment = $\frac{661.50}{1.05^2}$ = 600
   So initial investment = £600.00
   Interest = 661.50 – 600.00 = £61.50
   1 mark for correct multiplier; 1 mark for squaring this; 1 mark for rearranging equation to calculate initial investment; 1 mark for correct answer. Total 4 marks.

3. By midnight Tuesday: 0.89 × 1200 = 1068
   By midnight Wednesday: 0.89 × 1068 = 950.52
   Or, using square of multiplier, 1200 × 0.89^2 = 950.52
   Area covered = 951 cm² to nearest cm²
   1 mark for multiplier; 1 mark for calculation using repeated multiplication or square of multiplier; 1 mark for correctly rounded final answer. Total 3 marks.

4. 6 litres = 6000 ml
   Number of bottles = 6000 ÷ 300 = 20
   Amount received = 1.25 × 20 = £25
   Profit = 25 – 18 = £7
   Percentage profit = $\frac{7}{18}$ × 100% = 38.9% to 1 d.p.
   1 mark for calculating 20 bottles; 1 mark for money received and profit; 1 mark for $\frac{7}{18}$; 1 mark for correct rounded answer. Total 4 marks.

Pages 120–121, Speed, distance & time

Check-up box

1. **a** 2.3 × 60 = 138 min $\qquad$ **b** 60 + 14 = 74 min
   c 0.6 × 60 = 36 min
2. 30 min = 0.5 h
   Average speed = $\frac{18}{0.5}$ = 36mph
3. Bus arrives at 08:48. From 08:48 to 09:22 is
   12 + 22 = 34 min

Exam corner

1. From 13:42 to 14:40 is 18 + 40 = 58 min
   1 mark for 13:42; 1 mark for correct answer.
2. She should have used 1.5, not 1.3, to represent 1 hr 30 min.
   Distance = 3 × 1.5 = 4.5 miles
   1 mark for identifying 1.3 used incorrectly; 1 mark for correct distance.
3. No, he is not correct.
   Distance travelled at 70mph for 15 min = 70 × 0.25
   $\qquad$ = 17.5 miles
   so he will not have travelled far enough in 15 mins.
   Alternative reasoning:
   Speed needed to travel 23 miles in 15 min = $\frac{23}{0.25}$ = 92mph
   so he would need to travel at 92mph to get there in 15 min.
   1 mark for calculating either the distance travelled or the speed needed; 1 mark for valid explanation.
4. **a** 16 m/s = 16 × 60 × 60 = 57 600 m/h
   $\qquad$ = 57.6 km/h
   1 mark for either multiplying by 60 × 60 or dividing by 1000; 1 mark correct answer.
   b Using speed from part **a**,
   time taken = $\frac{120}{57.6}$ = 2.083 33... h
   0.083 33… h = 0.083 33... × 60 = 5 min
   Journey time is 2 h 5 min.
   9.03 + 2 h 5 min gives arrival time 11.08am.
   1 mark for calculating time using your value of speed from a); 1 mark for converting decimal fraction of hour into minutes; 1 mark correct answer. Total 3 marks.

Pages 122–123, Tackling shape calculations

Check-up box

1. **a** 70 mm $\qquad$ **b** 0.0015 m³ $\qquad$ **c** 300 mm²
2. 48 cm
3. 16π cm²

Exam corner

1. Square of area 14 400 cm^2 has side length
   $\sqrt{14\,400}$ = 120 cm
   Perimeter = 4 × 120 = 480 cm
    = 4.8 m
   *1 **mark** for calculating side length; 1 **mark** for correct perimeter in m.*

2. Volume of cylindrical tin = 5^2 × π × 12 = 942.4777961 cm^3
   5 litres = 5000 cm^3
   5000 ÷ 942.4777961 = 5.305 You would need 6 tins.
   *1 **mark** for volume; 1 **mark** for 5 litres = 5000 cm^3;
   1 **mark** for division to calculate the number of tins;
   1 **mark** for correct answer. Total 4 marks.*

3. 600 cm = 6 m
   Perimeter = 6 × 5 = 30 m
   $\frac{30}{1.5}$ = 20
   So 20 whole fence panels are needed.
   Cost of fence = 20 × 22.50 = £450
   Cost of labour = 60 × 4 = £240
   Total cost = 450 + 240 = £690
   *1 **mark** for perimeter; 1 **mark** for 20 panels; 1 **mark** for cost of builder; 1 **mark** for correct final answer. Total 4 marks.*

4. Cube has side length $\sqrt[3]{216\,000}$ = 60 cm = 0.6 m
   Surface area of cube = 0.6 × 0.6 × 6 = 2.16 m^2
   3 tins of paint need to be bought.
   *1 **mark** for finding side length; 1 **mark** for converting units; 1 **mark** for surface area; 1 **mark** for correct answer. Total 4 marks.*

Pages 124–125, Venn diagrams & probability

Check-up box

1. A = {13, 17, 19}
   B = {16, 17, 18, 19, 20}
   C = {12, 15, 18}
2. $B \cap C$ = {18}
3. $A \cup C$ = {12, 13, 15, 17, 18, 19}

Exam corner

1. a
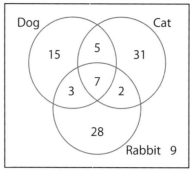

   *1 **mark** for Venn diagram with three intersecting circles;
   1 **mark** for 5, 2, 3 in intersections; 1 **mark** for 9 in universal set only; 1 **mark** for fully correct Venn diagram. Total 4 marks.*

   b $\frac{9}{100}$
   *1 **mark** for correct answer.*

2.
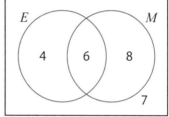

   *1 **mark** for Venn diagram with two overlapping circles;
   1 **mark** for 8 in M only; 1 **mark** for 7 in universal set only;
   1 **mark** for fully correct Venn diagram. Total 4 marks.*

3. From the diagram given: 6 × 12 = 72, 4 × 6 = 24
   Total cost so far = 72 + 24 = £96
   150 − 96 = 54
   Total for one person doing both activities = 12 + 6 = £18
   54 ÷ 18 = 3
   Three students signed up for both activities.
   *1 **mark** for calculating cost so far; 1 **mark** for calculating cost of both activities; 1 **mark** for correct answer. Total 3 marks.*

My notes

My notes

My notes

OXFORD
UNIVERSITY PRESS

Great Clarendon Street, Oxford, OX2 6DP, United Kingdom

Oxford University Press is a department of the University of Oxford.

It furthers the University's objective of excellence in research, scholarship, and education by publishing worldwide. Oxford is a registered trade mark of Oxford University Press in the UK and in certain other countries

British Library Cataloguing in Publication Data
Data available

978-1-38-200649-1

10 9 8 7 6 5 4 3 2 1

Paper used in the production of this book is a natural, recyclable product made from wood grown in sustainable forests.

The manufacturing process conforms to the environmental regulations of the country of origin.

Printed in the United Kingdom by Bell and Bain Ltd, Glasgow

Acknowledgements
Author: Katie Wood
Series Editor: Naomi Bartholomew-Millar
Editorial team: Dom Holdsworth, Matteo Orsini Jones (Haremi Ltd)
With thanks to Paul Hunt, Jemma Sherwood, Karen Gordon and Jane Roth for their contributions.

The publisher would like to thank the following for permissions to use copyright material:

Cover illustrations: Cristina Romero Palma / Shutterstock, Rachael Arnott / Shutterstock

Artwork by Q2A Media Services Pvt. Ltd.

Although we have made every effort to trace and contact all copyright holders before publication this has not been possible in all cases. If notified, the publisher will rectify any errors or omissions at the earliest opportunity.

Links to third party websites are provided by Oxford in good faith and for information only. Oxford disclaims any responsibility for the materials contained in any third party website referenced in this work.

MIX
Paper from responsible sources
FSC® C007785